ACCELERATE THE SALE

KICK-START YOUR PERSONAL SELLING STYLE TO CLOSE MORE SALES, FASTER

MARK RODGERS

Mc
Graw
Hill

New York   Chicago   San Francisco   Lisbon   London   Madrid   Mexico City
Milan   New Delhi   San Juan   Seoul   Singapore   Sydney   Toronto

To my precious wife, Amy;
all things are possible because of you.

1 2 3 4 5 6 7 8 9 10 11 12 13 14 15   DOC/DOC   1 9 8 7 6 5 4 3 2 1

ISBN   978-0-07-176040-9
MHID   0-07-176040-7

e-ISBN   978-0-07-176125-3
e-MHID   0-07-176125-X

Library of Congress Cataloging-in-Publication Data

Rodgers, Mark.
      Accelerate the sale : kick-start your personal selling style to close more sales,
   faster / by Mark Rodgers.
         p.   cm.
      ISBN: 978-0-07-176040-9 (alk. paper)
      1. Selling.   I. Title.

   HF5438.25.R623   2011
   658.85—dc22   2011008772

Interior design by Think Book Works

McGraw-Hill books are available at special quantity discounts to use as premiums and sales promotions or for use in corporate training programs. To contact a representative, please e-mail us at bulksales@mcgraw-hill.com.

This book is printed on acid-free paper.

Contents

Foreword

I n my early 20s, in the primordial stages of my sales career, the president of our company asked me how I saw the sales process. I felt I was in the arena with gladiators at the time, praying for a "thumbs up" from the sales emperor.

"Adversarial," I replied, with that proud look of thinking you know it all when you truly know nothing.

"Oh, oh," responded my fearless leader.

I've learned a lot since then, founding my own consulting firm and creating global communities of salespeople whom I mentor. Perhaps more than any other single jewel, the diamond I've mined from the hard work is that this is a relationship business—the antithesis of adversarial.

When asked, I gladly agreed to write this foreword for Mark Rodgers—one of those mentor community members I'm proud to have with me—because he's adapted my philosophies, mixed in his own and those of others, and achieved an alchemy of solid, reliable, pragmatic sales tools to apply immediately. I assume you're in sales if you've read this far, so you know how "in the moment" you must be, and that this profession is both art and science.

I believe wealth is discretionary time. It is not money, per se. Money can fuel wealth, but as we all know, it doesn't take the place of being at our children's recitals, sports events, or parties. It's no substitute for a great vacation with our loved ones. It can fuel these experiences, but it can never replace them.

Too many people are engaged in the pursuit of money to the degree that they are eroding their wealth. Mark will guide you to the creation of profit in less time, not more. A lot of salespeople work hard. I always wanted to hire the ones who worked smart.

I drive exotic cars, and it's an interesting coincidence (or perhaps not) that Mark talks about speed, acceleration, and roaring to the finish line. In superbly performing cars, you need both torque, to start you moving quickly, and horsepower, to propel you effortlessly at high speed. Mark provides this with practical examples drawn from real clients and conditions. This book is not a theoretical guide but rather a practical companion. It's a high-performance learning vehicle.

Running Through the Tape

In high school, I was a track star, specializing in the sprints. As in so many youthful pursuits, we acquire principles and techniques that stand us in good stead for a lifetime. In track, I learned to "run through the tape." Too many runners subconsciously let up as they approach the finish line, allowing a competitor to beat them at the tape. My coaches taught me to run as though the tape were 10 yards farther down the track than the actual finish line, so that I was still traveling at my maximum speed when I finished.

I won a lot of races with that technique and, metaphorically, I still do.

Occam's Razor is a principle that suggests that the easiest course of action is usually also the best. I've long advised people in sales to stop going around the block to get next door. We tend to make sales too convoluted, too doctrinaire, too reliant on aphorisms and bromides. Run straight and true, and run through the tape. Don't let up until your goals are met.

In fact, this is a relationship business where our goal is to find the real buyer (the "economic buyer" in my lexicon) and form a trusting relationship. You can't sell successfully to lower-level people who can say "no" but can't say "yes." You can't expect others to market for you, lacking your knowledge and passion. Most of all, *you must have the mind-set that says, "I have tremendous value to pro-*

vide, and I'd be remiss if I didn't try to provide it for every appropriate buyer."

The finest salespeople I've ever seen never talk of quotas, or closing, or hit rates. They talk of client improvement, customer satisfaction, and dramatic results. They focus on the output of the value they bring to the table and on what's in it for their customers. When others are served well through your actions, then you will be served well, too.

Rather than acronyms and shortcuts, learn here how to initiate, innovate, and incite buyers to buy. Place yourself in the buyer's shoes and devise strategies to persuade and influence. Learn from the interviews with sales executives that are included.

What you're about to read is a prime example of taking the great, attributed ideas of many thought leaders—amongst whom the author kindly includes me—and focusing these keen insights specifically on the sales profession. What emerges from the bright light hitting this prism of focus is an entire spectrum of great sales ideas.

I invite you to enjoy and learn from the journey as this power lights your way.

Alan Weiss, Ph.D.
Author, *Million Dollar Consulting*

Acknowledgments

'd like to thank my wife, Amy, for putting up with me for almost two decades. I've dragged her around the planet, we've worked around the clock, and she's endured a work schedule that would bring most Spartan warriors to their knees. Amy, I promise we'll take a weekend off soon.

Next, I'd like to thank my brother in letters and draft editor, Michael (Mike) Popke. He is Joe Perry to my Steven Tyler. (Does this reference work for anyone other than Mike and me?) He gets first pass at just about everything I write and lets me know when I've veered off course, which is to say, frequently.

The racing fuel for this work was my mentor, Alan Weiss. His no-nonsense, no-excuses demeanor provided early direction for this project and was its catalyst.

This project would still be on my computer if it weren't for my terrific literary agent, John Willig. His experienced hand has guided me every step of the way. John Willig is simply one of the best in the business.

And the project might still be on John's computer if it weren't for the top-notch professionals at McGraw-Hill. Acquisition Editor Stephanie Frerich's enthusiasm for the project was fast and enduring; in addition, she gave me the space to work, and for that I am eternally grateful. Thanks to Developmental Editor Ron Martirano, whose fast pace, sense of humor, and affinity for sports perhaps rivals my own. Nancy Hall, Senior Project Editor, made certain every *t* was crossed and that we stayed on schedule. The marketing and publicity duo of Julia Baxter and Pamela Peterson—crucial to getting the word out—who are polite enough to listen to my out-of-the-box marketing ideas. And of course, to the McGraw-Hill sales team, I salute you.

I'd also like to thank those who contributed to the book. This list, no doubt, will not be all inclusive and is in no particular order: Duane Sparks, Ken Fisher, Martin Seligman, Linda Newsted, Bill Davidson, Tom Bradford, Simon Moss, John Carroll, Bill Corbett, Andy Green, Brian Knutson, David Goldman, Shmuel Ellis, Anne Ponzio-Shirley, Ken Bowman, Chris Cibbarelli, Robert Cialdini, Chuck West, Dave Gardner, Eric Dorobiala, John Early, Doug Albregts, Doug Girvin, Doug Slotkin, Patricia Haneman, John Duffy, Jim Zimmerman, Malia Potts, Michael Murphy, Matt Unertl, Mike Bushinski, Mark Rossi, Mike Tatoian, Gary Ramey, Pete Scholovich, Wayne Glowac, Greg Cooper, Julie Terberg, and the Ed Hernandez family.

I must include a special note of gratitude to our clients. Through wonderful reciprocal relationships we've grown together, laughed together, and hopefully made the world a bit brighter as a result of our partnerships. Thank you.

I'd like to thank our small but close-knit family. You helped propel this book forward; heaven knows I didn't want to let any of you down. I'd especially like to acknowledge my brother, Jack Rodgers, also a writer, who gave me encouragement throughout the writing process (*80,000 words, how hard can it be?*).

Finally and specifically, I'd like to thank my parents, Jack and Alise Rodgers. My dad gave me his work ethic and sense of humor, my mom her love of language and writing. All I am and have I owe to you.

Introduction

THE ART OF ACC*SELL*ERATION

May I help you?"

Invariably drawing a "no-thank-you-I'm-just-looking" response, this question is probably the worst opening line a retail salesperson could ever use. While not exactly an earth-shattering insight, here's a question for you: Heard it lately?

Of course, you have—and that's the problem. Far too many sales professionals are stuck in neutral, and it's not just at the retail level. Countless business-to-business sales teams also suffer from a dearth of sales skills. Product pitches, sales scripts, and ridiculous notions like "Always Be Closing" are just a few reasons why salespeople and their organizations are going nowhere fast.

Fast Facts

Here are some startling statistics that prove this book is desperately needed. According to research conducted by The Sales Board, Inc., which studied more than 16,000 customers and 300 salespeople in 25 industries:

» 86 percent of all salespeople ask the wrong questions and miss sales opportunities.
» 82 percent of all salespeople fail to differentiate themselves or their products from the competition.
» 62 percent of all salespeople fail to earn the right to ask for a commitment from the buyer.

But the most frightening statistic for every senior executive, sales manager, and shareholder should be this: 82 percent of salespeople rely on discounting the price to make the sale. That's right: Most salespeople have to give it away.

To top it all off, the Internet has generated an explosion of consumer-to-consumer education via chat rooms, forums, and blogs. These platforms create dynamics in which customers get smarter—and get smarter *faster*—than salespeople. Executive vice presidents, sales leaders, and salespeople are desperate to reverse this trend.

Accelerate the Sale will help, enabling you to create, discover, and internalize distinct sales skills and approaches—quickly giving you an edge in the marketplace. Appealing to senior sales executives, sales managers, sales team members, and aspiring sales professionals, this book will help anyone who relies on sales to succeed. Simply put, *Accelerate the Sale* will result in you selling more, faster.

Time and Profit Relationship

When selling anything, a successful salesperson needs to grasp one concept immediately: Wine and cheese may get better with age, but deals don't. (See Figure I.1.)

Here are a few reasons why time decreases success and profit in so many sales situations:

» The buyer reconsiders his or her decision to purchase.
» Price negotiation plays sellers off one another.
» The natural ebb and flow of emotions can diminish buyer enthusiasm.

■ FIGURE I.1
Time and Profit Relationship

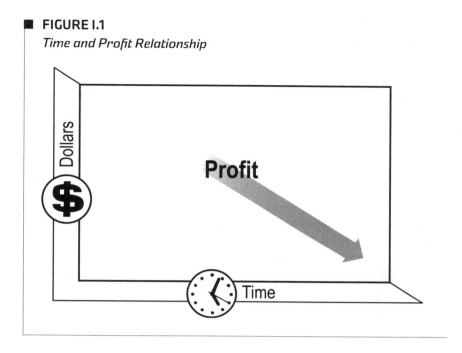

» Many products lose value over time.
» Inventory-carrying costs and interest on wholesale lines decrease profits.

Acc*sell*eration: Closing More Business, Faster

Acceleration may be Newton's second law of motion, but the art of acc*sell*eration—the act or process of closing more business, faster—is the first law of sales success. And with selling, it is an art form. There are guides, but no exact formulas. Ideas are presented, but left open to interpretation. So, get ready to be creative!

My definition of acc*sell*eration includes sharpening preparation, developing skills, and producing the mind-set necessary to operate in today's competitive sales landscape. This is a notion I will refer to frequently throughout the following pages; when I do, I use this unique spelling: acc*sell*eration. Keep an eye out for it; when you see it, you'll know that idea is of utmost importance.

In an attempt to enable you to go further, faster, I've also created "acc*sell*erators" at the end of each chapter. These are at-a-glance, priority takeaways; simply turn to the shortcuts to refresh, remind, and review.

In *Accelerate the Sale*, I will endeavor to provide practical, results-driven techniques. Some will be quick and simple, others more sophisticated. But all will be translated into pragmatic approaches. This is more important now than ever, because the traditional sales environment is rapidly changing.

I will, in most instances, present both a business-to-business (B2B) and a business-to-consumer (B2C) perspective. This is an attempt to broaden your view of the utility of these ideas and make them directly applicable to your specific situation.

The strategies and tactics presented in *Accelerate the Sale* will help with almost any sales exchange. Please keep in mind that some sales cycles are *extremely* long and can take six or nine months; others can take years. Certainly, ideas here can help in those unusually long sales cycles. Additionally, I also encourage you to read another terrific McGraw-Hill book, *The New Solution Selling: The Revolutionary Sales Process That is Changing the Way People Sell,* by Keith Eades.

In researching this book, I've endeavored to bring you diverse perspectives from successful sales practitioners in a wealth of industries: from motorcycles to marketing, forensics to firearms, computer technologists to consultants par excellence, from giants of academia to a giant of an alcoholic recovery mentor. These contributions are labeled as "Street Smarts" sidebars. (We had so many great contributions, in fact, that I've had to use the book's website to showcase them all!)

Accelerate the Sale also includes insights from prominent thought leaders such as Alan Weiss, Daniel Yankelovich, Martin Seligman, and Robert Cialdini, as well as references to "The Simpsons," Rush drummer Neil Peart, and my favorite Founding Father, Benjamin Franklin. Yes, I know. It's not your typical sales book.

As mentioned previously, bonus content is available at the book's website, www.AcceleratetheSale.com. Here, you'll find podcasts, videos, articles, and a forum to share your sales experiences. Think of it as an asylum for sales professionals.

Of course, there's no shortage of my own editorial comments. (I've been told I work in sarcasm the way Michelangelo worked with stone, and sometimes—just sometimes—I'm not exactly politically correct.)

Motors as Metaphor

Speaking of being politically incorrect, I know it's not PC to admit in 2011 that I *like* things that burn gas. But for me, nothing is as cool as the look and sound of a 1968 Chevy Camaro or a 1940s-era Harley-Davidson motorcycle.

There's just something about a finely tuned machine and the feeling it gives when you punch the gas or "twist the wick" (motorcycle-speak for rolling on the throttle). You feel the g-force as you're propelled down the road. It's almost the same feeling of exhilaration you experience when your buyer proclaims, "Yes!"

For the past 25 years, I've had the privilege of working with the Harley-Davidson Motor Company. After college, my sales career began in a Harley-Davidson dealership just outside of Philadelphia. I then moved to Milwaukee and spent years working for Harley-Davidson corporate. And for the last 14 years, I have operated a thriving consulting practice, of course, with the Motor Company as one of my favorite, long-term clients.

I've been engaged in almost every aspect of the sales profession—from helping dealership associates and managers improve their closing ratios to guiding phone reps through the handling of difficult customer-service situations, to assisting vice presidents of sales in creating and executing comprehensive sales-performance initiatives.

This has been an extraordinary experience. I've been able to hone and craft my sales skills, develop my distinct approaches with likeable and respectable people, and talk to individual customers about unbelievably cool products. It also has provided me with a different way of thinking about the world.

In one of the older Harley-Davidson buildings in Milwaukee, down a darkened hallway, an old Harley-Davidson V-Twin engine is on display. Some resourceful employee carefully removed portions of the various covers to reveal engine mechanics, and the model is used primarily for training dealership technicians and occasionally entertaining visiting consultants. With a flick of a switch, this cutaway comes to life at slow-motion speed. The pistons thrust up and down, the valves open and close in perfect time, and the crankshaft spins—enthralling all who see it. For me, watching that engine move in such orchestrated precision is both mesmerizing and clarifying, reminding me why motors are the perfect metaphor for business.

If that V-Twin model were a real, fire-breathing, fuel-burning motor, it would create that all-important force known as torque. Think of combustion as the sale, pushing the pistons and generating the force (or revenue) to power the rear wheel, which provides the propulsion to move you—and your company—toward your ultimate destination.

Some sales professionals—and some companies—just arrive there faster than others.

This book will help you reach the finish line first.

CHAPTER 1

The Checkered Flag

LESSONS FROM YOUR VICTORY LAP

'm going to see what the other guys have."

The customer, in his early 20s, had brought along his father for reinforcement. Dad didn't say anything. He didn't have to; his facial expression said it all: Don't mess with us.

If you've spent two minutes in the profession of selling, you've probably heard customers threaten to go somewhere else, to compare you with others, to see what else is available. This causes fear and panic in most salespeople, dejection and depression in others. But not in motorcycle sales manager Ken Fisher.

"Hang on one second," Fisher enjoined. "I have an idea."

He proceeded to the dealership locker room and changed out of his logoed staff shirt with nametag and into his street clothes—so he looked like any other person who might be running errands. When Fisher rejoined his stunned prospects back on the showroom floor, he announced, "I'll go with you."

"They looked at me like I was crazy," Fisher remembers. "I told them if the boy found a bike he wanted, who better to help him than a sales manager at a motorcycle dealership."

Fisher drove father and son down the street to the next motorcycle dealership. After five minutes in the store, no one had acknowledged them, so Fisher started to talk bikes using the *other* dealership's inventory. Ten minutes passed and still no one had acknowledged them. At the 15-minute mark, the son looked at Fisher. "Let's go back to your place," he said. "We want to buy from you."

Fisher didn't get frustrated. He didn't get angry. He used the natural flow of the sales exchange, more than a little creativity, and some chutzpah to win the business. He was confident he knew the product, secure in his relationship with his buyer, and, best of all, had no fear of failure. He had nothing to lose, so why not? He was unconventional and assertive while not aggressive.

What a great sales story.

Your Greatest Sale Ever

Think back to your greatest sales success.

What were the circumstances? Were you in your place of business or at your client's workplace? How did you comport yourself? What did you say, and how did you say it? In what manner did you represent yourself and your organization? What do you think ultimately compelled your customer to buy? And how did you ask for his or her business?

Maybe it was your first sale, or maybe it was your biggest. Perhaps it was the one for which you had to work the hardest or were forced to overcome the most daunting obstacles. Or maybe it even required a bit of serendipity.

Regardless of the circumstances, take a minute or two to jot down the following:

» What strategies and tactics did you employ?
» What were you feeling at the time you made the sale?
» What did you learn from the process?
» How did that sale compare to your other sales experiences?
» If there had been more money on the line, would you have handled the interaction in the same manner? What if there had been less money involved?

Whatever your specific sales success, chances are you're smiling right now, recalling that triumph. And you should be grinning. It's important to celebrate your achievements. (To listen to more great sales success stories, or perhaps even share your own, go to www .AcceleratetheSale.com, and click on "enhanced content.")

The problem is that most sales managers—in an honest attempt to improve their own skills and their organization's performance— focus almost exclusively on those sales situations in which they *weren't* successful. This follows conventional wisdom: When you make a mistake, scrutinize it and fix it.

Focus on Your Success, Not Just Your Failures

What if you concentrated your energies on those times you actually were successful? After all, that is the type of sales behavior that you're trying to understand and replicate. What if you reviewed both what you did well and what you could improve upon? And what if you did all that in the context of your successes, not your failures?

In 2005, Tel Aviv University professor Shmuel Ellis conducted a revealing study of after-action reviews with two companies of soldiers in the Israel Defense Forces. He demonstrated that soldiers performing successive navigation exercises learned at a significantly higher rate and improved their performance when they were debriefed on their failures *and* successes following each day of training. By comparison, soldiers who reviewed only their failed attempts did not perform as effectively. In a follow-up study in 2006, Ellis and his colleagues discovered that the group of soldiers who learned from their successes also developed richer "mental models," likely the reason for their increased performance improvement.

In a second study, Ellis similarly found that individuals who have experienced success also are more comfortable discussing their mistakes. Learning from mistakes after a successful experience is much more effective than learning from mistakes after a failed experience. People learn more from their mistakes if they feel psychologically safe.

In my work with thousands of salespeople over the past two decades, I've found Ellis's theories to be quite accurate. If you frame the examination of success and failure within the context of a winning sale, people are willing to speak more freely and probe more deeply, thereby discovering higher leverage and more meaningful revelations. ("I responded in this manner because I was afraid the customer would find out I didn't know more about the product," versus "I should have asked better questions.") But framed within the context of an *unsuccessful* sale, that examination will lead individuals to become defensive or create a revisionist view of what actually happened, neither of which is helpful.

Many times when I ask sales workshop participants to remember details of a glory sale, I see a roomful of smiles. Then, when I ask them to describe those success stories for others, their pride swells and the emotion rises in their voices as they recount the circumstances like a dramatic reading of "Casey at the Bat"—only this time with a happy ending. (For those of you unfamiliar with "Casey at the Bat," by Ernest Thayer, you should really look it up; it's a great poem.) They vividly describe the setting, everything from who was sitting where and to who was wearing what. They mention the objections the buyer raised and how brilliantly, confidently, and artfully they countered those objections—ultimately enabling the buyer to see things their way.

Perpetuating the Power of Closing

For most salespeople, successful selling creates an absolutely euphoric experience. It's that moment when the customer says, "Yes!"—the one word that drives so many of us to keep going in this demanding profession. Researchers of psychology and neuroscience believe this feel-good moment of goal attainment is facilitated by the secretion of the neurotransmitter dopamine. "Basically, dopamine brightens and highlights our connections with the world around us," says David Goldman, M.D., chief of the Lab of Neurogenetics at the National Institute of Alcohol Abuse and Alcoholism. "It's essential for associating something that happens with the feeling of pleasure."

STREET SMARTS

Choice and Commitment

Michael Murphy, Ph.D, is a former NCAA Division I wrestler who went on to earn his doctorate and is now sales director for Elanco, a global, innovation-driven company that develops and markets products to improve animal health and protein production. He considers himself committed to commitment. He recalls:

> I had a sales coach that talked about choice and commitment. Specifically, he said, we have a choice. We can decide if we want to make that extra call, or if we want to call on that client who wasn't very kind to us the time before. We have a choice. We can decide to do that or not, and that will affect our performance.
>
> The word *commitment*, I believe in it. I live the word *commitment*, because you're either committed to something, or you're not. There is no "kind of" committed. Choice and commitment are very important in my daily operations and in how I coach people.

Are you committed to your success?

In other words, dopamine chemically reinforces those behaviors that make us feel good. These are the moments of closing bliss that sales professionals seek again and again. And part of this positive cycle is looking forward to the next sale. (See Figure 1.1.)

Brian Knutson, assistant professor of psychology and neuroscience at Stanford University, theorizes that a significant component of happiness is looking forward to something. Using magnetic resonance imaging (MRI), Knutson studies the importance of anticipation.

Inspired by the classic work of Russian physiologist, psychologist, and physician Ivan Pavlov, Knutson replaced dogs with people and food with money. Test subjects received a small cash payoff

■ FIGURE 1.1

Perpetuating the Power of Closing

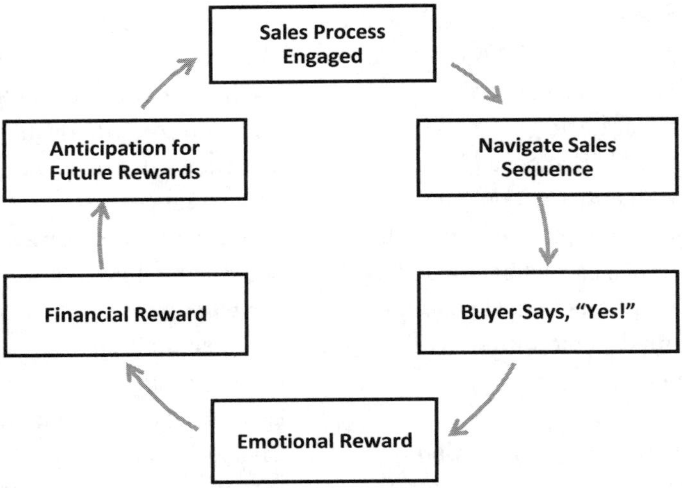

```
                    ┌─────────────────┐
                    │  Sales Process  │
                    │    Engaged      │
                    └─────────────────┘
      ┌─────────────────┐        ┌─────────────────┐
      │ Anticipation for│        │ Navigate Sales  │
      │ Future Rewards  │        │   Sequence      │
      └─────────────────┘        └─────────────────┘
      ┌─────────────────┐        ┌─────────────────┐
      │ Financial Reward│        │Buyer Says, "Yes!"│
      └─────────────────┘        └─────────────────┘
                    ┌─────────────────┐
                    │ Emotional Reward│
                    └─────────────────┘
```

if they won a video game. When Knutson's team of researchers looked at MRIs of the test subjects' brains just before they received the cash prize, they noted bursts of neurological activity, which indicated their anticipation of a reward. The bigger the prize, the bigger the burst. (Who says commissions don't work?)

According to Knutson, this increase in brain activity is associated with the happy feelings we experience due to the excitement of anticipation. Goldman reinforces this notion: "Research in the past decade has shown that *anticipation* [emphasis added] of reward is often the strongest releaser of dopamine in a key region of the brain known as the nucleus accumbens. Once a person learns to associate a certain stimulus with a pleasurable outcome when reexposed to the stimulus, they release dopamine and experience pleasure, as well as *craving* [emphasis added]."

Positively Addicting

Perhaps this is why, regardless of how tired we are or how numerous our other challenges, the elation of sales success reenergizes us. I've seen salespeople at the end of a 16-hour day who, hair sticking up and shirttail hanging out, receive a reaffirming "yes" from a buyer and immediately turn around and ask, "Who's next?" The rush is intoxicating and positively addictive.

I use the term *positively addictive* because in terms of the human condition, the pursuit of the pleasure principle is what makes you want to experience that moment of "yes" again and again. And guess what? There is not a single thing wrong with this kind of addiction—as long as you pursue deals legally, morally, and ethically (which I believe most sales professionals do). This is what makes our economy—and, some might say, our society—work.

Putting the "Bang" in Your Engine

Sales success is the combustion for your organization's engine. Without sales, there is no revenue. Without revenue, there is no cash flow to support capital investment, research, marketing initiatives, salaries, and a litany of other business expenses. (Yes, all this is common sense, but you'd be amazed by how many people outside of the sales department forget this chain.)

Your individual sales success also is the combustion that powers your personal life, providing the necessary income for you to pursue your chosen lifestyle. That's why becoming addicted to that sales rush can be seen as such a positive experience.

So here's a key question: How can you re-create sales success time and time again? The answer involves fully focusing on those things directly under your control. You can't control the economy, the weather, or the Federal Reserve. But you can make certain that you have the skills necessary to perform successfully when the moment presents itself. (I have little tolerance for so-called sales professionals who blame the economy for their lackluster performance when they're not even capable of responding to a simple price objection.) To acc*sell*erate your sales, you must make sure your engine is well tuned. You also may need to seek out new definitions of success.

Of course, the most important component of sales success is when a deal is closed and money is in the bank. But if you are truly going to improve your company, your profession, and yourself, you need to maximize all of the benefits of your sales exchanges. You need complete combustion. Or as racing enthusiasts might say, "You need a better burn."

To create the "bang" in an internal combustion engine, several factors must be in play. First, you need the right amount of fuel and the right amount of air, as well as proper compression and a well-timed spark to create the explosion that powers the engine. (Some engineers refer to this as "expansion," but "explosion" sounds cooler.) Your customers will bring the spark, and you bring the rest.

To really understand how to acc*sell*erate your sales engine, you also need to know how fuel-injection systems work. While I don't expect you to become a NASCAR racing technician, comprehending the basics of a system's mechanics will help tremendously.

The average person thinks that fuel injection enables better performance because it "injects" *more* fuel into the engine, but fuel injection actually injects the *perfect amount* of fuel into the combustion chamber. This, combined with other elements, is what leads to the most efficient combustion. Fuel injection won't make your engine rev at higher RPMs, but it will give you a better burn, maximizing the power available from each combustion event.

That's exactly what many salespeople need. They don't need to work harder or more hours; they need to simply maximize their existing sales. They need a better burn.

Putting Money in the Bank Isn't Good Enough

Yes, sales success is measured when a deal is done and the money is banked. But I suggest that if you want to maximize your return on effort (a new form of ROE, return on effort!), you must consider, explore, and communicate additional positive aspects of your buyer exchanges. I call these facets the "New Lessons for More Complete Sales Success"—guides that will enable you to carefully review your sales exchanges and identify successes that others may miss, thereby enabling you to further leverage, extend, and replicate your successes.

Ten New Lessons for More Complete Sales Success

To maximize your sales "burn," you must understand completely and be able to articulate for others the real value you deliver. The benefits of your sales efforts extend beyond money in the bank. The following list will help you identify additional forms of value inherent in your sales exchanges, and detail what you can do to maximize them for greater acc*sell*eration.

1. Cultivate Your Personal Reputation. Few things remain as important in selling as your credibility. Your positive personal reputation doesn't just happen; it requires your active management. When you're known as the person who keeps his promises, the one who finds out all the necessary details and delivers them, the professional who remains true to his word (even if the situation is no longer advantageous to you), you build your business and your career.

Do you call when you say you will? Do you acquire the information you promise? Are you able to bring information not previously known to the conversation? Pay fastidious attention to your buyers' requests and your responses to them, and watch your personal reputation soar. Given the current economic uncertainty, your ever-increasing positive reputation is what will earn you your second, third, and fourth sales transactions with the same customer. Your personal reputation communicates your consistent performance. Cultivate and keep it.

2. Harness Personal Energy. Few professions (commercial crab fishing, perhaps) require the kind of mental, physical, and emotional stamina that selling does. Commuting to your buyers' place of business, being enthusiastic *all the time*, and possessing the fortitude to survive inevitable ego shots require energy like nothing else. So you must harness all that available energy and put it to work for you. Here's how to break down your sales exchanges:

» Do you comport yourself well and make a positive impression on the buyer?
» Are you able to connect on both professional and personal levels?
» Do you use carefully crafted questions to make the buyer say something like this: "No one has ever really asked me that before. Give me a little time to consider it"?

As previously stated, once you've made a successful sale or reached a goal, your brain and your body undergo important neurological changes. But far too many salespeople start celebrating too soon. They're too quick to go for coffee or relive the exchange with anyone willing to listen.

Be cognizant of your small victories, sure, but then harness the energy they create. Practice what Stephen Covey calls "integrity in the moment of choice." Covey, most famous for writing *The 7 Habits of Highly Effective People*, states that there exists a moment between a person's response and his action in which that individual may choose the action.

When you've done something well, such as adhering to the examples above, don't use that energy boost to relive a small but important daily victory with colleagues over coffee. Instead, use that energy-filled moment to generate momentum for making one more phone call, sending one last e-mail, or visiting another prospective buyer. Don't waste that precious momentum.

3. Learn Something New by Asking Better Questions. One element of sales success is the notion of improving the state of your buyer. When your buyer learns something from you, thinks differently as a result of interacting with you, or acts differently as a result of spending time with you, you have improved his or her condition. When that person believes interacting with you is a positive thing, you suddenly become seriously valuable.

How do you do that? Often, the best way is to ask meaningful questions of your prospect and then listen—really listen—to the answers. This can give you deeper insight into how to best serve that customer with your sales offerings, and it also can teach you a thing or two about your industry—making you more informed now and in the future.

Ask probing questions like these:

» "I've seen a trend with other clients toward younger buyers. Are you experiencing the same pattern?"
» "Although revenues are increasing slightly with my other clients, what's really noteworthy is their increase in gross margin. Are you seeing this, too?"
» "What impact has the current economy had on your buying habits, or those of your customers?"
» "From your perspective, what are the two biggest trends currently happening in your business?"

A terrifically underutilized aspect of the sales profession is that if you pay attention, ask the right questions, and listen to the responses, you'll become incrementally better after each and every transaction. This sort of "snowball" improvement is exactly what you need in today's hard-nosed, competitive environment.

4. Create Lateral Connections. Another worthwhile consideration is to create lateral connections between your buyers and your prospective buyers. When you are working with someone in a B2B (business-to-business) situation (e.g., a marketing vice president or human resources director), how about exploring ways to work with that same organization's vice president of sales or customer service, the head of the call center, or even the general manager in charge of European operations? It's these sorts of lateral connections that can really pay off in terms of referral business.

In a B2C (business-to-consumer) conversation, these lateral connections typically are friends, family members, coworkers, financial planners, landscapers, and others. Even if you don't make the sale today, you gain a minor victory if you've obtained contact information for, were introduced to, or even were just told about a potential lateral connection.

5. Create New Methods of Customer Retention and Recovery.
It's been said that the phrase *customer retention* is the new "customer acquisition." Making this claim, I feel a bit like the fashion designer Isaac Mizrahi contending that silver is the new black. Nevertheless, examine your current sales exchanges, and find ways to retain clients and recover lost ones. In a B2B environment, this could include suggesting the use of employee surveys (and guiding management's understanding of the results), focus groups, and CEO roundtables. In a B2C environment, suggest that a client look into hiring personal shoppers, offering educational seminars, and providing a 24-hour customer-support service.

The idea for a new product, new service, or new program can be just the ticket for keeping current customers engaged and reaching out to new or inactive clients.

6. Burnish Organizational Repute. Every time you interact with a buyer on behalf of your organization, you educate that client about your company—and about you. Every phone call, every e-mail, and every conversation frames the way the outside world views your business.

Keep this in mind and endeavor to conduct yourself in a way that polishes your organization's "brand." Years ago, sales professionals believed that satisfied buyers told 2 people about their experiences, while unhappy customers aired their complaints to 10 others. Well, that was pretweet. Today, Twitter, Facebook, and countless bloggers allow dissatisfied customers to sound off to thousands (or tens of thousands) of people. Which is why taking steps to burnish your organization's repute is so important. Remember that every time you interact with the public, both professionally and personally, you really are representing your brand.

So, don't hesitate to revert back to the days of civility and decorum. Dress well, speak correctly, avoid clumsy etiquette, and understand that *please, thank you,* and well-placed compliments remain the lubricant of society's engine.

7. Identify Weaknesses in the Sales Offer. Another way to leverage your sales success is to use your moments of checkered-flag glory to identify weaknesses in your approach or your offering. Was

Can Salespeople Reinforce Your Brand?

Brand-building is Wayne Glowac's business. As CEO of Glowac + Harris, a marketing firm specializing in branding, he emphasizes the important role salespeople play in presenting their company's brand. In fact, "they are the brand, in many instances," Glowac says,

> Branding, in its holistic definition, is managing the feelings and expectations of all your stakeholders. The salespeople are the front line, and in some instances the only human that a customer or prospect will directly come in contact with. Because of that, they are living the brand everyday. It's vitally important that they understand the mission of the organization and merge that with their own personal mission and their customers' needs. When you can do all three, you'll achieve success beyond normal.

Doug Albregts also knows a thing or two about brands. As vice president of sales and marketing for Samsung Electronics America for the Enterprise Division, he opines,

> I think salespeople play an instrumental role in extending the brand to the market, as they must personify the company brand value in a way that reinforces the message and assures customers/partners alike that the company supports the brand promise. Brand statements should reflect a commitment on behalf of the company to the markets it serves. It's the sales organization's job to extend that credibility at a personal level on behalf of the company. I think this is something most companies overlook.

there something about your last offer that made it more attractive to some buyers than others? Buyers will let you know what they like and don't like, which makes it easier for you to examine how you present prices, product features, and delivery methods and times.

8. Create Ideas for Marketing Adjustments. An additional lesson to be learned from success results from an internal review of your marketing efforts. Are some components of your marketing more effective than others? Is your e-mail campaign more valuable than your print efforts? Are your e-mail subject lines provocative enough (but not *too* provocative!) to increase open rates? Are those buy-one-get-one-free offers compelling enough to stimulate purchases? Do people actually purchase products and services from your website? Or do they just go there for research purposes? (If you aren't already, become familiar with Google Analytics, an invaluable tool that tracks the number of page views on your website and the time spent on each page. You might not need a 30-second promotional video on your home page if visitors click away after seven seconds.) The point here is to query customers after the fact to find out what they found so irresistible.

Some people contend that sales and marketing are two completely different disciplines and should be treated as such. That's like saying you should be able to buy Oreos without the white stuff; it's just wrong. Sales and marketing must operate synergistically.

9. Identify Organizational and Communication Disconnects. Miscommunication or miscues related to ship dates, billing information, and other details beyond the actual sale should be addressed and fixed organizationally. After all, these are the things that most often aggravate customers. If harnessed correctly, salespeople can be one of the key elements offering continuous improvement in your organization.

Salespeople tend to blow a gasket when it comes to such mix-ups, especially when it involves valued, longtime clients. But here's the thing: Consider that mishap as the gift that it truly is. After all, this is an opportunity for you to make things right once and for all. More often than not, problems are addressed by taking adaptive action that rectifies the dilemma quickly. But steps to properly

STREET SMARTS

"Smarketing" Savvy

Gary Ramey, vice president of sales and marketing for Beretta U.S.A., the oldest manufacturer of firearms in the world (since 1526!), knows a thing or two about combining sales and marketing. In fact, he's even coined a term for it: *smarketing*. Ramey says,

> I think the difference between high-performing sales organizations and mediocre ones is the setting of goals and training of people. We see it fairly often, where people hire somebody's friend, bring them in, give them a price sheet, and tell them to go sell with a belief, a prayer, and hope that just by sheer will, they'll succeed.

Frankly, I believe the world has evolved to the point where salespeople who don't understand marketing aren't going to succeed. Sales *and* marketing really aren't two different departments. I think they're closely linked. If you have salespeople who don't understand marketing, you won't be successful. If you have marketing people who are developing things in a silo, you won't be successful. We try to make sure that everybody understands each other's challenges and works together.

Marketing attracts the buyer; a sale closes the deal. That's why I believe that sales professionals are perfect candidates to provide input about marketing direction and execution.

and permanently correct the problem are rarely taken. This is the automotive equivalent of continuously adding oil to a vehicle with a broken, oil-slurping gasket. Just fix the gasket!

10. Identify New Markets or Market Segments. Finally, review your sales successes and identify new markets or market segments to approach. If you've had success selling to retailers, how about adding wholesalers to the mix? Conversely, if you've been selling to wholesalers, consider retailers or suppliers. Then sit back and notice what you've accomplished. In addition to having money in the bank as a result of your successful sale, you and your organization now have the racing fuel necessary to perpetuate your success cycle. It's not enough to just get the sale in today's hyper-competitive market; you need a better burn.

In fact, it's worth examining these 10 lessons of sales success even when your exchanges *don't* result in money in the bank. You may not have made the sale, but at least you can learn something from the effort.

The winner of a NASCAR race is usually the driver with enough fuel or enough tread left on the tires to continue the race when others have pulled into the pit. If you enable yourself and your sales team to expand your definition of success by living these new lessons of sales success, you too might have enough fuel left to cross the finish line ahead of the competition more often.

Sales success is business acquisition. Identifying, replicating, and communicating these lessons will enable you to put more money in the bank, more often—thus acc*sell*erating your success.

CHAPTER 1 Acc*sell*erators

>> Reflect on your greatest sales success. What were the circumstances? What can you learn from your success? How can you replicate and augment your victory?

>> Learn something new by asking better questions: "With other clients, we've seen a trend toward younger buyers. Are you experiencing the same pattern?"

>> Creating lateral connections with existing buyers can often be the fastest way to garner more business.

>> Customer retention is the new acquisition. How can you keep more customers longer?

>> Every time you interact with your buyer, you educate him about your company, yourself, and how you do business. Use these opportunities to burnish your reputation.

CHAPTER 2

Fuel-Injection Connection

THE PARAMETERS FOR SALES SUCCESS

ave you tried the clutch?" I asked in a friendly tone.
Most Harley-Davidson dealerships encourage customers to sit on the motorcycles. That's the first step toward actually riding one. When astride the bike, they start pushing buttons, clicking switches, and squeezing levers, as they stare off into the distance and imagine themselves thundering down the road. It's obvious that's where this potential customer was heading.

"Have you tried the clutch?" I asked again.

Without saying a word, the customer began flailing away at the clutch lever.

"The clutch lever effort of this particular model has been reduced some 14 percent over the last several years," I informed him. "Harley-Davidson has achieved this improvement through a better throw-out ramp, a Teflon-coated clutch cable, and—this is amazing—a stiffer conduit that reduces the arc of the cable. These all combine to make the lever effort as easy as pushing a hot knife through butter."

"Wow!" The future rider stared at me in amazement. "I've never heard that before."

As a sales professional, I *live* for these kinds of moments.

"Well, that's just one of the reasons why people choose to do business with us!" I smiled sincerely and stuck out my hand to introduce myself, "Mark Rodgers."

The Art of Acc*sell*eration

This is an example of the notion of acc*sell*eration—blending talents, knowledge, and demonstrated skills all in a brief, simple, but extremely effective way. These are the parameters of sales success.

Any sales professional who conducts initial exchanges in a similar manner—regardless of the business—differentiates himself or herself from practically every other salesperson a prospective buyer has encountered. Note that in this example, I engaged the customer by asking if he had tried the clutch lever, then impressed him with some outside-the-brochure information and vivid descriptions. (Anyone can read the marketing materials; regurgitating them to prospects doesn't add value.)

When the customer expressed awe because he just learned something new, I exuded confidence—but not cockiness—by adding, "That's just one of the reasons why people choose to do business with us!"

Finally, the clincher: The official introduction, which usually always succeeds in capturing the potential buyer's name—a crucial step in any sales process. This example encapsulates how three dominant areas of sales skills—offering expertise, language skills, and process proficiency—work together to faithfully fulfill the sum of their parts.

I call this the "amazing fact" open. I use something interesting about the product or service to immediately engage the buyer. You may be thinking, *but what if he doesn't respond with "that's the greatest info ever?"* No problem, follow his or her lead. The other direction this "amazing fact" open can take is when the prospective buyer says, "It sure does look cool!"

"It sure does," I might reply. "What do *you* like about it?"

Immediately, it's obvious that this particular buyer isn't interested in the technical aspects of the motorcycle; he cares much more about the aesthetics—an observation that can prove to be a valuable one. But by asking the prospect another question, one geared away from the mechanics, the sales professional has turned the conversation toward what's most important: the buyer's perspective.

For me, this example crystallizes the competencies required for sales success. Talents are harnessed, knowledge is utilized, and skills are demonstrated. And it's an easy one to follow and adapt if you are in a B2C situation—selling cars, appliances, home-entertainment products, or motorcycles. But what happens if you work in a B2B environment?

Business-to-Business Applications

Let's say you're at a cocktail event with prospective buyers. Now, unlike in a Harley-Davidson dealership, social etiquette here dictates that you introduce yourself to others before mentioning anything about a clutch. (On second thought, don't even bring up the clutch.) Instead, find an appropriate time during the conversation to reveal an "amazing fact" about your company or your product: "Well, we have a bit of news. Our company just received the Stevie Award for customer service; it's like the Oscar of the sales business."

To which most people will say things like, "Congratulations!" or "Very cool." Or "Tell us more." If someone says that, tell them more: "We've joined the ranks of previous Stevie Award winners like McAfee, Toshiba, Office Depot, and Wachovia, and we achieved this through an almost-perfect customer-satisfaction index, one of the lowest customer churn rates in the industry, and a new client account hotline we call 'One and Done.' One call, and the customer's concerns are handled."

Of course, prospective buyers will probably respond with more affirmative comments, and you might say: "We're quite proud of this achievement. Clients tell us it is just one more reason why they choose to do business with us. But enough about us, what's going on with your company?"

At this point, what have you accomplished? You've shared good news about your organization and specifically and strategically positioned yourself with other brand-name winners. You've used language that differentiates yourself from the competition. And you've used your process skills to deftly turn the conversation toward the prospective buyer and encouraged that individual to talk about him- or herself and his or her business. Congratulations!

Building Your Engine for Success

In the last chapter, I suggested new ways for you to identify, evaluate, and amplify your sales success, thereby creating better sales "combustion." Now, let's develop the systems and skills that will enable you to create that combustion consistently and over the long haul. To illustrate, I want to return to the fuel-injection metaphor.

Building on your knowledge of combustion and fuel injection, let's turn our attention to "closed-loop" fuel-injection systems. These systems contain precombustion sensors that gauge everything from engine temperature to throttle position to ambient air temperature. Those readings are sent to an electronic control module, or ECM (in selling terms, think of it as an organization's sales manager), which determines how much fuel to inject into the combustion chamber. Then, postcombustion oxygen sensors measure the exhaust gases and report back to the ECM, which either confirms or corrects the fuel-air mixture. Essentially, a closed-loop fuel-injection system conducts a before/during/after performance analysis (Figure 2.1), which represents *exactly* the way your sales skills–development initiatives should work.

Your presales combustion sensors will provide you with a sense of what your buyer is thinking, what you're thinking (obviously), and your shared synchronicity of the buying and selling experience. (See Figure 2.2.) This gives you the information required to

■ FIGURE 2.1

Closed-Loop Fuel Injection

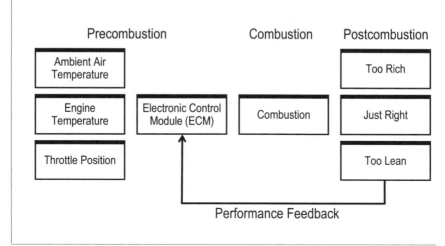

■ FIGURE 2.2

Fuel-Injection Connection

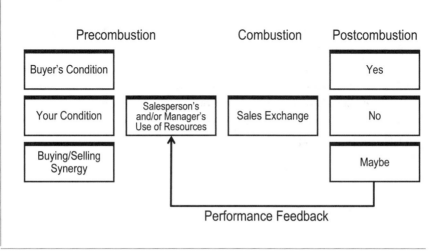

Be Bold, Not Belligerent

Some salespeople will demur when presented with selling suggestions like the ones suggested here. They'll say that they don't want to come across as cocky, arrogant, or braggy. (When people tell me they're uncomfortable talking about what's going on with them or their company, I can't help but think that they must not be very proud of what they are doing.) Is there risk involved with this approach? Sure. So, my suggestion is to be confident, not cocky, and assertive, stopping just shy of aggressive.

Besides, more buyers than you might think prefer to have someone steering them through the purchase process. Just as Lewis and Clark needed Sacagawea, like Sir Edmund Hillary needed Tenzing Norgay (OK, just as Bert needs Ernie), your buyers need a talented guide. That guide should be you.

Customers want to be aided in their purchase experience by someone who knows what he's talking about, someone who adds a perspective the buyer may not have considered, and someone who does so in a way that instills confidence. Your effective use of language and a self-assured demeanor assures your prospect that you're the right person for the job.

Just remember to be cognizant of your target audience, a given buyer's personality, and the culture in which you are operating. The publishing world is different from the construction industry, which is different from the software business. Additionally, be aware of regional and cultural differences. What's friendly conversation in Philadelphia could be perceived as overly aggressive in Fargo. What's considered a typical sales presentation in New Jersey might offend in Nebraska.

send the mixture into the sales combustion chamber. After you do that, measure the results, and then correct or confirm, as needed.

The biggest difference between the mechanical application of this model and the human one is feedback; more specifically, feedback quality and quantity. In the closed-loop fuel-injection system of a vehicle or motorcycle, the ECM receives thousands of inputs per second, with continuous monitoring of performance. (If only as sales professionals we had access to so much objective data on our efforts!) But we'll talk more about feedback later. Let's first turn our attentions to the mental models necessary for success.

Mental Models: A User's Guide

Mental models contribute to your effectiveness by helping organize thoughts about your experiences, but some models work better than others. The challenge is that the selling environment and the buyers who populate it are usually far more complicated than we can artificially establish on a double-axis chart. What follows is an attempt to help you better understand yourself and become a faster, more effective sales professional.

Try not to get too caught up in fitting all of the puzzle pieces together perfectly. That can be an exercise in futility—the mental equivalent of holding your motorcycle handlebars too tightly, which causes forearm fatigue and hand pain that makes you less responsive and your ride less enjoyable. Some of the suggestions that follow overlap intentionally. Use them as a general guide, without seeking perfect delineation between concepts, and I guarantee they will help you clarify and improve your condition. By "condition," I mean a combination of your innate talent, acquired knowledge, and skill execution. Your condition directly impacts your ability to succeed in a sales environment.

Three Realms of Success

I believe there are really three realms of sales success: innate talent, knowledge, and skills. Here's how I define each of these areas.

Innate Talent

Innate talent can be defined as "marked innate ability or an ability of superior quality." To me, that means possession of a highly functioning skill set in a given area: your inner drive to succeed, for example, or your ability to compartmentalize conflict. Now, this is not to say you can't cultivate a talent. Rather, I contend that at what level you perform is dependent on your natural predisposition toward that particular talent. Is the ability "hardwired" into your genetic code, or do you struggle mightily to become barely competent?

I'll refer to talents here as fairly fixed, meaning you might go from a −8 to a −5 on a performance scale. More than likely, you wouldn't go from a −10 to a +10 in a given area. For example, if you have precious little talent as a public speaker, you're probably not going to be able to completely reverse that and become a JFK-esque public speaker. Don't get me wrong: If you apply yourself, you can and will improve. You're just not predisposed to as high a level of competency in that area. (For proof, compare Michael Jordan's basketball career to his foray into baseball.)

If it helps, think of your innate talent as the engine and chassis. When you're considering performance modifications, you typically work within the framework of your vehicle. You rarely swap out the engine to improve performance, because it's fairly fixed—just like your innate talent. So you work with what you have.

Knowledge

Knowledge is considered to be the "state of knowing or understanding gained through experience or study." Although certainly able to be expanded or refocused, the definition is fairly firm. You possess, for example, a basis for understanding your market and your customers, but you still have the capacity to learn more or change your perspective. Knowledge differs from talent in that you can grasp your buyer's new strategic initiative more easily than you can change your own inherent ability to be resilient.

If your talent is the engine, then your knowledge is the cams, exhaust system, or high-performance electronic control module.

These components certainly can be swapped out, although it's not an everyday occurrence. After all, your exhaust system can be changed more easily than your chassis. But those components, like your knowledge, remain fairly firm.

Skills

Finally, *skills* can be defined as "proficiency acquired or developed through training or experience." I like to think of a skill as something that helps you obtain an objective by leveraging your innate talent and knowledge. Skills are fairly fluid. You can choose to use them or not—or change and adapt them—fairly quickly. For example, en route to your client's office, you might decide to alter your response to that potential buyer's anticipated objection based on a new piece of data or a new strategy. The competency continuum shown in Figure 2.3 displays a linear depiction of these three realms showing how each is more or less readily adaptable.

To round out the motor metaphor, think of your skills as the vehicle's driver. The driver uses the vehicle (engine and chassis) and the performance features (cams, exhaust system, and ECM) to reach an objective. Whether navigating around a racetrack or going to the grocery store, it's up to the driver's fairly fluid skills to determine how the vehicle is used.

■ **FIGURE 2.3**
Competency Continuum

Talent	Knowledge	Skills
Fairly Fixed	Fairly Firm	Fairly Fluid

Sales Success: Where Does It Come From?

Sales success really comes from the overlay and interplay of these important domains. The following overview for sales success is included to help you discover some of the larger components behind building your success. Although some of the finer points will no doubt be different from what some psychologists and scientist might argue, I have found this model to be very helpful in my understanding of sales success. (See Figure 2.4.)

Over the next several pages, I'll explore the fairly fixed, innate talents I believe are necessary for sales success. They include inner drive, communication abilities, action orientation, and resiliency.

Inner Drive

Exactly what talents are required to be successful in sales? The first one is an inner drive to succeed. Successful salespeople are a motivated bunch. I don't believe this is learned so much as it is an

■ **FIGURE 2.4**

Sales Success: Where Does It Come From?

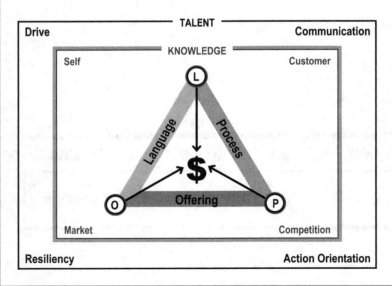

innate character trait. Psychologists like to refer to "achievement motivation" as a propulsion that makes us act out of a desire to show competence as it relates to others: "I'm better at this than you."

While not necessarily a malevolent trait, it's an inherent part of human nature to wonder how we compare with others in a given group. Despite the best efforts of the politically correct, self-esteem police in today's "everyone gets a trophy" society, people still want to know where they rank. If you pull aside the average eight-year-old at one of those "we don't keep score" soccer games and ask, "Who's winning?" he won't respond by saying, "Oh, we just play for fun." He'll say, "We are, 3 to 1."

The other side of the inner-drive coin is the desire to avoid showing incompetence toward others: "I don't want you to know I'm *not* good at something." This idea of being driven by the fear of failure (which by the way, often remains hidden because we're afraid of others knowing we're afraid) was addressed by Jerry Rice in his inspiring 2010 National Football League Hall of Fame induction speech.

"I'm here to tell you that the fear of failure is the engine that has driven me throughout my entire life," Rice revealed. "It flies in the faces of all these sports psychologists who say you have to let go of your fears to be successful, and that negative thoughts will diminish performance. But not wanting to disappoint my parents, and later my coaches, teammates, and fans, is what pushed me to be successful."

Rice seldom disappointed. Regarded by many pro football fans as one of the greatest to ever play the game, he ranks as the NFL's all-time leader in touchdowns scored (208), made 13 Pro Bowl appearances, and won three Super Bowls. Considering the success he's had, perhaps more of us should admit to being motivated by fear.

A third condition that psychologists suggest contributes to an inner drive is what's known as "mastery goals"—goals that remain focused on mastering a particular task. "I never tire of playing 'Tom Sawyer,' because it's difficult to play correctly," Neil Peart, the highly respected drummer for the veteran Canadian rock band Rush, said in the recent documentary *Rush: Beyond the Lighted Stage,* regarding one of the group's most-enduring hits. "And when I do, it makes me feel good."

This is an example of being driven by a mastery goal (and not just a fantastic song).

Communication Abilities

"How much of our ability to produce and comprehend language is genetically programmed, and how much is acquired environmentally?" This is one of the questions explored by Malia Knezek of Duke University. As Knezek pointed out in her 1997 online article, "Nature vs. Nurture: The Miracle of Language," language cannot be completely genetic. But there are some aspects of an individual's genetic makeup that help explain how language works and how it does not.

Citing the works of Howard Gardner, Stephen Jay Gould, and Noam Chomsky—"thought leaders" in their respective fields—Knezek does an exceptional job of outlining the issues of whether our use and understanding of language, at some level, may be innate (which is, of course, the heart of the nature vs. nurture discussion; are we born with some ability, or is it developed?). She refers to Gardner's work in *Frames of Mind: The Theory of Multiple Intelligences*, which also perfectly serves our discussion, because Gardner lists four uses for language:

1. to induce action in other people
2. as a memory aid
3. to transfer explanations or knowledge to another person
4. in metalinguistics, the study of language and its relationship to culture and society

To a sales professional, all of the above purposes of language are crucial. Inducing people to action is the primary objective of a salesperson. Using language as a memory aid keeps our sales offer front-of-mind with prospective buyers. Explaining and transferring knowledge is crucial to creating a valuable, successful sales organization, and metalinguistics allows sellers to reflect on sales exchanges and improve the way in which language is used to engage the buyer.

Knezek, to quote from her paper's title, states that language ulti-mately is a savvy blend of nature and nurture, which is why you will find language a recurring theme in this book.

Action Orientation

In his concise overview of psychological literature, Simon Moss, Ph.D., of Monash University in Australia, describes action orien-tation as the capacity to regulate emotions, thoughts, and behav-iors to fulfill an individual's intentions. This capacity is crucial to sales success. Your ability to compartmentalize personal conflict, workplace disagreements, and other distractions of postmodern life to focus solely on the tasks at hand (such as prospecting, sales calls, and territory management) is vital to keeping your career in gear.

Moss also hints at the innate characteristics of action orienta-tion when he states that "action orientation generally refers to the capacity of some individuals to regulate their emotions effortlessly, rapidly, automatically, and perhaps unconsciously. Accordingly, individuals with an action orientation seem to show more flexibility with the approaches they invoke, to accommodate the unique objec-tives and constraints of any context."

Does this mean that a person can never improve their action ori-entation? Certainly not.

As with other talents previously discussed, action orientation can be improved. When I sought permission to use Moss's work, he added: "Action orientation, although partly influenced by some innate factors or early childhood, can be developed over time, usu-ally by embracing challenging contexts."

Resiliency

Finally, perhaps one of the most important innate talents is the abil-ity of a sales professional to be resilient, to bounce back from nega-tive situations. Some might call it "persistence"; I prefer resiliency.

The sales profession is fraught with discouragement. At any stage of the sales process, a potential buyer can—and often does—blurt out, "No!" The reasons for the objection may have absolutely nothing to do with the salesperson, but rather are a result of pricing pressures, internal changes within the buyer's organization, or simply the ever-shifting landscape of business priorities. But the ability to bounce back rests squarely on the sales professional.

That said, is resiliency innate? Much like other innate talents, I believe it is fairly fixed, meaning we probably have some sort of natural predisposition to be either positive or negative. The most powerful salespeople typically are the ones hardcoded to think positively. And at the same time, the good news is that certain aspects of resiliency can and should be learned.

In his groundbreaking work, Martin Seligman, Ph.D., author of several articles and books, explores the topic of optimism. His *Learned Optimism: How to Change Your Mind and Your Life*, originally published in 1991, in my opinion, should be required reading for every sales professional.

Seligman initially concentrated his efforts on the habits of explanation, or how people explain what most frequently happens to them. Those who were pessimistic (and less resilient) when facing setbacks would blame themselves and might say something along the lines of: "I'm the reason this sale failed."

Optimists, on the other hand, being very predisposed to resiliency, would blame the circumstances and then move on to the next challenge, perhaps saying: "The buyer was in a bad mood, and there's nothing I can do about that."

Seligman noted that optimism won't change what a salesperson says to the prospective buyer; rather it will change what the salesperson says to himself after a negative exchange. Instead of telling himself, "I'm no good," he might rationalize that "the client was too busy to fully consider my offer."

In *Learned Optimism*, Seligman explores this perspective. What did he find out? In one series of studies, optimists outsold pessimists by 8 percent in the first year and by 31 percent in the second. And in another set of studies, they outsold the pessimists in one group by 21 percent during the first year, and by 57 percent in the second year! As an aside, this second group was special because they were initially people who did not pass the organization's "fitment" tests. Optimism matters, because it produces resilience, which in turn produces more sales.

The reason I included resiliency as an innate talent is because it is fundamental to sales success, and some people naturally are predisposed to it in greater degrees than others. But like other innate talents such as inner drive, communication, and action orientation, resiliency is fairly fixed. And that means improvement is possible.

Not only did Seligman discover that inherent optimism can be measured and linked to career success, he also determined that it is possible for people to obtain optimism over time, ultimately gaining better control of their lives.

STREET SMARTS

Fuel for Success

Doug Slotkin is the inside sales vice president for Zillow.com, a successful real-estate information website. There, you can find listings, agents, and just about anything you want to know about the process of buying or selling property. Slotkin, an insightful sales professional with more than 20 years of selling experience, has spent the past several years building an inside sales force at Zillow.com from the ground up. This talented group of 73 reps and 7 managers reports to Slotkin and sells advertising space to real-estate agents across the country. And they're good at it. Slotkin explains why:

The best indicator as to whether somebody's going to have success on my team is if they have energy. Do they have energy when I initially screen them on the phone and interview them? Do they have energy when they come in and meet with us? Because if they don't have incredible energy selling themselves—the thing they know the most about—how are they going to have incredible energy on the phone, selling something that they don't know as much about?

So, I'm looking for energy, first and foremost. I can teach a lot of other stuff, but if they don't have energy, it's a nonstarter.

31

The question remains: Does sales success make you optimistic, or does optimism make you a successful salesperson? Well, our innate talents overlap and operate in tandem with one another, not separately. So, the only way to answer this question is with a simple but powerful "Yes."

Your talents are diverse and interrelated, and your inner drive for success is connected to your action orientation: "I must not let others know that I'm incompetent at cold-calling, so I'll squelch my emotions and improve." Your ability to communicate depends on your ability to be resilient, and your ability to speak with others about your sales exchanges (meta-talk) enables you to see how circumstances (not you) led to failure. And so it goes, in a constant loop of nearly constant combinations.

Might you choose other talents to include in a sales success model? Sure, but in my opinion, the four we've discussed—inner drive, communication, action orientation, and resiliency—will acc-*sell*erate your sales like no others.

Once you are aware of and acknowledge your innate talents, you can move to traits that are less inherent—namely, knowledge. In the next section, we will focus on four dominant types of knowledge: know yourself, know your buyer, know your market, and know your competition.

The Four "Knows"

This section covers the fairly firm areas of knowledge required for sales success. They are the classic four "knows": know yourself, know your buyer, know your market, and know your competition.

Know Yourself

We've explored in previous sections of this chapter the significance of talents and abilities. Now it's time for a bit more reflection. When you really understand yourself—your purpose, your goals, your strengths and weaknesses—you will discover some previously unarticulated advantages. To get started, ask yourself these questions:

» **Who are you?** Not in the existential sense, but are you aware of your innate talents and preferences? And most importantly, how can you use those to benefit others and, ultimately, yourself?

» **What resources can you offer?** And do you clearly understand the resources—be they physical, professional, social, or personal—at your disposal?

» **When and where do you perform at your best?** In one-on-one situations? In front of large groups? At your office? Out in the field? On the phone? Or behind text messages and e-mails?

» **Why do you do what you do?** Are you aware of what you truly value in your life and in your career, and does your daily behavior reflect that? For most of us, doing something other than what we truly value causes stress and angst.

» **How do you strive to achieve your objectives?** Do you know your own communication style? Are you aware of the critical path you must travel to attain your goals?

» **At what age in life do you plan to have accomplished your personal and professional goals?**

Know Your Buyer

After getting to know yourself, the second-most-important person you need to know is your buyer, the one who has the power to purchase what you are selling. Whether that's because he or she is the one who can authorize funding, approve the purchase order, or swipe the credit card, this is the person on whom you need to fully focus. Here's how:

» **Identify who can buy what you're selling.** Can you describe and group them demographically—by race, gender, income, education, home ownership, employment status, physical location, and even travel distances?

» **Know what interests your buyers.** What are their activities? What do they value? Can you describe them psychographically—their personality traits and their attitudes, for example?

» **Recognize where and how you can reach buyers.** Can you connect with them via trade associations, community events, or certain media outlets? What sort of places do they frequent, and why?

» **Realize when your potential buyers exhibit particular behaviors.** Are they influenced by the changing seasons, for example, or by something else?

» **Understand why buyers buy.** Are your buyers driven primarily by price? Value? Creative problem solving? Can you identify specific, idiosyncratic buying triggers?

» **Know how your buyers buy.** Is the decision to purchase made individually? By committee? By RFP (request for proposal)? By fiscal year? Is it based strictly on need? Are there influencers with no authority but plenty of sway?

Know Your Market

Americans are frequently accused of being an insular group. We don't, it is claimed, know what's going on in the world around us as much as we should. There may be a regrettable amount of truth to that. With some people, unfortunately, that insularity carries over to their professional lives. Face it: Many people know what's going on in their company, but not all of our colleagues know a heck of a lot about the industry in which they sell. Change that by knowing the answers to the following questions:

» **Who are the primary players that make up your market?** How many companies are involved? What are their dollar volumes? Their profit numbers? Their specific niche? And how does that niche differ from others?

» **What are the current trends in your market?** Is the market in a period of growth? Decline? Stagnation? Is there an influx of new ideas and people? Or is talent leaving?

» **When do buyers in this market typically make their purchasing decisions?** Is it during a business cycle? A specific time of year? The fiscal calendar? Are there other timing considerations, such as tax and holiday seasons?

» **Why are the players positioned in the market as they are?** Is it because of specific product superiority? Savvy marketing efforts? A competitive differential?

» **How does your market organize itself?** Are trade associations active? Do factions exist within those trade associations? Are there other marketplace leaders? Is the market fractious and loosely organized, or is it tight-knit?

Know Your Competition

Creating a strategic profile for each of your competitors can help you better acknowledge your inimitable superiority in the marketplace. I'm not suggesting that you spend an inordinate amount of time worrying about the so-called other guy, but taking a little time to think about your buyers' other options can help you formulate an even more effective strategy. When doing so, consider these questions:

» **Who are your existing competitors?** How are they perceived by your shared buyers? What are their strengths and weaknesses? And who might be your future competitors?

» **What drives a particular competitor?** Do you know, or can you speculate on, that competitor's long- and short-term business objectives? What is that competitor's greatest cash cow?

» **When did your competitors enter the market?** What was their last major move, and when was it made? When do you anticipate more such moves?

» **Why do your competitors behave as they do?** Why do they target specific buyers?

» **How are your competitors organized, and how do they market themselves?** What incentives are their employees offered? How have they reacted to past industry trends, and how might they respond to new ones? How might they retaliate against your initiatives?

The next section covers the fairly fluid areas of sales skills. The three dominant areas of sales skills needed for success are offering expertise, language skills, and process proficiency.

Skill Acquisition and Execution

Earlier in this chapter, we identified skills as "proficiency acquired or developed through training or experience." I also added another dimension to the definition, suggesting that your skills help you reach your objectives.

Three dominant skill areas are required for sales success. First among them is offering expertise, often called product knowledge. I prefer use of the term *offer*, because it encompasses more—including products, services, and even such specifics as company history and reputation. The other two major skill areas are language and process proficiency. As you master each of these disciplines, you will tap into previously undiscovered sales potential.

Offering Expertise

First and foremost, you must know what you're talking about. Sounds like common sense, right? Your offering expertise is the codification and communication of what you're selling. Where does that product or service fit in the marketplace? What are the forms and functions of that product or service? And what do you need to know about its cost, financing options, and delivery methods?

This is what I mean by offering knowledge. This is all about understanding the needs of your buyers in your specific business segment and establishing your inimitable superiority in the marketplace. (Don't worry if you have yet to achieve inimitable marketplace superiority; I'm going to help you do just that!)

Language Skills

Also crucial are superior language skills. The words you use and the phrases you choose will have a huge impact on your success, for better or for worse. Language affects both a listener's conscious and unconscious impressions of the individual speaking, which is why the success or failure of a potential sale depends on your ability to match the language style of your prospect.

Process Proficiency

Finally, you must possess a firm grasp of your own sales process. Always know what's next. Many salespeople erroneously believe that there is some singular "big moment" that occurs in the midst of every selling situation that leads to their success. But really, what we call success is a series of small agreements reached throughout the process that propels you to "yes" with the greatest speed: "Yes, I'll take your call." "Yes, we can get together." "Yes, I'll share our priorities." You need to be aware of what the next "yes" will be, and you must understand the development and deployment of effective sequences. This skill set pertains to all aspects of business, including acquisition, managing buyer relationships, and referrals.

Accsellerate by Getting More— and Better—Feedback

Now let's revisit the topic of feedback and how you can improve these things we've covered. Performance feedback can come via three different ways: (1) your assessment of your own performance; (2) your manager's assessment of your performance; or (3) your buyer's assessment of your performance.

Unfortunately, most people receive feedback in a haphazard and disjointed manner, meaning they wait for someone to provide it. This raises many issues, as you'll soon see. For the moment, concentrate on new strategies for soliciting feedback.

Joseph Luft and Harry Ingham obviously were on to something when they created the now-renowned Johari Window while researching group dynamics at UCLA back in 1955. The often-cited four-quadrant model has stood the test of time as a way to delve deeper into understanding what you and others know (and think) about you. (See Figure 2.5.)

Here are the four quadrants:

1. What is known to you and to others about yourself
2. What is unknown to you about you, but known to others
3. What is known to you about you, but unknown to others
4. What is unknown to you or others

Sales professionals can generate plenty of analysis with this model. But for right now, if you really want to get there fast, focus

■ FIGURE 2.5

Johari Window

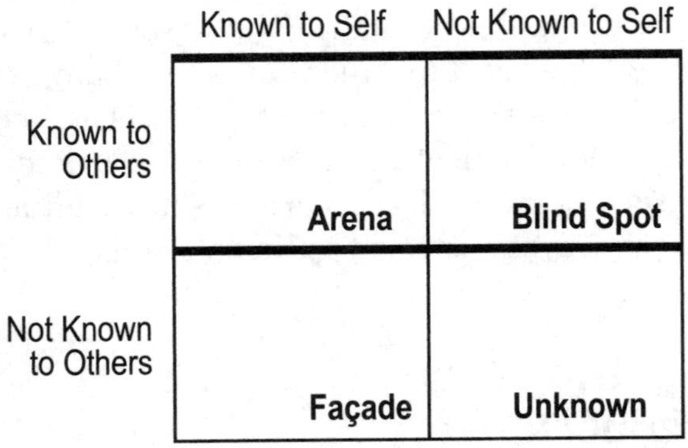

	Known to Self	Not Known to Self
Known to Others	**Arena**	**Blind Spot**
Not Known to Others	**Façade**	**Unknown**

on discovering what is unknown to you about you but known to others. The best way to do that is through feedback filters.

Filter Your Feedback

As mentioned earlier, the major difference between a mechanical, closed-loop fuel-injection system and your human system is really one of meaningful, frequent, and objective feedback. In the mechanical system, the feedback is predictable in its frequency. With humans, it's much more complex. As the adage goes: Machines are neat, people are messy.

It is incredibly difficult to obtain and leverage feedback because most of us simply don't receive it well. By that, I mean we get defensive if feedback is negative—or we do not take any action at all. The key is to determine and understand what is meaningful and what isn't. I make no claims at being an expert on this (for myself, let alone for you!), but I can confidently state that I've gotten better at it over the years. To help yourself, consider creating the following feedback filters:

» **Feedback filter 1: People you don't know.** I give feedback from this group little credence; many psychologists say the feedback people in this group provide really is meant for their own benefit, not yours.
» **Feedback filter 2: Coworkers.** You work with them, and they may seem like friends. But, again, I rarely give much weight to feedback from coworkers. There are too many competitive pressures and workplace dynamics to create much value.
» **Feedback filter 3: Family and friends.** This is an important group. Although they don't always see things through the same lens as you do, these people presumably (barring dysfunction) are the most important people in the world to you and have your best interests at heart.
» **Feedback filter 4: Trusted advisors.** Individuals you respect for their accomplishments, and who you truly believe have no agenda, are the ones who have your best interests at heart. This will be your most valuable group to cultivate and from which to seek feedback.

Now, let's look at the basic building blocks of sales success.

In this chapter, we've covered the parameters for success by understanding the closed-loop fuel-injection analogy, exploring innate talents, reviewing acquired knowledge, and developing skills execution. At its essence, this chapter attempted to answer the age-old question: Are great salespeople born or made?

The answer: They're made, and with some really strong building materials.

STREET SMARTS

Two Biggest Mistakes

Pete Scholovich, principal of the Retail Ready Group, has worked with Iomega and Office Depot. One of his favorite claims to fame is placing at least nine SKUs in Wal-Mart's cellular phone and mp3 technology accessories areas; some of those items were still on shelves after three years, an impressive track record in technology retailing. Scholovich says he often sees salespeople make two major mistakes:

They fail to really map out a plan prior to going in and actually making a presentation or a call. It's the old adage about aim, ready, fire. Plan the work, and work the plan. If you establish an order of events that have to take place, and set a goal at the end of that order of events, you're in a much better place to be successful as a salesperson in any field.

The second biggest mistake is not having some thick skin and taking things personally. It's very easy for salespeople, if they're really passionate about what they do, to let things get under their skin. It is a business transaction. Not everybody's going to love you; not everybody's going to hate you. You try to put your best foot forward and to demonstrate competence, credibility, and positive intent in the selling situation. Do the best you can, and go from there.

CHAPTER 2 Acc*sell*erators

» When you can get your buyers engaged, either experientially or figuratively, you're creating acc*sell*eration—a blending of your unique skills, abilities, and talents that speeds you further along in the sales process.

» Similar to how closed-loop fuel-injection systems work, sales skills are acquired by taking precombustion measures (your skills, your buyer's attitude, and synchronization of your selling process with his or her buying process), engaging in a combustion event (the sales exchange), and then obtaining feedback. Monitor and adjust.

» The inner drive to succeed is fundamental to sales success and is comprised of three areas: (1) the need to show competency relative to others: "I'm better than you," (2) the fear of revealing incompetence: "I don't want you to know I'm not good at this," and (3) the desire for self-mastery: "It's hard, I did it, and that makes me happy with myself."

» The capacity to regulate emotions and behaviors to fulfill intentions is known as "action orientation." Terrific salespeople have this in spades.

» Resiliency is perhaps the most important talent. How do you explain what happens to you, positively or negatively? Optimism matters, because it produces resiliency, which in turn produces sales.

CHAPTER 3

Crawling Under the Hood

REALLY UNDERSTANDING YOUR OFFERING

n a city that will remain nameless, at a Harley-Davidson dealership that also will remain nameless, a salesperson who (surprise!) will remain nameless made a feeble attempt to greet a prospective customer: "May I help you?" he squeaked.

"Sure," I replied. "Where are your V-Rod motorcycles?"

"Over there," he said and pointed to a dark corner of the store that looked like it hadn't seen customer traffic since Ronald Reagan was in office.

"What do you know about them?" I prodded.

"Not much," he said quickly. His attitude was probably part of why these gorgeous machines were relegated to some less-than-stellar square footage. He added condescendingly, "I don't think they're very good."

Not very good?! I almost lost my *mind*!

A liquid-cooled Harley-Davidson V-Rod motorcycle may not be everyone's cup of espresso (it gravitates away a bit from the classic 45-degree, air-cooled configuration), but let's not kid ourselves. This motorcycle boasts a hydro-molded frame, which reduces the number of welds required, which substantially increases the frame's rigidity—a crucial consideration that radically improves a motorcycle's ability to corner aggressively. It also makes for a nicer-looking frame that (as far as I know) is only found on certain models of Aston-Martin cars, Chevrolet Corvettes, and Ford F-150 trucks. Furthermore, the V-Rod's liquid-cooled 120-horsepower Revolution engine, designed in close collaboration with Porsche (but not *by* Porsche), seems to be a favorite of Formula One racing hero Michael Shumacher, who owns *eight* of these motorcycles! It goes fast and stops fast with Brembo 4-piston front brake calipers. The bike also boasts 43-mm inverted front forks, lowering the unsprung weight, which helps keep more tire contact with the road (not an unimportant detail). And I'm really just getting warmed up here!

For a salesperson to say this motorcycle is "not that good" is exactly what should be keeping CEOs, CMOs, and sales executives tossing and turning at night. Imagine the research, engineering, and marketing dollars spent—only to have the final three yards to a sale be blocked by a salesperson's ignorance and indifference. (By pulling out the motorcycle, showing off the exquisite design, and relating some of the engineering behind this marvel of modern motorcycling, I was able to convince the wayward salesperson to change his thinking!)

Knowing something about what you sell is a bedrock skill in today's selling environment. With the preponderance of information available from countless media sources, salespeople need to be more diligent than ever in their pursuit of offering expertise. "Don't just spew facts," proclaims one sales book. "Features and benefits presentations are dead!" reports another doom-and-gloom expert.

OK, that's fine. I certainly understand and appreciate the marketing-based need to appear contrarian and cutting edge. At the same time, however, I'd like to watch you try to interact with a prospective buyer *without* referring to facts, features, and benefits. As it goes with many endeavors, the key is in how you *use* those facts, features, and benefits. Little Leaguers, for example, may throw the exact same size and weight of baseball as that used in the Major Leagues, but few of them possess a Sandy Koufax curveball. How are you and your sales team throwing the ball?

The Three Most Important Product Questions

Whether you're selling tangible or intangible items, buyers are typically interested in how their condition will be improved as a result of acquiring what you are selling. The cliché is that no one buys a drill because she wants a drill; she buys a drill because she wants a hole. Similarly, no one buys a Harley-Davidson motorcycle because he is looking for a means of convenient transportation; he's usually making some sort of personal statement (or perhaps looking for a date). And no organization is buying your company's consulting services because you use the Herzberg model of organizational hygiene; they hire you because they want to attract and retain talent. In order for buyers to understand why they're buying an item or service, you first need to know why you're selling it.

Here are three questions to ask yourself to help you better understand your offering, be it a product, service, or brand:

1. What do you have, do, or offer?
2. How does it work?
3. How is the buyer's condition improved as a result?

Most products and services can be analyzed by reviewing the model shown in Table 3.1.

You can explore your offering two ways—from macro- and microviewpoints—examining its fit, form, function, and financial components. Some of these components may be more robust than others, given the nature of what you sell, and some components might overlap. In both cases, that's fine. The idea is to create a method for which you can more completely understand your offering.

Don't get too hung up on specificity, either, by trying to determine an exact delineation between macro and micro. Just start working through each component of your offering, and you'll

■ TABLE 3.1

Offering Constructs

	Fit (Marketplace)	Form	Function	Financial
Macroaspects (Broad Strokes)	History Brand Market Share Recognition Contributions	Style Culture Gestalt	Components	Price Payment Terms
Microaspects (Detailed Analysis)	Good Better Best	Design Visual Appeal Qualitative Ownership Aspects	Specifications	Nuances Specifics Promotions

quickly discover what you know and don't know about what you are selling.

These component categories are designed to help you and others in your organization think more deeply about what you do. This might be a challenge for some people, which is actually a good indication that they are thinking about things differently than they have in the past. Most salespeople never endure this sort of intellectual heavy lifting. If you and your staff do, however, you will come to know your offerings more completely than your competitors know theirs. And it won't be too long before your sales numbers reflect that.

What Do You Have, Do, or Offer?

When considering what you have, do, or offer, ask yourself, *How can I analyze things from the broadest perspective possible?* Then you can break everything down into microdetails and look at even the smallest components of your offering to identify compelling aspects.

Where Do You Fit? To get to that point, begin with evaluating where your offering fits within the marketplace. From a macro-perspective, does your company have the benefit of 150 years of existence, or is it fresh and new? As a result of that history, does your offering have a strong brand or a developing one? Does the mere mention of your company or product connote an expectation of quality, or does it conjure something else? Are you the market leader, or are you leapfrogging your way up? Has your offering received some sort of third-party recognition? Have you won an award or received positive media attention? Has your organization been recognized by others for its contributions to your field, discipline, or community?

If one of your macroperspectives here is market share, the microperspective might be consideration of your performance within a particular market segment. For example, Apple keeps an incredibly close eye on where its iPhone ranks in the smartphone category. You may even want to think about this in terms of how you would rank your own specific offerings. Are they the good, better, or best of what is available in the market? Is your offering the Les Paul Studio, Les Paul Standard, or Les Paul Custom? You get the point.

What Form Does Your Offering Take? Another category to explore is the form of what you sell. Think both style and design. What type of product do you sell? Is the furniture you sell categorized as Mission style? Is your insurance coverage all-inclusive? Is your consulting style collaborative? Does your offering boast individuality by possessing a combination of distinctive features?

You also could apply these concepts to organizations by exploring the culture or gestalt of a given group. What are the predominant attitudes and behaviors of your team? How do you collectively accomplish things? What do you value? What is your focus? Is your company more like Google or IBM? Goldman Sachs or Zappos?

Microperspectives on your offering's form might include insights about your product's design. Has it been structured for aesthetics, function, or both? For example, Harley-Davidson motorcycles typically have an exhaust crossover hidden neatly behind the exhaust pipes. This exposes the gorgeous V-Twin engine *and* aids in the evacuation of exhaust gases that is crucial to maximizing performance. What aspects of your offering might benefit both form and function?

Intangible microperspectives could be feelings induced by owning or participating in your offering. While some sales authorities consider this the "softer" side of the selling business, I think they also are significant and speak highly to the power of your brand. As a client, how might it feel to acquire McKinsey & Company to help you develop a bold new business strategy? How does it feel to own a Harley-Davidson? How do you like being in good hands with Allstate?

***How Does Your Offering* Function?** When most salespeople try to better understand their product or service, they think about how it functions and what it accomplishes for the end user. Go further; break down each element as completely as possible. When considering a Harley-Davidson motorcycle, for example, you should include the engine, fuel-injection system, exhaust, transmission, drive system, wheels and tires, brakes, frame, paint, and controls and instruments. But there are subsets to each of these elements, too: the bore of the cylinders, the stroke of the pistons, and the compression ratio—all of which add layers of specificity.

And we haven't even gotten to the microperspective yet. Can you identify component specifics? To wit: the Harley-Davidson Super Glide motorcycle has a 96-cubic-inch, 45-degree, air-cooled V-Twin with a bore and stroke of 3.75 in./4.38 and a compression ratio of 9.2:1. Now, that's pretty specific. It's also a very impressive representation of the offering.

For intangible offerings (such as consulting services), consider whether you provide strategic direction, conduct employee focus groups, design performance evaluations, deliver training sessions, execute personality testing, study technology needs, or create customer satisfaction scores. These are all valuable inputs.

Let's say you're a consulting firm using the ubiquitous DISC survey (one of the most commonly used personality surveys) to provide workforce personality assessments. The DISC model of personality profile testing includes a 25-question survey boasting

A Fast Route to Expertise: Google Alerts

I f you don't know what a Google Alert is, conduct a (what else?) Google search for the term. You will be taken to a Web page that will show you how to create an alert for specific keywords, then you'll receive notifications about news, blogs, videos, and other content posted on the Web that meet your keyword criteria.

This method is, without a doubt, the fastest way to find out about your buyers, your market, your competition, and even yourself! I have done this on many occasions when working with clients, and they never cease to be amazed at how much I know about them and their business—thanks to Google Alerts.

a forced-choice construction, which makes respondents choose between a given set of descriptors and evaluates their frame of mind in particular social settings: work, home, with friends. Again, these are just the functions, not the client improvement. We'll get to that momentarily.

What About Your Financials? No exploration of your offering knowledge is complete without examining the financials. Price, value, and payment options are all of utmost importance. Are buyers able to finance your offering, or is up-front payment required? Can they break up the payment, paying half now and half on delivery? These are the basic, broad-brush strokes that make up your understanding of your offering's financial implications.

Then there are the specifics, the microdetails. Are there nuances to how someone might pay for your product or service? Is a credit-history review or some other sort of approval process required? If so, what specific things should prospective buyers know about that process? Are there parameters regarding down payments and installment plans? Are promotional considerations available, such as a price reduction for full up-front payment?

These are all ideas that should be explored in a complete grounding of your offering education. It's crucial to look at your offering and identify every aspect that may—or may not—appeal to buyers, and then it's important to be able to explain how the constructs of your offer work and the advantages they provide.

How Does It Work?

You must be able to describe your offering and any of its components in at least one, if not all, of the following three categories: mechanical, procedural, and biological.

» **Mechanical.** Can you explain your offering from a mechanical perspective? Think back to my example of the 96-cubic-inch, 45-degree, air-cooled V-Twin engine. And can you translate what, exactly, that means for the rider?

» **Procedural.** Maybe your offering is not mechanical in nature. If this is the case, can you describe something procedural about it? Try something like this: "We're ranked number two in the industry. This ranking is determined three times per year by industry associations via an anonymous survey." Procedural descriptions also can enable buyers to more clearly understand how your processes can match their needs: "What we must do first is clearly understand your objectives, then set out to understand the metrics that can be used to identify success, and finally determine exactly what the return is for you, your team, and your organization." Here's one more procedural explanation: "The culture of our firm is completely customer-centric. We say that because prior to starting any project, we will visit your site, speak to your employees, survey your best customers *and* the ones you've recently lost, and then we'll work collaboratively to design a solution to meet your objectives. This often takes anywhere from two weeks to two months."

» **Physical or emotional.** Perhaps your offering can best be explained physically: "Our preworkout drink is considered a hemo-dialator. This means that it dilates the blood vessels, enabling a greater amount of nutrients and oxygen to be transported to your muscles while you're training." Oh, I know what you're thinking: *Mark, I sell financial services. How would any-*

thing physical or emotional apply to me? When selling a financial services product, I'm certainly going to tap into the potential client's emotions by suggesting the sense of security and calm that comes with knowing that client's family will be on solid financial footing in a time of crisis. Or, back to the Harley-Davidson dealership, how about reminding the customer of the way his pulse will quicken every time he revs that throttle? Get creative, and you'll be surprised by how many products can be incorporated into conversations about physical well-being and emotional enjoyment.

How Will Your Buyer's Condition Improve?

This is, without a doubt, the most important question. Does your offering make the buyer better off financially, psychologically, spiritually, and/or socially? Does it enable the buyer to do something faster, such as reduce sale cycles or shorten a project's duration? Is your offering more affordable than others, either in a onetime payment or by dint of long-term use? Does it reduce mental or physical effort?

STREET SMARTS

Don't Get Stuck in the Weeds

Doug Slotkin, sales vice president for real-estate website Zillow.com, issues an important warning to salespeople pitching their products and services:

It can't be too feature-laden. You can't get into the weeds about features; you've got to talk benefits. The features are only a means to the benefits. I think a lot of reps make the mistake of making their pitch very feature-laden, and not enough benefit-laden, and then they lose momentum on the call, they lose steam, they lose the prospect's interest. The prospect wants to know, "How is this going to help my business?"

Perhaps your offering is simply "nicer." A taxi can get you to the airport, but when you take a Lincoln, Mercedes, or Cadillac you *arrive*.

Or is your offering just "different" from the others? For many buyers, that is reason enough for further investigation of you, your organization, and your products or services. Your stats and specifications don't always have to be better; sometimes different will do. What's important here is not just that you possess a general understanding of how your offerings improve the state of your buyer; you must be able to articulate those improvements in a clear and compelling manner.

Sales Acc*seller*ation Exercise

Here's an offering expertise exercise. (Like physical exercise, this will only produce results if you actually do it.) Take a blank sheet of paper and create three columns across the top of the page:

What We Have, Do, or Offer	How It Works	How the Buyer Is Improved

Then list as many items as possible under each column. Push yourself, and you'll be shocked—shocked!—at what you'll discover. Also, think about what might be typical uses for your offerings, as well as extreme uses and even unusual, unconventional ones. There's no telling what sort of products, services, or sales offshoots can pop up from this sort of freeform thinking. A flute in a rock band? Jethro Tull did it and won a Grammy!

When asked to participate in this activity, some misguided salespeople declare, "I know what we sell; I don't need to do that." To them, I say, "Do you *really*? Do you really understand as many facets of your offering as possible?"

In the race for sales success, the winners are usually the ones with the most finely tuned engine. Put me in a competitive sales situation with the woeful V-Rod salesperson from the beginning of this chapter, and I like my chances. I've done the preparation necessary to succeed. Extraordinary expertise about a seller's offerings cannot be underestimated anymore. It's far too important.

You can do this exercise individually, but it produces much more powerful results when conducted in a group setting. I also suggest you consider having this exercise become part of the conversation with some of your best clients and customers. Their compelling reasons for why they chose you and your offerings may be radically different from your own perspective.

(If you'd like printable forms to aid with this exercise, visit www .AcceleratetheSale.com to download them.)

Knowledge Is King

I don't want to brag, but I can dramatically improve the offering knowledge of Harley-Davidson dealership staff members in as little as 20 minutes. Through guided activities and a bit of prompting, we as a group can take any tangible product (such as a motorcycle or a leather jacket) or any intangible product (an extended service plan) and create anywhere from 20 to 120 macro- and microaspects of that particular offering.

Of course, those salespeople aren't going to spring all 120 microaspects on the next person who walks through the dealership's doors looking for a new leather jacket. But the more they know about what they sell, the better their odds of persuading that next customer to leave wearing some new leather.

Self-confidence skyrockets, too, after participating in a sales exercise like this. The more you know about something, the more likely you will be to engage others. Once that's accomplished, the next thing most salespeople need is a better understanding of language.

Compelling Communication

Because the effective use of language is so important to boosting sales, I'll be covering it a lot throughout this book. In fact, the entirety of Chapter 4, "Making Your Engine Purr: Language Is the

Key," is dedicated to it. For now, let's round out this chapter about offering expertise by focusing on how to effectively fire up all of that intellectual horsepower you've just created.

If you've given serious thought about your offering and participated in the sales exercise, you now have a ton of useful offering expertise. Now, harness it for the time-honored sales skill of communicating features, advantages, and benefits. (Of course, I'll put some twists on these sacred cows.)

A feature is any attribute or a characteristic of your offering. The advantage is what the feature enables and, of course, the benefit is what's in it for the buyer. So, sticking with some of our previous examples, upon discovering that my prospective motorcycle customer likes to ride fast, I might say this: "This motorcycle has a 96-cubic-inch engine, and it delivers 86 foot pounds worth of torque. What this means to you is it's an absolute blast to ride."

Note that the feature here is the 96-cubic-inch engine, the advantage is the 86 foot pounds worth of torque, and the buyer benefit is that the motorcycle is an absolute blast to ride.

You can, of course, use this same communication pattern with any offering: "Our consulting firm custom-develops every survey instrument. They are sensitive enough to track nuanced cultural differences between departments or even locations. What this means to you is you'll have the best information possible on which to base your strategic decisions." (When you use the phrase, "What this means to you . . . ," it compels you to add a meaningful buyer benefit while piquing the interest of said buyer.)

A twist on this basic pattern is to add some component of proof to the communication string: "This motorcycle has a 96-cubic-inch engine, and it delivers 86 foot pounds worth of torque. What this means to you is it's an absolute blast to ride. And I should know; I put 2,000 miles on one last month." The sales professional's personal experience here is being used as persuasive evidence.

Here's another example:

Our consulting firm custom-develops every survey instrument. They are sensitive enough to track nuanced cultural differences between departments or even locations. What this means to you is you'll have the best information possible on which to base your strategic decisions. We know this, because the last firm we worked with experienced a 27 percent reduction in employee turnover.

Feel free to use third-party proof, too: "And we're not the only people to think so. *Motorcycle Consumer News* made the same observation in its review of this model last month."

Once you feel comfortable adding proof statements to your basic features, advantages, and benefits communication, begin playing around with the sequence of this communication pattern. Just like musical scales, when you start to experiment with different sequences and timing, you create new sounds. (Do you know that only seven natural musical notes exist? And look at what some of history's greatest composers were able to do with those seven. Heck, look at what AC/DC was able to do with just three!)

Here are a couple examples:

Harley-Davidson motorcycles boast a 3-micron-thick powder-coated clear coat. This keeps your paint looking newer longer, and it protects against scratches. It's so thick that most surface scratches can be easily buffed out, keeping that showroom look. This is a distinct advantage over some other brands, because their paints are only 1 or 1.5 microns thick.

Our consulting firm uses only custom-designed survey instruments. These are so sensitive they can determine nuanced organizational differences between locations and even departments. It's a huge advantage over firms that use off-the-shelf systems.

Note that the climax of the above communication patterns comes at the end of the statement. What if you tried putting the "power" up front? Here are some examples:

If you're looking for a motorcycle that is an absolute blast to ride, this model cranks out 86 foot pounds of torque via a 96-cubic-inch engine.

If you're looking for the best data on which to base your strategic decisions, we are often able to determine nuanced organizational differences between locations and even departments with our custom-developed survey instruments.

Here are a few more ideas to accelerate your understanding of what you sell.

» **Review your product literature at least once per month.** Yes, that means contracts, too. You'll be surprised by how many details you can inadvertently overlook when you breeze through your own company's materials. Someone took the time, energy, and effort to compile all that data, so don't give them short shrift. I know a lot of salespeople who haven't even read their own organization's literature, let alone studied it. I also encourage you to review any and all contracts or agreements. Again, it can be surprising how many customer policy and procedure questions can be answered within the text of those agreements.

» **Read product reviews.** As you well know, the media plays a huge role in our daily lives. It's awfully hard to escape, so you better figure out how to understand the role of influencers in your business. Long before Facebook, experts hypothesized that less than 1 percent of the population writes, reviews, and publishes. Yet that 1 percent influences the other 99 percent. So be a media hound, looking out for what the media is saying about you, your offerings, and your industry. More than likely, what they're saying is influencing your buyers.

» **Check out online forums.** Online forums exist for practically every group and subgroup of customers out there. Peer-to-peer communication is more prevalent and prized than ever, but keep in mind that people who populate forums tend to be in the vocal minority. Still, online forums will help keep you updated on what your customers (and potential customers) are talking about.

» **Use personal experiences to deepen your offering knowledge.** If your company custom-designs survey instruments, you should know how to use those instruments. If you sell training workshops, you should attend one or more of the sessions. If you sell guitars, you should be able to strum a tune. You don't have to be Eddie Van Halen, but to not even play is disrespectful to your buyer, yourself, and the profession of selling guitars.

» **Use designers' comments to communicate your product's attributes.** "Willie G." Davidson, senior vice president and chief styling officer at the Harley-Davidson Motor Co., has often said that a Harley-Davidson motorcycle is like "rolling sculpture." And let me tell you, I've used that descriptive language on more than one occasion—and given credit for it to Willie G. My favorite designer comment from the auto world comes from Enzo Ferrari, who famously said, "Aerodynamics is for those who can't build engines."

» **Use product managers' stories, too.** People involved in the development of a product or service possess all sorts of insider information. As long as it passes the company's "OK to use" test, that information is fair game in sales conversations. For example, Harley-Davidson engineers once got so excited about the design of a cool new motorcycle that they neglected to think through delivery logistics; the bike was too long for any of the company's existing shipping crates. They scrambled to make a crate that would accommodate the new model, but it was still a close call. Today, buyers of that motorcycle love this inside scoop.

» **Realize that you're the expert.** Never underestimate the persuasive power of your personal (albeit often qualitative) take on your own offerings.

Why Work So Hard?

"Every buyer is different." How many times have you heard that in your career? The more you know, the better you can service your buyer and match his or her needs with your offering. If you only know four aspects of your offering, you're forced to find a buyer who is looking for at least one of those four attributes. If you know 25 variations, you'll be able to match more buyers more consistently. When it comes to understanding your offering, the more you know, the faster you'll go.

CHAPTER 3 Acc*seller*ators

» Little Leaguers may throw with the exact same size and weight baseball as that used in the Major Leagues, but few of them possess a Sandy Koufax curveball. How are *you* throwing the ball?

» Buyers are interested in how their condition will be improved. No one buys a Harley-Davidson simply as a means of transportation. Why are people buying what you're selling?

» Three critical questions you must ask yourself: (a) What do you have, do, or offer? (b) How does it work? (c) How is the buyer's condition improved as a result?

» When exploring what you offer, focus on the four *F*s: fit, form, function, and financials. Knowing these areas will make you a more complete sales professional.

» The following is *the* (small word, big implications) critical question to be able to answer regarding your offering: How will your buyer's condition improve?

CHAPTER 4

Making Your Engine Purr

LANGUAGE IS THE KEY

Don't worry, fellas," I assured them, "You two will have your knees in the breeze and be bustin' bugs in no time."

The two 30-something accountants from the city were grinning like kids who had just been given keys to the candy store. They shot mischievous glances at one another as they took their new vernacular out for a test ride.

"Knees in the breeze!" the first one repeated with a smile so big it looked like he could eat a banana sideways. "Bustin' bugs!" beamed the other, who delivered his line with an almost musical quality while nodding like a Derek Jeter bobblehead doll.

Perpetuating Culture Through the Effective Use of Language

In the Harley-Davidson world, we talk a lot about the Harley-Davidson culture. Whenever I'm working with dealers or anyone involved in the Harley-Davidson business, I mention the importance of perpetuating that culture, and I always receive prideful acknowledgment and agreement.

Then I ask, "What is that culture?"

Blank stares.

Eventually people start shouting out, "Freedom!" "Adventure!" "Being bold!"

Then, silence.

"Yeah, I don't know what it is, either," I always say. "But we better figure it out."

Of course, Harley-Davidson has figured out what the culture is and does a great job of perpetuating it. A *culture* can be considered the expression of a particular community. What people do, the way they dress, and the way they speak all play a role. When I use the patois (definitely *not* a motorcyclist's term) of the biker culture and teach it to others not yet engaged in that culture, it enables them to instantly feel a part of it.

Subversive Prestige

Some linguists refer to this as "subversive prestige," which is typically used to describe the fairly common phenomenon of middle-class suburban kids who adopt the language of urban street gangs. It makes them feel cool or tough, as if it elevates them somehow.

So, while I'm not trying to prepare new motorcyclists for roles in *Sons of Anarchy*, I do share worthwhile elements of the biker lexicon with prospective buyers, who can use them immediately. It's fun—and it's also me using subversive prestige. Logic makes you think. Emotions make you act. This language is emotional.

Insider's Prestige: Your Key into the Club

How can you incorporate subversive prestige into your sales process? Well, every industry I've ever encountered has its own jargon. When you use that vocabulary correctly, you communicate that you are "in the know," that you have knowledge of how that company or that industry works. Insurance people speak of "captives," "floaters," and "churn." Computer professionals talk of "authentication," "solutions," and "root directories." Not as cool as "bustin' bugs," but you get the idea.

I call this gaining "insider's prestige"—demonstrating that you know a bit of how things work on the inside. This is just one way that you can use language to acc*sell*erate your sales success. Let's take a look at others.

Language: An Important Part of the Sales Success Model

Superior language skills build the confidence needed to engage more people, more effectively—be they customers, colleagues, or family members. As it relates to selling, communicating well enables you to effectively discover your buyers' dominant purchasing motives, make your sales offer, and rebut sales objections. Plus, improving your vocabulary has even been said to help improve your IQ!

People sometimes suggest to me that language isn't really all that important; after all, it's just a bunch of words. Much like the sound of a perfectly tuned engine rev or exhaust note can quicken your pulse (and apparently increase your testosterone, according to a United Kingdom study reported in *The Washington Times* in December 2008), so, too, can language.

Have you ever been present when someone uttered a racial slur? (Stand-up comics often do this for effect, and it works!) When that happens, do you feel the collective energy in the room instantly become emotionally charged? That's the power of language.

You may be familiar with the term *fighting words* or, as it's more commonly used, *fightin' words*. These terms are usually uttered in old Westerns and "Bugs Bunny" episodes, but make no mistake about it: fightin' words are very real. There is even a fighting words doctrine in U.S. constitutional law, a limitation to the freedom of speech granted in the First Amendment. In 1942, the Supreme Court established the doctrine and held that "insulting or 'fighting words,' those that by their very utterance inflict injury or tend to incite an immediate breach of the peace" are among the "well-defined and narrowly limited classes of speech [which] the prevention and punishment of . . . have never been thought to raise any constitutional concern." They are of "slight social value," the court added. And although the interpretation of the fighting words doctrine has changed over time, this is evidence enough to understand—and respect—language's potentially powerful and often negative impact.

The age-old way to test the power of words is by asking yourself if you would refer to your wife as "the first day of spring" or "the last day of a long, hard winter." Either way, it's the same day. But the language you use to describe it is significantly different and will likely yield two extremely disparate responses. To improve your chances of selling more quickly, start with your objective, and then choose your words carefully.

Another language lesson is detailed in Andy Green's 2007 book, *Creativity in Public Relations*. Green relates the story of Rosser Reeves, 1950s adman extraordinaire and creator of such timeless gems as "Melts in your mouth, not in your hands," "How do you spell relief? R-O-L-A-I-D-S," and the political slogan "I Like Ike." Reeves and a colleague were walking down the streets of New York City one glorious spring day when they encountered a panhandler holding a sign that read: "I am blind."

"I can immediately improve his response rate," Rosser confidently proclaimed to his companion before walking over and introducing himself to the panhandler. He then added three words to the man's sign. As Rosser and his friend stood back to observe, passersby stopped, looked at the sign, glanced around them, and then complied with the panhandler's implied request for donations. What were the three magic words Rosser added to the sign?

"It's springtime and . . ."

When coupled with the sign's original language, the panhandler's message read: "It's springtime and I am blind."

Why would this have such an astounding, immediate, and persuasive impact on people minding their own business on a busy New York City street? Because it created within everyone who saw it an instant identification with and understanding of the panhandler's unfortunate plight. In short, it inspired empathy. When you can understand the world, or at least certain circumstances of that world, from the perspective of another individual (say, a potential client), you are much better positioned to use effective language.

Great Sales Advice—Do You Really Understand?

Gary Ramey, vice president of sales and marketing for Beretta U.S.A., says this is the best sales advice he's ever been given:

Understand your customer, and understand your consumer. You can't go in and meet a customer [for the first time], and start explaining what they need to do in business. You have to understand the competition, how products are merchandised, and the price point. You have to do significant homework before you ever sit down with a customer and have a sales presentation, because once you've done all your homework, once you understand the marketplace, and you present to them your brand, it's not really even a sales call. It's a program review with a recommendation that any customer would appreciate, because you're providing them with valuable information that they most likely had not compiled. You're almost doing the buyer's work for them.

Make Yourself More Interesting

As a salesperson, you want to—nay, you *need* to—engage with prospects. The problem is that many go about this process in completely the wrong way. Most salespeople, in an attempt to quickly establish rapport, will ask innocuous personal questions: "Do you play golf?" "Do you like tennis?"

At some point, you may have conversations with your buyer that include those exact questions. But if you're looking to acc*sell*erate sales results, that kind of banter should be saved for later. So should talking endlessly (and usually aimlessly) about yourself. Instead, ask provocative questions about your buyer's opinion regarding the business at hand. Here are some B2B examples:

» "How will the recent drought in the Southwest affect your expansion plans?"
» "Will the bankruptcy filing of your competitor's transportation unit have any consequences for your organization?"
» "How might the financial regulatory reform impact your business?"
» "Will the continued elimination of landline phones in favor of mobile phones alter your marketing campaigns?"
» "How will the closing of the London office impact your division?"
» "What do you like about what's going on right now in your industry (or your organization)?"
» "What would you change if you could?"

Note that these questions can be categorized as either current events or related to competition, government regulation, social trends, organizational issues, or experience. With a little intellectual effort, you can apply the same model to retail sales. As you might suspect, I'll provide examples about selling Harley-Davidson motorcycles.

» "Do you think we'll ever see 'green' motorcycles? You know, environmentally friendly bikes? (Not ones that are actually green.)"

» "Have you seen the new model the other guys just introduced?"
» "How do you think the exhaust decibel restrictions will impact your riding?"
» "Would you endorse hands-free mobile devices for motorcyclists?"
» "Have you been to our newest location on the north side of town?"
» "What do you like about our dealership?"
» "What do you wish we would do differently?"

These questions will do more to acc*sell*erate your sales than any personal questions about golf, or tennis, or family vacations. First of all, these probing, thought-provoking inquiries provide you with important details about what your prospective buyers are thinking and how you might be able to help them make up their minds. But even more importantly, they make buyers think more highly of you, because you've asked questions that were out of the ordinary, questions that prove you know what's going on in the industry and the world. They probably will boost your credibility, too, because you're asking for buyers' opinions—a strategy that suggests *their* opinion is most important, not yours. After all, if you've got the good sense to ask for their opinion, they can't help but like you. It's as immutable as the law of gravity.

Controlling Conversations

As mentioned earlier, many buyers are looking for someone to lead them through the ambiguity of the sales process. One way to guide them is by leveraging the power of your position. People have a tendency to defer to the experts. When you are in a selling situation, and armed with the knowledge covered in Chapter 3, "Crawling Under the Hood: *Really* Understanding Your Offering," your buyer will view you as an authority. Make the most of this by using what I call "expert language."

The words *recommend*, *suggest*, and *advise* all carry a sense of clout. So when you're with customers whom you'd like to move in a particular direction, work these powerful terms into the conversation. When the buyer says something like, "What do you charge?" and you're not yet ready to talk price (perhaps because you don't have all the necessary information you need to give him or her a quote), you might respond this way: "Great question. Here's what I'm going to *recommend*. Let's take a few minutes to talk more about your objectives. Then, within 48 hours, I'll send you a proposal outlining options from which you can choose."

Don't be surprised when this verbal approach works. And the terms can be used almost interchangeably: "Here's what I'd like to *suggest* . . ." "Here's what we *advise* in this situation . . ." These are powerful words that help you subtly direct your buyer toward more productive conversation.

Another way to use language in a meaningful but understated manner is through what I call "consent questions." As an example in this case is better than a definition, award-winning journalist Ann Compton of ABC News used a consent question during a news conference with President Barack Obama when she asked, "Mr. President, may I ask you a question about race?" To which the president said, "Of course." This softened the question, gave the POTUS a moment to think, and Compton received a thoughtful response.

You can do the same thing in your selling situations. If you have a difficult question to ask, try presenting it with a consent question in which you first seek permission to ask another question: "May I ask you about budget?" "May I inquire about approval authority?"

I like the use of general consent questions in sales conversations, too: "May I ask you a question?" "Would you do me a favor?" "May I make a suggestion?" These types of inquiries are viewed as polite, especially in the early stages of a sale. When the prospect responds with a "yes," he or she is agreeing to do something, and that is persuasive psychology.

That said, you also can ask consent questions rhetorically—that is, without really expecting an answer. In those cases, a mental agreement exists between both parties that just naturally segues to the actual question you want to ask.

Increasing Your Persuasive Horsepower

Without reaching for hyperbole, vivid descriptions can make your sales offer more enticing. Here's a primer on some aspects of language you may have forgotten about since high school English class.

» **Adjectives.** Use adjectives, which modify a noun, when appropriate. Here are some examples: *gleaming* chrome, *sparkling* paint job, *magnificent* motorcycle, *elegant* design, *gifted* salesperson, *compelling* point. Compare these sentences: "The software program has a graphical interface" versus "The software program has an elegantly designed, graphical interface." "You have a point; we should discuss it further" versus "You make a compelling point; we should discuss it further." Don't go overboard, but the thoughtful use of a well-selected adjective—one word!—can boost your persuasiveness.

» **Examples.** Provide examples, regardless of how difficult it may be to find ones that prove your point or explain why you're saying what you're saying: "The significant torque provides the necessary acceleration to confidently pass other vehicles." "The parallel path technique used by our consultants helps to identify parts of the project that can be worked on simultaneously, enabling you to get to market sooner." Your reward will be increased commissions.

» **Metaphors.** These paint visual images for your buyer. A metaphor is a figure of speech in which a word or phrase that ordinarily designates one thing is used to designate another, thus making an implicit comparison: "The management team is the heart and soul of this company." "This marketing campaign is a diamond in the rough."

» **Similes.** Similarly, similes—the comparison of two unlike objects using the word *like* or *as*—can help create a mental picture in the buyer's mind: "His yearly bonus was as big as a bus." "Her word is as strong as steel." "Buying from him is as easy as A-B-C."

» **Analogies.** You also should be comfortable using analogies to compare two dissimilar items: "Hitting second gear at 6,000 rpm on a V-Rod is like launching an F-11 fighter jet off an aircraft carrier." "Transitioning to the new EAP program will be as smooth as Tiger Woods's golf swing." "We've hired a guy we refer to as the Michelangelo of website design."

Did She Really Just Say That?

We'll revisit the topic of language repeatedly throughout this book; it's *that* important. But let me bring this brief language primer to a close with a quick story. I was attending a hectic conference of business managers and executives not long ago when I approached a doorway at roughly the same time as a sharply dressed woman in her late 50s or maybe even early 60s.

She was wearing a gray business jacket and matching below-the-knee skirt, expensive shoes, and a tasteful pearl necklace. As we arrived at the doorway simultaneously, I paused to let her pass first (as I was taught to do). She paused as well, looked at me, and like some sort of street thug, gave a bit of a head bob, did a double-tap on her sternum, and said, "My bad," as if we were attending a meeting of the Latin Kings.

You could have pushed me over with a feather! Hearing those words come out of her mouth was such a contradiction in terms it was unbelievable. It's fascinating to observe how the language you use can so quickly change someone's impression of you. (Looking back, the thought occurred to me that the nicely dressed woman might have been eyeing me up and chosen her words carefully, based on what she thought was the best way to communicate with me; I *am* much younger than her!)

Some Language Dos and Don'ts

Some language should be avoided at all costs. For example, *at the end of the day* has no purpose in your communication arsenal, as if your opinion is the absolute last word on any given topic. Also, the overuse of *like* (as in "I was, like, really trying to convince him that he looks good on that bike") has got to stop. It's almost as if Frank Zappa's daughter, Moon Unit, re-recorded her infamously irritating '80s-era single "Valley Girl" for the 21st century. Try to be a bit more descriptive: "I'm intrigued . . . ," "He is smitten . . . ," "They are ecstatic. . . ." And then people who are, you know, like, out of junior high will have higher opinions of you. Here are some others:

» **Stop the spread of the insidious "I'm just sayin'."** I'm unclear as to when or where this turn of a phrase came into vogue, but its usage seems to have increased in recent years— usually as the universal get-out-of-bad-behavior line. What I mean by this is that people think they can make rude or inappropriate comments as long as they preface or conclude them with, "I'm just sayin' . . ."—as if that makes everything OK. Here's what *not* to say in business situations: "I'm just sayin' that your guy isn't the sharpest knife in the drawer." "Your team is unskilled and incompetent; I'm just sayin'." "Is that your daughter in this picture? Not too flattering. I'm just sayin'."

» **Master the art of digital conversation.** We tweet, we text, we IM. Today, e-mail almost seems quaint. You must embrace emerging forms of communication if you are to excel in sales in the 21st century. Spend some time learning, understanding, and getting better acquainted with the platforms and applications with which you're least familiar. Make sure you've got a grip on how and what you are saying, because each method of communication is ruled by its own idiosyncrasies. I know one person who sends all of his e-mail communication in capital letters, because he thinks it's easier to read. His 20-something recipients think he's lost his hearing, because he's continually "shouting" in his e-mails.

» **Be careful with abbreviations.** When you're using digital methods of communication, always make sure you know what you're saying when you abbreviate. I can't remember where I read the story—it might have been *Reader's Digest* (we motorcycle guys read *RD*)—of a mother who was text-messaging her teenage daughter's friend, whose own mother had recently passed away. In an attempt to comfort her, she signed off on one piece of correspondence with *LOL*, thinking it meant "lots of love." She was horrified when she found out it didn't.

» **Listen to your inflections.** When you finish your statements on an up inflection, you either turn wha*tev*er you are saying into a question or make yourself sound unsure. A down inflection at the end of a sentence, on the other hand, conveys confidence.

» **Watch how you say what you say.** Remember when your mother told you that it's not what you say but how you say it? Try adding vocal emphasis to different words of the following statement: "I did not say you lost the sale." When you do, it creates dramatically different meanings. (Go to www.Acceleratethe Sale.com to see and hear this one in action.)

» **Practice saying things three different ways.** Language is like anything else; it requires practice. I try to verbally convey my point on three different levels. One uses simple language (*happy*), another involves slightly more elaborate language (*elated*), and the third encourages the use of multiple syllables and/or the creative side of your brain (*exuberant*). Or how about the trio *help*, *comfort*, and *assuage*. Practice using these three levels of language based on what is appropriate for a particular buyer or prospect. It's fun, isn't it? Or amusing. Or mirthful. So is seeing how fast you can make the sale.

Situational Sales Success Stories (S³ Stories)

Would you like to learn about one of the most successful sales communication approaches of all time? Sure, you would, and that's why a portion of this chapter on language is dedicated to the time-honored tradition of storytelling.

Storytelling is one of the oldest, most effective forms of human communication. For thousands of years before Twitter, Facebook, and even the printing press, humans informed and instructed others via stories. It probably started with members of the species *Australopithecus africanus*, some three million years ago, making wild hand gestures while sitting around a tree. Communication then progressed to the first cave drawings, no doubt thanks to some braggart talking up his huge and likely exaggerated aurochs kill to all his friends.

My point is this: Storytelling as a communication art form has stood the test of time. Why? Because it's compelling. Just try listening to only half of Jim Croce's "You Don't Mess Around with Jim," Gordon Lightfoot's "The Wreck of the Edmund Fitzgerald," or Harry Chapin's "Cat's in the Cradle." It's almost impossible. Even if you've heard these songs before, you still want to know how the story ends.

To acc*sell*erate your success, consider developing what I call "situational sales success stories," or S³ stories. These are precreated retellings of how you helped buyers improve their condition in given situations. These are an elevated skill set that can yield tremendous speed in your sales efforts. If you want to get good fast, become a great situational sales success storyteller. In so doing, you will:

» **Create a nonthreatening way to share information.** In many sales situations, your potential buyer can be on hyperalert, wanting to avoid feeling silly or uninformed. And if the conversation is focused on him or her, personal defenses are often heightened. But if you make your point via storytelling that does not involve the individual to whom you are speaking, it's much easier for that person to relax and focus on the conversation.

» **Allow buyers to insert themselves into the role of your situational sales success story's main character.** The best sales stories are ones in which the main character is someone other than you, the sales professional. Inserting yourself into the lead role could send the wrong message, suggesting that you are self-centered and your story is contrived. So don't be the hero in every story; make the main character someone else.

» **Entertain while you inform, educate, and persuade.** Perhaps it stems from childhood, but adults (especially adults) want to be entertained. Oh, sure, there are those stalwarts who claim they're only interested in a spreadsheet, a Gantt chart, or scientific findings, but even hard-nosed types enjoy a good story every once in awhile. S³ stories contain three subtle but distinct objectives: inform, educate, and persuade. When you inform someone, you make that person aware; when you educate, you bring about understanding; and when you persuade, you enable your buyer to embrace a particular point of view. Say you'd like to inform a customer about a change in your company's financing policy. You may choose to educate that buyer about the benefits of a new product system, or you could opt to persuade him or her as to why continuing to use your company will provide a competitive advantage in the marketplace.

» **Provide a "social proof" component.** As one of my professional heroes, Robert Cialdini, Regents' Professor Emeritus of Psychology and Marketing at Arizona State University, claims, "We follow the lead of similar others." That's right; when we hear that "all the kids are doing it," that has a profound impact on us. Using situational sales success stories leverages this idea of social proof, or informational social influence, and makes what you're talking about seem even more compelling to your prospect.

» **Break through the surrounding informational noise.** In his book, *Data Smog: Surviving the Information Glut*, author David Shenk states that the average American in 1971 encountered 560 daily advertising messages. By 1997 (the year *Data Smog* was published), that number had swelled to more than 3,000 per day. And the Newspaper Association of America recently published a piece on its website proclaiming that the average American today is exposed to 3,000 advertising messages before breakfast. Is the latter hyperbole? I certainly hope so. But the point is that there's a *lot* of noise out there, and to cut through it you must have a compelling story to tell.

The following are elements of a compelling situational sales success story:

» **The story should have a point.** Whether it's how a buyer surmounted financing difficulties to make a purchase or how another client decided to take a risk despite the economy's ambiguities, you tell situational sales success stories to fit a particular set of circumstances. That's the point, and your stories should have one, too.

» **The story should contain telling, vivid details.** Describe the type and time of day, maybe the main character's fashion sense, and one flattering physical trait. Recount the way in which that person considered an idea, and relate a detail of the offer or a complicating factor in the transaction. When selling a Harley-Davidson motorcycle, I might say this: "She was the quintessential corporate executive: well-dressed, articulate, comporting herself as if about to call to order a board of directors meeting. And she was eyeing up a radical custom-painted, candy-apple-red Super Glide with one of the most sinister skull paint jobs I've ever seen." Get the picture?

» **The story should use a repeatable phrase.** I love using language to color stories, and (as this book confirms) I also enjoy incorporating motor-speak into my conversations. Phrases like "Chrome won't get you home," "Go fast or be passed," and "To boost or not to boost, *that* is the question" all can color your situational sales success stories and make them memorable. There are plenty of general business phrases that work well, too: "You can't save your way to success," "Lead, follow, or get out of the way," and "Even if you're on the right track, you'll get run over if you don't move." In your next conversation with a client or potential customer, try working in just one of these phrases. When you finish your situational sales success story with something along the lines of ". . . and that's when Steve Buyer, senior vice president at ABC Corporation, discovered that chrome won't get you home," see if your prospective buyer doesn't smile and repeat your clincher: "Chrome won't get you home."

» **Beginnings are crucial.** Don't open your situational sales success story with a cliché. Instead, develop creative ways of getting started. If your prospective buyer says this: "We just don't know what's going to happen with our industry and the economy," you might begin your situational sales success story like this: "That's exactly what Steve Buyer said, not more than two months ago." Bingo! They're listening—because they want to know who Steve Buyer is and how he managed to overcome a similar situation.

» **The story should contain at least one unexpected element.** People love the unexpected in stories. Think about the plot turns in books, movies, and even songs. If you know exactly how things are going to turn out, why stay tuned in? Let's pick up with our Steve Buyer example above:

That's exactly what Steve Buyer said, not more than two months ago. His company was struggling, its stock value had sunk, key managers ditched the organization, and all rational indicators told him not to make any big decisions. Then, his firm experienced a product recall. That's when Steve and his colleagues decided to invest in their business instead of cutting back. We put together a performance initiative designed to keep revenue flat but increase margins. Morale improved, the company attracted some talented new people, and now, although not completely back to business as usual, it's well on its way—all because Steve and his team turned left when others would have turned right.

Storytelling Stumbling Blocks

Just as dynamic situational sales success stories require certain elements to work, they also need to steer away from the following stumbling blocks:

» **Too much attention to nonessential accuracy.** Why doesn't this work? "Well, wait until you hear what happened to one of our favorite customers, Michael O'Dell! It was last Thursday . . . er, no Wednesday . . . no, OK, it *was* Thursday. He came in around 10:30 in the morning; no, it was really closer to 11, and . . ." You've lost the customer at "er." It doesn't matter what day of the week it was or what time of day. If it's not absolutely crucial to the story, no one really cares. Make your point, and keep moving. (Don't misunderstand my point: If a detail enhances the story, by all means, use it.)
» **Too disjointed.** Try following this story: "We had one client recently who wanted to go ahead with a particular project. Well, it was a problem at first, because he didn't think his company

could afford it. But now he's glad he partnered with us for the project. See, the company was just a small start-up eight years ago, and then they ultimately went with our best offer. . . ." If, in your situational sales success story, you flit from the client buying your offer to the client having a problem, to the company enjoying the results, to how you helped solve the problem, your story will be more confusing than an episode of the dearly departed network television series *Lost*. Consider first introducing the character (your buyer), then his dilemma, then how you helped solve that dilemma, and, finally, how the buyer and his company are now living happily ever after.

» **Too long.** If you're talking for more than 15 or 20 seconds at one time, stop.

» **Inauthentic.** Make sure your situational sales success story doesn't appear corporately vetted or brand-controlled. Today's consumers are very cognizant of ideas being packaged. This is why the current trend of posting testimonials on company websites, which in the old days (18 months ago or so) was considered a great idea, is now losing steam. If customers read nothing but positive product reviews and glowing company testimonials, they suspect that whatever they are reading has been pasteurized by spin doctors and thus lend less credence to that information.

Delivery Methods

Today, there are so many more options involved for telling your S^3 stories than our cave-dwelling predecessors enjoyed. You can share stories face to face in one-on-one situations, of course, but they also work in larger group settings (such as a business meeting), as videos, and via e-mail or even text message. Then there's Twitter, which should challenge even the strongest tellers of S^3 stories, as well as blogs, Facebook posts, and that old-fashioned device we used to call a telephone.

Here are five must-have situational sales success stories to keep in your arsenal at all times. I'll provide the bones; you flesh them out:

1. A buyer who never used your company's products or services is now one of your biggest fans.
2. A client who faithfully used the "other brand" until you showed him or her the light.
3. A customer who was loyal to only one method until you showed him or her another option.
4. A buyer who couldn't afford your best offer, but you helped his or her company figure out a way both of you could still do business together.
5. A customer who initially wanted to delay purchasing until you proved why buying now was a wiser decision.

Now that you have some ideas for situational sales success stories, consider ways to rev them up and fine-tune them. Take the model, create one great, truth-based story for each of the five situations, and write them down using the guidelines suggested earlier. Make them all capable of being told in less than 25 seconds—preferably quicker. Require every salesperson on staff to learn the five stories and be able to recite them. Test employees; they'll enjoy this process and internalize high-quality S^3 stories in an organizational learning exercise. Next, begin monitoring client conversations with sales staff to ensure situational sales success stories are used in the appropriate situations.

More Great S^3 Stories

In business, you're typically acquiring customers, engaging them to do more business with you, or attempting to win them back (I call this "recovery"). Table 4.1 creates a matrix you can use to develop stories based on each part of the grid. Then you'll have a situational sales success story for just about any selling situation.

Here are some examples of how you can apply this model. (The numbers correspond to Table 4.1.)

1. Inform/acquisition:
   - B2C example: You let customers know your store now offers personal shoppers, and they come and experience it for themselves. Now, they're believers.

TABLE 4.1

Storytelling Specifics

	Acquisition	Engagement	Recovery
Inform	①	④	⑦
Educate	②	⑤	⑧
Persuade	③	⑥	⑨

- B2B example: You let a prospective buyer know your business now provides organizational insight through employee and customer surveys. That buyer opted for your services, and now he's one of your loudest supporters.

2. Educate/acquisition:
   - B2C example: You showed a customer how to properly fit a helmet. Now, he's committed to you and says he'll never buy online again.
   - B2B example: You showed a customer how to properly interpret market trends. Now, that client comes to you for all of her market-research needs.

3. Persuade/acquisition:
   - B2C example: You spent two hours on an evaluation ride with a customer of another brand of motorcycle. Now, he's purchased one from you.
   - B2B example: You provided a prospective buyer a day's worth of free onsite workshops, which resulted in you being hired to conduct all of her company's training in a specific area.

4. Inform/engagement:
   - B2C example: You let customers know about the cool Friday night get-togethers at your store. Now, most of them are regular participants.
   - B2B example: You informed a client about your new manager's round-table meetings, in which other clients gather while you facilitate current business problem solving. Now, that client, once a potential candidate for taking her business elsewhere, participates consistently.

5. Educate/engagement:
   - B2C example: You showed a customer how to winterize his motorcycle. Now, he brings his friends to get their bikes winterized, too.
   - B2B example: You showed a manager in your client's company how to better interpret employee feedback. Now, she wants you to help other managers understand feedback better, too.

6. Persuade/engagement:
   - B2C example: You taught a customer previously opposed to group riding how to do so safely. Now, he is a frequent participant in your dealership rides.
   - B2B example: You demonstrated to a customer who was previously opposed to crashing projects (shortening duration) how to do so safely. Now, when prudent, she does so to her advantage.

7. Inform/recovery:
   - B2C or B2B example: You informed an inactive customer about your new personal guarantee. Now, he's decided to come back and give your business another try.

8. Educate/recovery:
   - B2C example: You calmly and rationally showed all of the OEM communication to an unhappy customer with a back-ordered part and educated him regarding how the system works. He didn't love the fact that the part was out of stock,

but at least now he understands that it wasn't your fault—
and is willing to give you another shot.
- B2B example: You calmly and rationally walked a disgrun-
tled ex-client through a communication error between your
company and hers by pointing out where the breakdown
occurred, accepting blame, apologizing, and then asking for
an opportunity to regain her trust. She took you up on your
offer.

9. Persuade/recovery:
- B2C or B2B: You won back a previously dissatisfied customer by giving him your personal cell-phone number,
conveying that you'll be there when you're needed. He did.
You were.

These are just examples to get you thinking. Other areas that
might prompt the creation of situational sales success stories
include increasing revenue, decreasing costs, improving internal
communication, improving sales processes, enhancing customer
loyalty, and boosting employee retention. (For more examples of
how the S³ model can be applied, go to www.AcceleratetheSale.com
and click on "enhanced content.")

Concentrate on who you helped (with that client's permission,
if you're using actual names), and what you did—but not how you
did it. If you talk about the how—"We've helped ABC Corporation
increase fourth-quarter revenue by almost 55 percent through
targeting current customer opportunities, crafting new approach
methods, creating new closing tactics, and tracking accountability"—your buyer might be thinking, *We already tried those things,
and they didn't work.* As a result, he or she is mentally checking off
reasons why his or her company shouldn't do business with you.

Instead, mention what you did, with whom, and share the credit:
"We've helped ABC Corporation increase its fourth-quarter revenue by almost 55 percent. The firm has credited our insight with
identifying and taking advantage of new opportunities. We think
it was really its ability to partner and collaborate that made the
results possible." The likely response from your prospect: "Can you
do that for me?"

This is how you truly acc*sell*erate the sale.

Experiment with these ideas, and develop your own situational sales success stories. Then you'll join a long and, well, storied tradition of communicating via storytelling. And when you use the right story in the right situation, the story you'll be telling others is how much—and how much faster—you've been selling.

CHAPTER 4 Acc*seller*ators

>> Lose the tired questions ("Do you play golf?") and replace them with interesting questions ("How will the recent weather affect your business plans in the West?"). You'll be more interesting to your buyer and learn crucial information to help you sell more, faster.

>> Control conversations by using expert language. Use terms like *recommend*, *suggest*, and *advise*, and you'll find people will follow your lead.

>> Practice saying things three different ways. It will build your vocabulary and your language repertoire. Think basic, intermediate, and sophisticated.

>> You can't always win in your stories, or you'll appear inauthentic. No one *always* gets the business or saves the buyer relationship. Tell the occasional misstep story, and your prospective buyer will find you more credible.

>> Work to develop stories around client acquisition, engagement, and recovery, and you'll have a story for just about every situation.

CHAPTER 5

One Down, Four Up

THE POWER OF PROCESS

*eople were starting to stare. I fired up the 15-year-*old Harley-Davidson for the third time and tried to get it moving without kicking, bucking, coughing, and ultimately shutting down again. And I could tell that spectators of this unfolding scene—customers and employees alike— were starting to question two things: the integrity of the motorcycle the store had just taken on trade and my ability to ride it.

The old sage in our dealership stood off to the side and just smiled. He enjoyed my enthusiasm for the business, but he probably enjoyed teaching me lessons even more. After satisfying his desire to watch me squirm like Mike Tyson in a spelling bee, and knowing that I was absolutely helpless in this situation, he ambled over, leaned in, and said, "First is up."

"What?" I said over the roar of the big machine before it sputtered out again.

"First gear on this bike is up," he whispered into the now-deafening silence. "First is up; second, third, and fourth are down."

My mind reeled. How could this be? No motorcycle I had ever seen had a shift pattern like that. First gear is always down. That's the way it works: one down, four up, or one down, three up. First gear is *always* down.

The sage smiled, recognizing by my facial contortions that I was trying to compute what he just said. "It's the only time Harley ever did it."

Deferring to his experience, I kicked the bike *up* into first and roared off, hopefully saving my reputation—and that of the motorcycle. (The sage was correct: This particular model, the 1971 FX, appears to be the only Harley-Davidson model ever manufactured with such a shift pattern. It reportedly was a holdover design for a heel/toe shift configuration of the previous model year.)

That experience left a lasting impression on me as well as giving me a memorable metaphor for the sales process. All the conditions can be right: compression, fuel, spark. But if you don't know how to get out of first gear (or into first gear, as the case may be), you'll never go anywhere.

So far in this book, I've covered how to more fully leverage sales success, uncovered the mysteries behind sales success, explored how to create offering expertise, and discussed how to become more proficient with language. Now we need to focus on understanding sales processes.

There is perhaps no topic covered as thoroughly in the world of interpersonal selling as the sales progression. Sales processes have been analyzed, codified, proselytized, and sterilized to the point of pabulum. I hope to change that perception during the course of this chapter.

Standard Sales Models

Many approaches to selling include a five-, six- or seven-step sales process that is often overly conceptual and fails to guide salespeople of any skill level toward success. Such processes can be as deficient as a moped competing against an NHRA Top Fuel dragster, and they typically include the following generic sales steps:

1. Approach
2. Interview

3. Demonstrate
4. Handle objections
5. Close
6. Follow up

There are many variations on this theme. Ron Willingham's AID, INC. (Approach, Interview, Demonstrate, val-I-date, Negotiate, Close), or Neil Rackham's SPIN (Situation, Problem, Implication, Need-Payoff) selling are just two examples. There are hundreds, maybe even thousands, of others, including company-customized models.

The biggest challenge with many general approaches is that the focus is often on the task, not on the result. If I'm a sales manager working with a salesperson, and I ask for an update of his performance, the salesperson might say, "Well, I've talked with several potential buyers, and I'm building rapport with them now."

OK, that sounds good. If our organization is using one of the aforementioned general sales models, then as a sales manager, I might accept this response as proof of progress. Unfortunately, many sales managers fall into the trap of thinking that this constitutes action. And who can blame them? It's what we've all been told for years. But here are some of the most egregious problems with such an approach:

1. There is no observable behavior or outcome. The sales manager needs room to say: "Show me the rapport you've established with your buyers today."
2. The salesperson doesn't have a defined next step. Instead, he is going to "understand" these hot prospects any day now.
3. Managers have no way of evaluating the process, and the sales team has no way of acc*sell*erating the sale.

Performance-Based Selling

My take on this very old topic is one that views sales and sales management from a performance-based perspective, one that asks what the desired performance outcomes of your actions are. It is based on two simple, timeless premises:

1. **No one buys a saw because that person needs a saw.** Somebody buys a saw because he needs a shorter board. This is a performance-based mind-set that focuses on the results to be obtained, not on the methods used to obtain them. (Your ethical, principled, and moral approach to selling; personal integrity; and commitment to your organization and career prevent those results from being underhanded or manipulative.)

2. **Milestones are the best way to evaluate progress.** When you identify observable, performance-based milestones in your sales process, you can easily recognize when you've reached them, then move on to the next agreement in the sales process, which would be your next "yes." This is essential to effective management of the process and dramatically reduces sales-cycle time. Therefore, performance-based selling can be defined as a method of selling that focuses on results and milestones, constantly moving salespeople and customers toward the next agreement in your sales process.

Don't skim over that definition. Read it again slowly, carefully analyzing what it means to you. Let's deconstruct it further to clarify what we are describing:

» "A method of selling" implies a step-by-step approach to *actively* pursuing sales. Funeral directors wait for business; successful sales professionals don't.

» ". . . that focuses on results and milestones . . ." provides a defined, often provable, or observable performance indicator. Again, you don't buy a hammer because you want a hammer; you buy a hammer because you want to drive a nail (or perhaps fix your 1979 Harley-Davidson Sportster, the product of a notoriously bad year in Harley history).

» ". . . constantly moving salespeople and customers toward the next agreement . . ." suggests that sales success is not one big "yes." Rather it is a series of small, ever-building commitments, affirmations, and agreements. When you break down your sales process into small, "next agreement" chunks, you can continuously move forward, looking not to the end of a long, unknown road but at the next turn right in front of you.

» ". . . in your sales process." That's right; I said "your sales process." I don't believe there is an ultimate sales process that

"Go Make Rain Happen"

Anne Ponzio-Shirley, a 15-year veteran of technology sales and now a partner at the inScope Consulting Group, understands sales processes. She closed a $15-million consulting contract for her firm in 2009, and inScope launched www.goelectricdrive.com, the Internet resource for everything related to electric vehicles. The client, the Electric Drive Transportation Authority, is a Washington, D.C.–based consortium comprised of major car manufacturers, utilities, and Fortune 500 companies. Says Ponzio-Shirley,

You've got to get people the tools in order to succeed. Having a defined sales process that supports the ongoing strategy, vision, goals, and objectives of the organization is critical. Then, making sure that it is audited and refined over time ensures continuous improvement. But it all has to be linked and tied together. There is nothing worse than having the CEO communicate a vision but no way to get to that vision. A strong sales process, defined with customer input and the goals of the organization in mind, lays the foundation for a successful salesperson. Hiring a salesperson and having them try to go make rain happen with no process to follow will never be effective. There are really four things to keep in mind with sales processes: (1) They must be measurable. (2) They must be effective. (3) They must be repeatable. (4) They must align the goals of the organization to customer needs in an easy-to-understand manner.

works for everyone, and I'm not going to give you "Mark Rodgers's seven quintessential steps to sales success." Instead, I'm going to provide you with the major building blocks to create your own process. What you really need is an understanding of what's important in *your* sales process, how you can verify that your objective is obtained, and what's next in your sales progression.

When you create your adaptation of these suggestions and make them your own, the results will serve both you and your organization. And you, no doubt, will work harder, smarter, and longer to make it successful because, well, it's *yours*.

Sales Process Basics

The following are some typical components of an effective sales model. Keep in mind this set of steps is not comprehensive nor is it ordered in a sequence for how they might best work for you. They are intended to be fairly representative and give you a sense for the idea behind developing your own performance-based sales process.

Get Your Prospect's First (and Last) Name

What? What kind of useless advice is that? I will bet you, right now, there are salespeople in your organization who are speaking with prospects and not capturing this most basic of information. And yet they will be the ones with the audacity to say, "I can't understand why we're not selling more!" Occasionally, I'm asked how to obtain a prospective buyer's name. (I'm not kidding.) So I say, "Stick out your hand, introduce yourself, and look expectantly at the other person. If they don't tell you your name, you say, 'And you are?'" Other advanced techniques include: "I'm sorry, I didn't get your name . . ." and the always-popular, "Do you have a business card?" You may also acquire this information via a third party, such as a referral (a great idea we'll get to later) or through a list (a terrible idea, unless it's very specific and well-maintained).

Capture Surface-Level Information

You need to know the basics of what's going on with your potential buyers. What brought them to you? What's their current employment or business situation? What's the general nature of the exchange?

(For more ideas on how to do this in a quick, subtle, and sophisticated manner, see Chapter 7, "Torque vs. Horsepower: Fast Starts and Getting There First.")

Match Your Buyer's Purchase Cycle

Much like you have a sales process, your prospect has, consciously or not, a *buying* process. The key to your success is finding synchronicity between the two. When does your prospective customer want to buy? What, in particular, prompted him or her to take action now? What is important to him or her, both personally and professionally? Where else has this buyer received information? And just what kind of information is it?

Buyer Continuum

Buyers come in all descriptions. I believe there is a buyer continuum that extends from the impulsive purchaser on one end to the research extremist on the other. (See Figure 5.1.) You've probably witnessed this in action. One customer will spend a fairly sizable amount of money with what appears to be very little forethought,

■ **FIGURE 5.1**
Buyer Continuum

Impulse Buyer   Research Extremist

while another will take weeks to analyze options, create spread-sheets, and perform regression analysis to determine the right cell phone plan. (When you think about it, perhaps that's the kind of effort required to actually figure out most calling plans.)

Driven either by want or need, buyers explore their potential purchase a number of different ways. (See Figure 5.2.) They ask opinions from their friends, rely on trusted media sources, read online product reviews, and take long hard looks at what they are considering buying. In addition to researching the product, pros-pects might research the sale, too, checking out the organization and the salesperson. (I've been told many customers determine what brand of car they drive based on their previous dealership experiences, as in "I buy Lincolns because they treated me well at Garbo Motors.") Buyers then ultimately examine their findings, assess all the information, and make a purchase decision. And, as I noted earlier, some people spend way more time on this process than others.

■ **FIGURE 5.2**
Buyers' Purchase Process

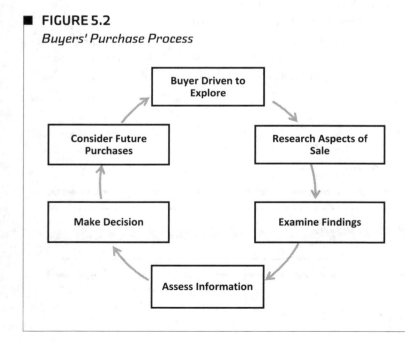

Obtain Meaningful *Background Information*

How do you know where your buyer is in the purchase cycle? Try asking questions like these:

» "If I may inquire, how long have you been thinking about this?"
» "What prompted your research for this (car, computer, consultant)?"
» "You sound informed; where have you done your research?"
» "What do you know about (some feature, product, or approach)?"
» "Have you determined a reasonable budget for this purchase?"
» "Are you hopeful to have this done by (this quarter, the end of the year, after the snow melts)?"

These questions will give you a fairly solid idea of where your buyer is in his or her purchase cycle. Don't be afraid to ask for specifics. If the buyer says, "I've looked online," you can come back with, "Where, specifically?" The idea is for you to augment his or her online research with your own knowledge, company information, and other services and to obtain enough background information to help move you to the head of the pack in terms of being able to help this buyer.

A jumbled, incomplete account of a prospect's history—"The company is thinking about maybe hiring a consultant to help with employee stuff; not sure what made them call us; sounds like they've talked to some other firms; they think they have budget and are planning to do something sometime next year"—does no one any good.

The prospect's history, as obtained by a high-performance salesperson, should read something like this: "Mack & Howe are looking for a consultant to help reduce employee turnover; they came to us because they read about our company in *Forbes*; they have already talked with two other firms: Deloitte and Stevens & Associates; they are looking to spend between $50,000 and $75,000; and they want to have an initiative in place by the first quarter of next year."

Or this: "Prospective buyer is named Kathryn Samson and is currently driving a 2007 Lexus; she has heard great things about the new Lincolns and wanted to check them out; she's considering

Cadillac's new coupe and has visited both local stores; customer is working at the medical center as an anesthesiologist; she doesn't want purchase to cost more than $500 per month but is also open to leasing."

In both of these sample profiles, the salesperson has gathered the prospects' names and interests, as well as key details about employment, what prompted them to consider the salesperson's organization, where else they're looking to buy, their purchase time frame and a good deal of info about financials. All of these details should be recorded in the organization's customer relationship management system, on a spreadsheet, or even in a notebook. They will likely be referred to time and again before the deal closes.

As a salesperson armed with this information, I know with whom I'm potentially competing—and high performers don't just know *of* them; they're actually familiar with their operations. Combine this knowledge with other information I've acquired about the prospective buyer, and I now possess very specific details that will help me best serve the customer. And when my sales manager— who lives by the motto, "Inspect what you expect"—inquires about the crucial information I've obtained from a prospect, I can emphatically answer in the affirmative and show the information. This is performance-based selling.

Obtain Crucial Contact Information

Again, noting such nuggets as a prospective buyer's direct phone number (extension or cell, with area code) and e-mail address (not website) seems like a no-brainer. But this concrete step—opposed to simply approaching a client or establishing a basic rapport—is frequently overlooked early in the sales process. Once you've captured a phone number and e-mail address, enter it into whatever database you're using. After all, if a prospect likes you well enough to provide crucial contact information, that's proof right there that you've already established some type of rapport. This model takes that "rapport step" and makes it subservient to the performance-based result: obtaining full contact information.

Additionally, if at all possible, make certain the potential customer's direct phone number is for a cell phone. This will obviously bypass any other "gatekeepers" and will give you the ability to send text messages (when appropriate). Text-messaging, once a skill mostly limited to teens and 20-somethings without jobs, has come into its own as a legitimate form of business communication. For various reasons of immediacy and time savings (namely, less small talk), I know many people who will respond more readily to a text message than to a voice-mail message or even an e-mail. Typically employed later in a sales relationship rather than earlier, it's an important tool to have at your disposal.

To obtain your prospective buyer's phone number and e-mail address, simply find a way to provide value early on in a sales conversation: "I've enjoyed our discussion. In case I find out additional information, how might we best stay in touch?"

If you've done your job correctly up to this point, you'll more than likely be provided all of the contact information you desire. In addition, you've created a sequence of small agreements.

Realize a Little "Yes" Leads to a Bigger "Yes"

This is a huge piece of the sales puzzle. The scientific, psychological evidence is clear: People are more willing to take you up on larger requests later if they've said "yes" to smaller ones first. Consider how many times your buyer has said "yes" in one form or another, even at this early stage in your sales process:

» "Yes, I'll tell you my name."
» "Yes, I'll tell you when I'm thinking of buying."
» "Yes, I'll tell you what aspects of your offer interest me."
» "Yes, I'll tell you where else I've gotten information."
» "Yes, I'll tell you my phone number."
» "Yes, I'll tell you my e-mail address."

This is powerful sales psychology. Ignore it at your commission's peril.

Get Expectation Agreement

Another component of an effective sales process is one that frames the customers' expectations of your exchange or relationship. It also should set the stage for you to ask for referrals, which I'll cover in depth in Chapter 9, "The Power of Referrals: Nitrous Oxide for

Your Sales Engine." For now, simply realizing that you should be prepping the prospect for a referral request sometime down the line is enough: "Well, Juan, we're thrilled that you're considering doing business with us. Just so you are aware, our objective here will be to make you so deliriously happy with your experience that by the time we're done, you're going to feel compelled to tell your friends and family about us. Sound good?"

Of course, feel free to use words that fit your style and that of your business and your prospects: "Dana, we're glad you're thinking about working with us. We want you to know our commitment is to work so hard for you that when we're done, you're going to want to refer your friends and family to us. Fair enough?"

Saying that this step is a powerful addition to your sales process is like saying Hurricane Katrina was a bit of storm. So many objectives are accomplished here: It states your commitment to your buyer's experience, it communicates your confidence in being able to help your buyer, and it sets the stage for you to receive referrals later. Explaining what to expect early in the process will dramatically increase the likelihood that customers will cooperate, making the transaction a much more mutually beneficial deal.

Also worth noting: All of the above pieces of information can be obtained at any time during the sales conversation, wherever you and your client might be. This exchange of information is not manacled to your retail establishment, the prospect's office, or a business luncheon.

Right about now is when some anxious sales managers must be asking themselves, *How do I know my salespeople are actually doing all of this? I need proof.*

Well, we're talking about performance-based selling, and all of the results should be provable. Could someone circumvent this step? Sure. Someone probably could circumvent a lot of steps in your organization. But that individual would just be cheating himself. You will know if referrals are being captured at the end of your sales process. If they are, this "experience frame" is likely being used. If referrals are not generated, you'll know that, too.

If, as a sales manager, you still have doubts, ask each member of your sales team to practice on each other the language, questions, and conversation examples provided here or to develop some of their own that attain the same objectives. Then do a "ride along" with your salespeople as they make calls or interact with prospects. You'll either hear these statements being used, or you won't.

Solution Suggestions

After discovering a prospect's purchase motivation, needs, and wants, an acc*sell*erated salesperson will be able to use his expertise to direct the prospect toward the best offering solution. This solution must solve the buyer's problem or satisfy a need or a want. It should fit the buyer physically, aesthetically, and financially. If you're talking about a piece of furniture, for example, the solution should be the right size for the room, look good in that room, and match the buyer's budget.

This is the point where buyer options come into play. Can you configure your product, service, or intangibles so that they make attractive packages for your buyer? For example, computer retailers often package the computer with software, a carrying case (if it's a laptop), numerous cables, and technical assistance. Cars feature various maintenance plans. Furniture is packaged with home delivery, warranties, and stain-protection options.

Package selling is not a new idea, but it remains a great idea. Here's why:

> » It provides a more comprehensive solution for your buyer. In fact, most buyers are happier when they buy multiple items: "I'm more satisfied when I buy a pair of pants, a belt, and a shirt than if I just buy the pants."
> » It simplifies the decision-making process and helps the buyer think more clearly about things. Instead of having to make one decision after another—"Do I want the car? Do I want the navigation system? Do I want the roadside assistance?"—the customer can simply choose between package one, two, or three.
> » It helps the buyer make the decision faster.
> » It puts the buyer in the picture (more on that in a minute), because it gives him or her all the control.
> » By providing your customer with a number of package options, you'll sell more items.

This solutions package idea works in both B2C (as just described) and B2B situations. For example, include consulting services in one of your proposal packages, and see what happens.

Take It for a Test Drive

Regardless of whether your offering is a product or a service, whether you sell B2C or B2B, you should encourage your prospective buyer to take your solution for a test drive. Now, if you're selling a tangible item like a car, a computer, or a guitar, that's a pretty basic proposition: Let your prospect give the product a try, and then answer any questions or amplify any interests. This gets a little trickier with an intangible, but it can still be done using language to achieve a similar experience.

Test drives should be an integral piece of your sales process. A test drive accomplishes one or more of the following:

» It helps your buyer begin to "see" him- or herself owning your offering.
» It maximizes and amplifies such emotional states as surprise, happiness, excitement, and pride.
» It conveys the perceived value of your solution.

Put Your Buyer in the Picture

When interacting with your buyer, make every attempt to mention how your offering will help him or her professionally and personally. In a B2B situation, you might say something like this: "As you can see, Julia, if we go this route, you'll be able to spend less time breaking up squabbles and more time concentrating on the real work of your operation."

In a B2C situation, try something like this: "As you can see, Ian, these chrome-plated covers resist dirt and grime, and they clean up quickly so you can get back out there and ride."

Another way to put your buyers into the picture involves you and your buyer collaborating on the solution. A great way to get this conversation started is to say something like, "Max, how would you describe an ideal solution to your situation?"

Transfer Skills and Knowledge

Engage your buyer by teaching him or her something he or she doesn't already know. This might range from helping a consulting client understand how your organization can quantifiably measure the results of an initiative (for example, "We go beyond training smile sheets to actually tracking workshop participants' performance when they return to the field") to simply sharing with him or her something different about your offering ("Many firms apply *their* process to you; we find out about your needs and build a process to suit *you*"). When you've improved your buyer's condition during the course of your sales process, that person will feel like he or she has more of a stake in the process.

Click the Pic

You also can *literally* put your buyer in the picture. In the Harley-Davidson business, I tell retailers to take a digital photograph of their prospective buyers when they are considering which model to purchase. This is a fantastic opportunity for the customer to see themselves on the motorcycle of their dreams (without having to invest in gigantic mirrors for the sales floor). A photo positively differentiates that salesperson and that dealership from the competition, makes the prospect feel like he's part of a fun family, and gives the salesperson a wholly legitimate reason to capture contact information and follow up.

This idea works in practically any face-to-face B2C experience. Working at Guitar Center and you've got a hot prospect eyeing a new Les Paul Custom? Shoot a photo of him with that piece of musical art in his hands with the digital camera in your pocket. Employed by an art gallery? Snap an image of the prospective buyer standing next to the piece she's considering. Selling furniture? Take a photo of the family kicking back on their sofa of choice. Make sure you use your own (or the store's) camera; this won't work with the customer's camera. The idea is for you to have possession of the photo, obtain the contact information, and then follow up.

I've also seen the picture method used with some degree of success in B2B situations. One company, for example, was considering buying a well-known author's business books and training materials for its employees. While the corporate buyer was having dinner with the author's representatives, the celebrity author surprised the buyer by joining them at the table. Naturally, the author's rep snapped photos of the buyer and the author together, and the corporate buyer wound up giving the writer his company's business. Was that solely because of the pictures? Of course not. But they didn't hurt.

Think about how you might incorporate a famous employee, cool logo, or unconventional office building into photo opportunities for your customers. I can't tell you how many Harley-Davidson

Building Pipelines and Using Facebook

Doug Slotkin, sales vice president for real-estate website Zillow.com, is quick to identify one of the biggest problems with real-estate agents:

Most agents don't have sales experience. About 80 percent didn't have prior sales experience before they got into real estate. So, they don't know about building and working a pipeline. They don't know that they should be building a future pipeline of business, and not all of it's going to happen right away. That's not a dynamic they're aware of, so we're there to help them on that front.

We give advice on how important it is to respond quickly and try all avenues. For example, if you've got an e-mail address and a phone number from somebody, you should call them. If you don't reach them, e-mail them to let them know that you're trying to provide them with the information they requested. If they're not responsive, it doesn't necessarily mean that they're not going to do business in the next six months or nine months. It just means that maybe they went on vacation. Who knows what happened?

So, we teach our agents to be patient. Some of the people are warmer, some are going to enthusiasts pose next to the company's iconic bar-and-shield logo each year at the corporate offices in Milwaukee—regardless of how much snow is on the ground.

These kinds of photographs aid the psychological phenomenon I call "ownership transference." When someone sits on a motorcycle (or slips on a dress or kicks back on a recliner), that person really is taking mental ownership. And having a digital photo to look at and share with friends enables that person to relive and reinforce those positive feelings of ownership. Putting your prospective buyer into the picture, both figuratively and literally, is a crucial step in your sales process.

respond quicker, some may not respond at all. But it doesn't mean that, eventually, you won't have an opportunity to work with them. You just need to let them mature a little bit.

Facebook is huge right now. So, if you've got a lead from somebody, and they didn't respond to your voice-mail message and your e-mail message, take their e-mail address, go to Facebook, and put that e-mail address on Facebook to see if they've got a Facebook page. If they've got a Facebook page, maybe they are somebody who's just more likely to respond to a Facebook communication than they are to e-mail or phone. So, go on their Facebook page and introduce yourself: "You had asked me for information in regards to buying a property in Delafield. And we haven't been able to connect, but I happen to see that you're on Facebook and thought maybe we could connect in the next day or so. When you have a chance, I'd love to show you what's available and see if it matches your needs."

That's the kind of on-the-ground advice that agents are not getting from their brokers. It's a value-add to what our sales rep brings to the table in terms of helping that agent be more successful. We're giving advice like that all the time.

Following Up with Real Value

If your sales cycle takes longer than a day (and whose doesn't!), make sure you continue to add value for your buyer, providing him or her with important information along the way to help make an informed purchasing decision. How? Deliver out-of-this-world value. On a regular but not annoyingly frequent basis, e-mail your prospect various items of interest: an article, a white paper, recent research findings, or anecdotal information he or she might find valuable. Those items can be relevant to the purchase conversation or something more personal that reflects, say, the prospect's interest in sports or theater. This enables you to stay in touch, keeps you at the forefront of the prospect's mind, and is dramatically more effective than mass mailings done by your organization.

Here's a business-related example, followed by one that's a bit more personal:

» "Hi, Megan, I thought you'd like to see this new article about the differences in personality-profile instruments we were discussing. I'll give you a call in a couple of days to see what you think."
» "Hey, Sean, I know you're a football fan, so I was wondering if you've seen this article about the Cardinals' program. I'll call you in a couple of days to see if you agree!"

Do not send daily e-mails that read: "Hey, Joel, do you want to do business or not?" If you do, count on hearing the latter response.

Be Able to Handle Tough Questions

No matter what you sell, customers are going to have questions and objections. Be aware of those objections and recognize that they can come from several different angles—no need, no money, no hurry, and no trust.

Handling objections is such a large part of the sales process that Chapter 8, "Accelerating Through the Curves: Rebutting the Toughest Objections," is dedicated entirely to this topic.

Trial Closes: The Difference Makers

What's the difference between a trial close and an actual close? A trial close asks for an opinion: What do you think about what we've talked about so far? An actual close asks the buyer to make a purchasing decision, to make a commitment, and sign on the line. Let's face it: Commitments are scary. In fact, commitments are terrifying.

I contend that at an appropriate time in your sales process, when you feel you've provided real value and real direction to your buyer, you should casually throw in the question, "So, what do you think?" This is the perfect trial close question. It's easy, conversational, and never appears out of place. And it will tell you *exactly* what the next step should be in your process.

If you say, for example, "What do you think?" and your buyer hesitates, then you know you have more work to do. You either didn't show the solution he or she liked or failed to present a compelling-enough case. So it's back to work for you.

On the other hand, if you say, "What do you think?" and your buyer says, "I *really* like it," you've just been given permission to go ahead and officially ask for his or her business.

Close Like a Pro

I'm tempted here to just tell you to ask for the business, then move on to the next segment. But there really is more to this process. First of all, when you ask for the prospect's business, start with your most extreme offer. Pick the most comprehensive or most expensive solution, and work down from there. Do this because you truly believe it is your "best" solution for this particular buyer. (If you don't believe that, and you suggest it anyway, you've just crossed an ethical line.) Offering the best solution first also acc-*sell*erates your sales conversations; if you present your least expensive option first and move up, you'll frequently repeat yourself. Plus, this approach provides the perfect setup if your buyer declines.

Here's what I mean: In the world of negotiation, there is a technique known as "rejection and retreat." Robert Cialdini, arguably the world's most-quoted sociologist on the study of persuasion, calls it "concessional reciprocity." If you offer your buyer your most comprehensive offering first, he may just say, "Yes!" If so, that's frost on the beer mug for you.

If, however, the buyer says, "no," you still have options—always a good thing. You can retreat after this rejection to your next, less expensive option, significantly increasing the likelihood that the buyer will now say, "yes!" After all, he recognizes that you've made a concession by offering something less extreme or expensive. Research also proves that customers feel better about their final decision and are more willing to fulfill their obligations by returning to you with repeat business and suggesting referrals, because you made a concession and they directed the decision. It works like this:

You: "What do you think?"

Buyer: "I really like it."

You: "Great! Should we move forward with Option A?"

Buyer: "I like it, but not *that* much. It seems too expensive."

You: "Then there is always Option B."

A note about this rejection-and-retreat method: It only functions properly when the first option is not a red herring, or something that you've artificially inflated. Also, retreating to your second offer must be done the moment the customer refuses your first offer. Don't come back two days later with that second option. (For more on leveraging opinions and the concept of rejection and retreat, see Chapter 11, "Trouble at High Speed: How Not to Lose Control of Your Buyer.")

Sometimes salespeople ask me what to do when the customer says no to *everything* you offer. Shrug it off: "Well, I'm sorry we weren't able to be of more help. But I'm glad I met you and hope we part as friends. But before we do, if I may ask, what specifically prevented you from going forward with us?"

With this approach, you may not get the business, but at least you'll leave on good terms—and perhaps find out something you need to adjust going forward.

Get Referrals and Testimonials

All sales professionals know they should regularly obtain referrals and testimonials, but this is one area of the business in which I think everyone can perform more effectively—myself included. Don't leave this task to some third-party call center from the Cayman Islands; just look your customer in the eye and ask.

Acquiring referrals is such an important component of acc*sell*-erating sales that I've devoted Chapter 9, "The Power of Referrals: Nitrous Oxide for Your Sales Engine," entirely to the topic. For the moment, suffice to say that after you've closed the transaction with either a signed contract or receipt of money, you should move the conversation in an alternate direction: "We're glad we've been able to help. As you and I discussed earlier, we are always trying to spread the good news about our clients and our services. Do you know anyone who might benefit from what we do?"

Pause. Do not be afraid of silence.

You can also use this opportunity to ask for a testimonial instead. If referral business is the gold standard on which you can build your business, testimonials are certainly silver. Asking for testimonials is similar to requesting referrals, with a slight twist.

You: "Well, we've certainly enjoyed working with you and look forward to our continued relationship. How have you liked the process?"

Buyer: "I thought it was great!"

You: "Excellent. As you and I discussed earlier, we're always trying to spread the good news about our clients and our services. Would you be willing to write down in a short e-mail what, specifically, you thought was great about your experience? I'd like to share that with others."

I guarantee (but only if you've done your job correctly) you'll receive a more-detailed e-mail than you expect. When customers have a positive experience with a store, company, or organization, they want to share that experience with others. Help them.

Continually Impress Your Customers

Many sales models focus on maintaining contact with past customers, keeping the relationship intact somehow. Wow. What an incredibly mediocre attitude. I mean, that's all well and good, but it's not necessarily what you need if you're going to create an acc*sell*erated sales cycle.

So what should you do?

Continually impress your customers. Remember their names, let them know they are important (even when you're not asking them to buy something); keep sending follow-up information after

Every Picture Tells a Story

What do O. J. Simpson's murder trial, Kurt Cobain's suicide, and Anna Nicole Smith's death all have in common? NMS Labs. They serve clients with DNA testing for criminal cases and identification of illicit substances, and they do an enormous amount of forensic toxicology work. Pat Haneman, national sales manager for the forensic business unit at NMS Labs—as well as the strategic business leader for forensics—is a firm believer in structure. In her line of work, she has to be. "I tend to be an individual who leans on processes very heavily," Haneman says:

I think it's critical that you have a structure to your sales approach with a client and also a structure to your sales call when you're in front of the client. It doesn't mean that you have to be paro-chial in how you approach your business, but I think it's important that you go in there with a plan, and you understand all of the tangents that can occur while you're in a sales call and know where you're going.

I'm a big believer in structure, to the point where I will diagram it with individuals before we go in to do a sales call. And when we come out, we go back to that diagram and say, "OK, let's do a bit of a postmortem on that sales call and see where it went." I particularly think that's important for new sales reps that do not have a lot of experience, because having that structure gives you a handhold so that you can, in a smooth fashion, move through the sales call. It allows you to, in a soft way, control the progression of that sales call.

they've made a purchase; and ask about their family, friends, and other interests.

Please don't treat this as a trivial suggestion, because it isn't. Impress your buyers to such a degree that they return to buy again and again from you and they send their friends to you, too. That's all the evidence you'll need to know your performance-based selling process works.

The idea behind a performance-based selling process is to make it results oriented. Again, people don't buy drills because they need drills; people buy drills because they need holes. Consider the output, not the input, and customize this process. In order for it to work, it's got to be *yours*! There are a lot of examples of process phases here. If you like them, use them and perfect them. If not, create your own. Just keep in mind that whatever you add must culminate in an observable result, not an intangible concept.

Diagram Your Process

Break down your sales process, as you currently know it, into easily digestible chunks. Then identify phases from this chapter you can employ, language you can use, or outputs you can show as that sales process progresses. Find greater efficiencies, and don't be afraid to ask: "Is there a better way?"

Be Prove-able

The idea here is to formulate specific direction markers that show you are moving toward a decision with any given buyer. You want to be able to say to your sales manager or your peers, "Let me show you where I am with this prospect."

CHAPTER 5 Accsellerators

» No one buys a saw because he needs a saw. He buys it because he needs a shorter board. Focus on the results to be obtained, not on the methods to obtain them.

» Don't focus on the big "score." Rather, think about small acceptances and agreements along the way. "Yes, I'll give you my contact information" is a great start.

» It's important to match your buyer's purchasing cycle. A big mistake many salespeople make is focusing on their own selling process, not on the buyer's purchasing cycle. Match that, and you'll be in sync.

» Understand the buyer continuum. Buyers can span the spectrum from spontaneous purchasers (even for such intangibles as consulting services) to research zealots (spending weeks deciding what cell phone plan to choose).

» Questions are good. Good questions are great. "You sound informed. May I ask, where have you done your research?" and "Are you hoping to move forward by the end of the quarter?" are two of my favorites.

CHAPTER 6

The GPS of the Sale

YOU NEED INSIGHT, NOT A SATELLITE

'm directionally challenged. I once got lost driving my car to my home in *my* city. My excuse was that I was thinking deep thoughts about selling more, faster. This geographic disability is why I was so excited when global positioning systems became readily available.

My first GPS was like an oracle sent from the heavens. I couldn't stop admiring its brilliance. A big, clunky gray box complete with large buttons and a *huge* two-inch lighted screen. It simply must have been something created either by former "Star Trek" set designers or James Bond's Q, the enigmatic scientist who developed all those awesome spy gadgets.

I marveled at this newfangled system's ability to provide directions to anywhere I wanted to go. *Imagine*, I thought, *never being lost again*—as the slogan for one such GPS proclaims. I smiled and sometimes cheered as my digital navigator, in her calm, confident voice, guided me into the unknown. But sometimes she scolded me. "Return to the highlighted route! Return to the highlighted route!" I didn't mind, because she knew the way. And I did not.

I also remember the crushing blow I felt when I realized the system wasn't infallible.

"Turn right in one-quarter of a mile," I heard my digital friend say one day, only to look around, assess my surroundings, and quickly discern that if I made a right-hand turn in one-quarter of a mile, I would be parked in the proverbial Lake Wobegon! It was like discovering Santa wasn't real, the Easter Bunny was my mom, and Barry Bonds *may* have used steroids—all in the same instant. How could this glorious technology let me down?

Now, of course, time and experience have shown that GPS systems are far from infallible. Some roads aren't incorporated, new residential developments sprout up, and manmade lakes are filled. And sometimes, just *sometimes*, to the delight of the Luddite, humans are more directionally accurate than computers. The question here is this: What is your sales destination, and what technology will you use to get there?

Technology You Can Use

Whether you are selling B2C or B2B, technology can help. Sort of like GPS systems for your sales efforts, contact management systems, process management systems, performance management systems, and the ubiquitous customer relationship management (CRM) systems are all part of the technology supporting contemporary business. But one of the most intriguing of all management systems is sales force automation (SFA), sometimes referred to as sales and field force automation (SFFA). PCMag.com defines this software program as "automating the sales activities within an organization. A comprehensive SFA package provides such functions as contact management, note and information sharing, quick proposal and presentation generation, product configurators, calendars, and to-do lists. When sales functions are integrated with marketing and customer service, it is known as 'customer relationship management.'"

A slightly different definition is offered by the Bridgefield Group's online glossary. The supply chain management consultancy defines SFA as "software and systems that support sales-staff lead generation, contacts, scheduling, performance tracking, and other functions. SFA functions are normally integrated with base systems that provide order, product, inventory status, and other information and may be included as part of a larger customer relationship management (CRM) system."

What's the difference between SFA and CRM? CRM systems are customer-centric systems that track purchaser or likely purchaser information, company interactions, purchase specifics, and similar data. SFA systems, on the other hand, are salesperson-centered and often track such things as lead management, sales forecasting, and the day-to-day tasks required to achieve a sale. SFA systems often, as already suggested, fit within a larger, more expansive CRM system—although some people use the terms interchangeably.

Doug Girvin, chief executive officer of Stantive Technologies Group, an IT programming partner of salesforce.com, makes the following distinction:

> I look at sales force automation as a subset of CRM. The CRM process begins with marketing, and that generates leads, which generate accounts, contacts, and opportunities, which generate sales that would be contracts. And then you have customer support on the postsales side. The sales force automation component, to me, really starts at the lead area and goes through to the closure of opportunities, and that's where CRM takes over: How do I manage that overall customer relationship going forward, beyond the transactional level, beyond the sales force automation element? So I see SFA as a very strategic component of an overall CRM strategy.

(Listen to my complete interview with Doug Girvin at www.Accel eratetheSale.com.)

However you define it, sales force automation is alive and well. In 2000, InformationWeek.com estimated the SFA software market to be a $2-billion-a-year industry; new projections from Global Industry Analysts, Inc., estimate the market will exceed $16 billion annually by 2015.

History of SFA

The evolution of sales force automation parallels that of personal computing. Some experts link the first iterations of SFA software systems back to the initial wave of contact management systems, which came into play in the early 1980s. Although the programs have changed immensely over the years, the objectives for why individuals and organizations continue to rely on these systems remain unchanged.

The first objective is to make sales practitioners more productive. By organizing appointments, contact information, buyer reaction, purchase order information, and other key details, SFA software allows sales professionals more time to accomplish the real task of selling—interacting with buyers. The second reason the SFA movement has gained momentum is that sales managers and sales executives needed a more comprehensive way to monitor sales force activities and share information with other departments within their organizations.

I was first convinced of the power of data in professional relationships years ago. I was speaking at a worldwide Harley-Davidson dealer convention with my wife (who also has worked for Harley-Davidson), and at the time I had been experimenting with the most basic of contact management systems. We were having a conversation with a few attendees when I recognized a dealer coming toward us. I politely excused myself from the current conversation, leaned out of the group, and greeted him.

"Happy birthday, Larry."

He took two steps forward. Then he stopped, turned, and with a stunned look on his face—as if he'd just seen the Loch Ness Monster and a leprechaun walking across the street holding hands—stammered, "What did you say?"

"Happy birthday!" I grinned like a five-year-old who just scored his first soccer goal.

Larry stared at me as if I were some sort of prophet, and stammered, "How did you . . . ? Who told you . . . ?" His voice trailed off. Finally, he said, "That's *amazing*. My children haven't even wished me happy birthday yet, and here you are."

For two years, Larry Brooks told everyone he met about this personal exchange. We've been friends ever since.

I knew then that data was important to cultivating relationships and sales. (Of course, John Naisbitt knew it before most of us, when he authored *High Tech/High Touch: Technology and Our Search for Meaning* in 1999.) But today's SFA systems do much more than simply collect names and remind you about customers' birthdays.

Basic SFA Features

Any sales force automation system will have as a component a comprehensive contact management database that stores names, addresses, phone numbers, e-mail addresses, and fundamental background and company information. Data for contact management can be input manually as well as through scan technology (like a business-card scanner, which reads the information and puts it in the system), blogs, and social-networking sites.

SFA systems also manage activities. For example, did you send your prospect an introductory e-mail, mail a hard-copy letter (people still do that, on occasion), or place a phone call? That kind of information—and its subsequent results—also can be captured. The details of all your customer interactions can and should be recorded for easy reference. Did you have a face-to-face meeting? Did you demonstrate your offering? Did the buyer have questions or objections? How did you respond to them? For me, this is the lifeblood of understanding where you are in your sales process with any buyer.

Other basics include e-mail functionality, which either interacts with your existing e-mail client (such as Microsoft Outlook) or operates on its own Web-based e-mail system. This enables you to quickly contact prospects after identifying a communication need in your activities log. And the most basic SFA system wouldn't be complete without a valuable scheduling component, which provides a method to organize calls, meetings, travel, buyers, and activities.

Much like anything else these days, SFA systems span the options spectrum, from mundane basic to dizzyingly detailed. If your organization operates under a formalized sales process—and it should—SFAs with a feature called "process workflow" will come in handy. This component allows users to customize all phases of the sales process while marking their progress with particular buyers and organizations. Consider it a guide or a method of accountability. I like the fact that it can help test the critical elements of the sales process and allow you to understand what's working and what isn't. Additionally, "automated lead capture" notifies you when a customer completes a contact information form on your organization's website. That information then is automatically added to your list of contacts.

Of course, these leads must be managed. Depending on volume and expertise required, a sales manager typically will assign each salesperson the responsibility of maintaining his or her own data. Whether it's scheduling time after your calls to input and update your systems, or setting aside time daily, this sort of disciplined approach is what can really make a CRM/SFA system work wonders.

Paperwork hassles can be minimized, too. Some systems configure the products and services that best match the needs of your clients, based on the information you input. Additionally, quotes, purchase orders, and contracts are generated automatically. This enables you to work more quickly, sometimes without even leaving your buyer's office. Systems also allow users to request a price concession (yikes!) via the system; e-mail a sales manager, who can evaluate the profitability of the deal; and confirm or counter. All quotes, purchase orders, and contracts can be managed and tracked.

Sales performance management is easily accomplished and enhanced, which makes the acquisition of an SFA system an easy one for decision makers. Closing ratios, profitability, and salesperson ranking all can be obtained simply and quickly, and management also can see what's in the sales pipeline to help forecast revenue targets and report to other areas of the organization. Programs can be optimized to assist sales managers in realigning territories or evaluating geographic trends, and others provide call-center integration. Did your prospect or someone from his company call your customer service representatives about a particular issue? If so, you'll know. And you won't walk into a buyer meeting and be blindsided by some unresolved customer service issue.

Advanced SFA systems also aid with sales-training solutions. Of course, I'm not talking about the face-to-face variety, but some programs are so sophisticated they can—depending on where you are in your sales process—provide tips about the next step in that process. Heading to a meeting with a buyer? Don't forget to stress your three-tiered marketing plan. Prepping for a group review? Check

Security and SFA

According to Doug Girvin of salesforce.com, the concerns over information security have gone by the wayside:

The cloud vendors [those supplying Internet-delivered software] have responded incredibly forcefully with very strong certifications, and places like salesforce.com have over 100 external security audits a year because of the Sarbanes-Oxley requirement [a U.S. law impacting data protection]. I would rank those vendors as much more secure than the traditional IT shops.

I think, organizationally, SFAs do a number of things. The first thing is they provide an automated way to roll up the activities and the production of the sales organization in a very simple way, so that you can see the numbers from a historical perspective and track trends, as well as do things like production and cash-flow planning in the case of manufacturers who have a supply chain to manage, or in the case of a small to medium-size business, in which cash flow is always important. The ability to see where you are, and where you've come from, and what the potential is for the future with some analytics tools, is a really powerful part of the sales force automation process.

out these online presentation pointers. Smart systems can handle this sort of heavy lifting and certainly are worth considering.

As you might imagine, all of this activity can be conducted and monitored through an application on your smartphone. Often referred to as mobile sales force automation (mSFA), these apps are still evolving through different iterations as users and programmers work to understand how to maximize their value.

Not all SFA systems—or users!—are as sophisticated as the ones above, but you have to admit, it all sounds enticing. There are hundreds of providers of SFA programs, off the shelf and custom built. They can be acquired through software installed on users' laptops or via the Internet.

The Bright Side of SFA

Unfortunately, because many field sales teams are on the road and not frequently seen by the home office staff, their productivity sometimes gets called into question. A huge benefit of SFAs, from this important political and productivity perspective, is that they make your sales team's actions more visible to others. Perhaps this is why Mike Bushinski, director of sales operations for a multinational corporation that deals in foreign-exchange-traded investment instruments, uses salesforce.com as his SFA of choice. His rule of thumb: "If it's not in the system, it didn't happen." His people understand this and use it accordingly. (Listen to my complete interview with Mike Bushinski at www.AcceleratetheSale.com.)

These powerful systems enable more accurate sales forecasting, which in turn enables better inventory controls, cash-flow management, and a host of other important organizational functions. They can also help with skills development, providing managers and salespeople an opportunity to review where and when a sale may have gone wrong and to collaborate on what might be done about it.

In addition, SFAs can assist with transparency and sales acc-*sell*eration, offering a template for what's next in your sales process. Practically all SFA systems boast the ability to customize phases of the sale, allowing you to use what's right for you and your industry.

When your buyer says, "Just do what you did for us last year," you'll want to respond with something like, "No problem, happy to help"—not, "Sure. Um, what was that again?" This brings us to another important component of an automated sales system: Every buyer interaction can be recorded, so repeat business can be captured quickly and easily. Plus, your buyers feel important because you will remember them and their particular situations.

Peer-to-peer mentoring, in which your staff helps each other, is yet another significant byproduct of SFAs. In fact, Bushinski now realizes that peer-to-peer mentoring is one of the main benefits of the system. "That's something we do a lot," he says. "Our sales team is in two different locations, New York and London. Now people in both locations can share notes and let each other know the dos and don'ts for any given client meeting."

The Dark Side of SFA

An oft-quoted statistic is that 50 percent of SFA initiatives fail to meet the desired business objectives, primarily because of low sales-team adoption rates—either as a result of the system being overly complex or the added responsibility of data maintenance. Sales managers also tend to overrely on them, opting to spend less time in the field and more time at corporate headquarters because they suddenly believe they don't need to actually see what's going on to know what's going on.

Additionally, because members of the sales team ultimately are responsible for documenting their actions, they typically report positive actions—regardless of whether they're accurate. Think about it: Would you really note that you blew the demonstration or mishandled a buyer's objection? Probably not.

Individualized Goal Analysis

Just as it is unwise to rely solely on your vehicle's GPS system, it's similarly ill-advised to rely completely on your organization's SFA system, no matter how sophisticated. As exciting as SFA systems can be (and they are), it's important to understand where their limitations are and where the human element takes over.

For example, say each salesperson on your staff has a goal of meeting with each of their accounts three times per month. Sounds perfect, right? This is one of those SMART (Specific, Measureable, Attainable, Relevant, and Time-Bound) goals that almost every company's management training program ardently supports. Plus,

---

STREET SMARTS

Why Bother? And Why Most Salespeople Don't

Respected business-execution expert Dave Gardner, president of Gardner & Associates Consulting, enjoys a successful career that has spanned some two decades. He suggests that the most compelling reason a sales professional or sales manager would want to adopt a CRM system is for organizational purposes:

Having this knowledge in a central repository that is backed up safeguards a company's investment in acquiring critical information. A sales practitioner can benefit from having all information in one place: contacts, pipeline, history of calls, e-mails, notes. One of the most powerful components a CRM system can provide is a dashboard of what deals are in process. If you have more than a handful of deals that you are working on, it is too much of a burden to try to remember everything, particularly if you are involved in a complex selling environment.

The second most-powerful reason to have a CRM system is to provide a status and chronological history of a deal or relationship with a customer—"Did I call him earlier this week or late last week?" "What, exactly, did I ask her?" This unburdens you from having to remember everything about a deal. The CRM system helps a salesperson stand tall. If you use CRM dynamically, it just becomes part of your

it's easy to set and measure using your SFA system. Merely monitor your call reports, and—presto!—you're complying with the new directive.

But this objective may not be what's required for your business. Some of your clients might need more than three meetings every month, others less. And still others may not require meetings at all; instead, they could probably use real-time problem-solving support.

routine—rather than a pain in the butt to deal with as a back-office reporting tool.

Adoption of these systems is the challenge. There is better adoption of CRM systems by inside-sales folks than field-sales folks. Why? Field-sales folks are generally working fewer and much larger accounts. Inside-sales folks tend to use CRM systems more effectively. Perhaps it is because their computer screens are in front of them all day. Field salespeople are, by nature, lone rangers—they really don't like people looking over their shoulders. They are also resistant, because they fear management may want to jump into the middle of deals that are in process in order to accelerate sales. The salesperson fears this will undermine his relationship with the account. Also, salespeople are a bit paranoid. They see their personal relationships as theirs, and don't want to make it easy for someone else to step into their specific role.

Finally, salespeople in the field—mistakenly, I think—don't see value in following a business process. They are there to close business, not capture information in a business application. But if they did, perhaps more would truly be successful. (Listen to my complete interview with Dave Gardner at www .AcceleratetheSale.com.)

Here's the rule: If it's easy to implement, the results are often hard to take.

It's no sweat for a manager to set the "meet with accounts" objective and use your organization's SFA system to monitor performance en route to that goal. The results, however, might be bothered clients, diverted resources, frustrated salespeople, and an overall reduction in production. Those subsequent downturns will definitely be hard to take.

The inverse is true as well. More meaningful objectives stem from actions with greater degrees of difficulty: spending the right amount of time with the right clients, providing the right information about the right offering. Is this harder? Yes. Does it require individualized attention? Yes. It is the right way to manage? Yes.

Regardless of how difficult individualized salesperson goal analysis may be, the resulting buyer satisfaction and loyalty will be easy to take. So while meeting with buyers is certainly important—and easy to track with your SFA—arbitrarily placing an across-the-board number on those meetings (or any other objective) may not be the wisest way to achieve an objective.

Even though I've used account visits in my example, this sort of arbitrary, across-the-board goal-setting wreaks havoc in many areas. What's really required here—and what your SFA can't do—is individualized goal analysis. This, thankfully, requires human intervention.

Performance Analysis

Your SFA system can tell you what has been done and what hasn't. Has a salesperson finished his call report and entered it into the system? Has she followed up with a buyer about a technical question? Has he asked for a particular client's business yet? What SFA systems can't do is tell you why something is (or isn't) happening.

Could your salesperson do what you're asking—finish a call report, say—if his life depended on it? Sounds extreme, but consider this: Perhaps a particular employee isn't entering his call report because he's not comfortable using the database. If necessary, give the user a tutorial, allow time for him to become familiar with the process, and then provide feedback on that employee's performance. Identify what he is doing well and what needs improvement. Or maybe the problem is not a technical issue, but one revolving around awkward seller-client conversations. Examine the source of the problem—something your system can't do for you.

If the performance issue isn't related to skills, that means the salesperson is blatantly refusing to accomplish the tasks at hand, which suggests you have a whole different set of challenges to work through. Does the employee feel his autonomy is being curtailed by you requiring call reports to be documented? Does she think she sells more, and sells faster, by *not* using the SFA system? Or maybe it's just a hassle to get to a computer and enter the data?

Jim Morrison had it right when he wrote the song "People Are Strange." People do and don't do things for many various reasons. This is why sales managers can sleep at night, knowing that there will be no computerized takeover of their responsibilities anytime soon.

Relationship Analysis

One plus one plus one equals three ($1 + 1 + 1 = 3$). There is no arguing that. It is the quantitative view. But this calculation also is used to demonstrate the limitations of a quantitative perspective.

Granted, one plus one plus one does equal three. It's also the mathematical representation of a man meeting a woman, falling in love, and having a child. And, of course, no equation can possibly display the breadth of human emotion involved in that kind of relationship. Think human emotion has no role in the world of selling? Think again; it's humans who *buy.*

What your SFA can't express adequately is the affinity your customers feel for your brand, your product, your organization, or even you. Yes, you can add customer comments in the "notes" section of your SFA. Yes, you can attach a letter of recommendation from that buyer to a file. But I would argue that without standing face to face and hearing the intensity in a buyer's voice or witnessing the look in his or her eye, you will never truly understand how that person feels.

This subjective perspective is part of what should go into your decision-making process when it comes to interacting with a particular client. What are you willing to do (work late or make special trips to his or her office) or not do (adjust prices or make program exceptions) to make the buyer happy?

Harder to measure but no less important are qualitative sales objectives, such as building outstanding relationships, contributing to brand awareness, exemplifying organizational culture, demonstrating corporate values, and becoming a trusted advisor or valuable partner. A quote from Albert Einstein (someone who knew a thing or two about quantitative analysis) ends this conversation: "Not everything that counts can be counted, and not everything that can be counted counts."

Understanding Personal Chemistry

Chemistry. It's a difficult term to define when referring to personal relationships. Often characterized as people having mutual attraction, rapport, or an emotional bond, chemistry is a distinctly human trait that cannot be interpreted by any SFA system—even the high-end ones!

Sure, an SFA system can capture such personal details as a buyer's avocation, family information, and other relevant data. But what it can't do is guide you through interpersonal interactions with your buyer. You can ask about a hobby or a family member when conversing with your buyer, as prompted by your SFA in your premeeting preparation. But the SFA can't tell you how to emotionally react to his or her response. Should you be sympathetic or empathetic? Should you be engrossed or merely interested? Should you be happy or ecstatic? Do you ask a follow-up question or move on?

Similarly, your e-mail analysis program may inform you how long a person takes, on average, to reply to your e-mails, or the time of day he or she typically replies, but it won't speculate as to why your client's e-mail habits are that way. Does she send you e-mail responses at 2:25 A.M. because she suffers from chronic insomnia? Do his replies consistently come through around 6 A.M., suggesting that he's up early to get work done or help the kids prepare for daycare?

How and why is this important to you?

Well, the insomniac could be prone to knee-jerk reactions as a result of sleep deprivation (come to think of it, having daycare-aged kids could result in sleep deprivation, too). So keep that in mind when communicating and interacting with this individual. Buyers with small children may be less willing to take risks when considering your offers and subsequent solutions to their situations. Instead, they may seek stability and safe options.

Naturally, these observations and insights can be included in the "notes" section of your SFA program. But if you're working on a two-year, $25-million deal, you'll likely have pages and pages of notes from numerous personal interactions. Reviewing all of those notes prior to each meeting could become laborious. You'll just want to review the critical issues and blend that with what you know about your client on a human level.

Understanding Group Dynamics

As a sales professional, you regularly interact with two primary groups at any given time: your selling organization and your buyer's organization. Let's concentrate on the latter.

A *group* is two or more people with common goals, norms, or a shared identity, while *dynamics* can be defined as the social, intellectual, or moral forces that produce activity and change in a given sphere. Individuals behave differently, quite often more conservatively, in groups. Whether the group is informal (friends accompanying another friend who is looking for a new car) or formal (a company committee organized to make buying decisions), group dynamics are always at work. Correctly evaluating and taking subsequent actions based on these dynamics is well beyond the realm of an SFA system. This is where *you* come in.

To understand group dynamics, you must understand the group roles people assume when operating in that type of environment. Some group members are initiators, suggesting actions or ideas. Others are information seekers or givers, while still others are evaluators who share their perspective on things. You can also add energizers, collaborators, collectors, and influencers to the list. Recognize that these roles are fluid; one person may play a specific role with one group and a completely different role with another. That said, I've been taught there is really only one role you should concentrate on: that of *the buyer.*

But the world is a complicated place, and many people will influence your buyer. To get a handle on this dynamic, one of the first things you should ask yourself is this: *What might a given person's position on your offer be?* Next, remember the adage, "Where you stand depends on where you sit." That mind-set will consistently provide you with a great starting point for determining the answer to your question.

If you're in a B2C situation and selling to spouses, for example, one partner may feel differently (read: negatively) about the purchase than the other. (In the Harley-Davidson world, we call this "spousal resistance.") If you are selling in a B2B situation, where group members sit will dramatically influence their perspective on a given issue. Marketing staff members may feel one way, members of the legal department may feel another way, and the people in accounting won't like whatever it is that's on the table because, well, they never like anything.

Another group dynamic difficult to capture and take decisive action on is a person's organizational influence. What weight does that individual carry within the group? You can certainly record job titles in your SFA as well as who reports to whom, but that will never accurately tell the entire story of a person's influence.

Finally, interrelationships are at the heart of group dynamics. People have positive and negative relationships of varying degrees. Do you have a positive relationship with the senior VP but a negative one with the director who reports to him? Does the manager in another department support your initiative? Understanding those relationships—even just a little—can help significantly acc*sell*erate your sales. (Although most SFAs can't help with group dynamics, I can. Go to www.AcceleratetheSale.com to obtain a free buyer's organizational mapping tool.)

Understanding Situational Dynamics

Even if you update your SFA as often as possible, you're still missing out on real-time data. As a result, you must continually be on the lookout for situational dynamics occurring with your buyer.

The "rule of contrast" for a particular buyer states that whatever has come before colors, influences, and shapes all that comes after. In other words, if someone is exposed to a less-expensive offer prior to yours, your price might seem even higher. If an individual is given a poor demonstration by a competitor, yours will look even better. When possible, be aware of what has already happened when interacting with your buyer. Think of yourself as a journalist, always on point and seeking the who, what, when, where, why, and how of what is happening with your buyer and his or her organization.

Another situational dynamic could, in fact, be a static situation. Consider the likelihood that somebody will change his or her mind about a given product or service that you're selling. Some individuals or groups will readily alter their opinions when provided with the right kind of information. Others remain entrenched in their positions, and—no matter what information is presented—will not reconsider.

Finally, you must assess whether your situation is objective or emotionally charged. People, obviously (and organizations, not so obviously), experience hundreds of moods per day, and those moods can play a material role in their decision to buy. This means that you, as the sales professional, should be able to discern a given mood and then act accordingly. If, for example, you sense that your client is having a rough day, suggest picking up the sales discussion another day, and ask what time is good for him or her.

Insights and Satellites

There is no question that SFA systems are here to stay, and that is fantastic. Centralized information, improved collaboration, and enhanced accountability and management functions improve sales-force and salesperson productivity.

But there is simply nothing that can speed a sales professional or his organization toward a destination more effectively than being armed with the proper sales insight: A well-designed SFA and a finely tuned skill set are the one-two punch of a most-effective sales effort.

Exclusive reliance on either could leave you all wet.

CHAPTER 6 Acc*sell*erators

» Whether you are selling B2C or B2B, CRM/SFA technology can help you do more, faster, by organizing contact information, buyer reaction, and purchase information.

» While it seems contradictory, incorporating computer systems into your sales process can actually help you develop better personal relationships with your buyers. You'll minimize the chance of over-looking details or forgetting personal preferences.

» Good performance is about accountability. As sales director Mike Bushinski says, "If it's not in the system, it didn't happen." In order for your SFA to work, you must enter all your activities, opportunities, and data as soon as humanly possible. Then everyone can see the important work being accomplished by you and your sales team.

» Jim Morrison had it right when he wrote the song "People Are Strange": People do and don't do things for many various reasons. Is it a skill or a will that's hampering the adoption of CRM/SFA systems? Either can be rectified with solid sales management.

» What CRM/SFA systems can't do is evaluate the qualitative side of your buyer relationships. More difficult to measure but no less important than hard data are qualitative sales objectives, such as building outstanding relationships, contributing to brand aware-ness, exemplifying organizational culture, demonstrating corporate values, and becoming a trusted advisor or valuable partner.

CHAPTER 7

Torque vs. Horsepower

FAST STARTS AND GETTING THERE FIRST

Wearing a polo shirt, gabardine trousers, and tasseled loafers, the wary customer moved carefully through the entryway like a rabbit suspecting a hungry fox to appear at any moment. *Definitely a "citizen,"* I thought to myself, employing biker vernacular for someone who isn't yet engaged in the motorcycling lifestyle.

Realizing he faced no impending doom, the citizen straightened his back and feasted on the sensory stimulation coming at him from all angles. The dealership was state of the art, expertly organized, and almost operating-room clean. Rows of gleaming Harley-Davidson motorcycles stood like sentinels, protecting their century-old legacy as rolling sculptures. The symmetry of their formation and the jewel-like paint jobs amplified their magnificence.

An intoxicating aromatic mix of rubber, leather, and a hint of cosmoline (the petroleum-based substance used to keep new motorcycles new) filled the citizen's nostrils. I smiled, recognizing the physical manifestations of something being switched "on" deep in the primitive regions of his brain. He scanned the 25-foot-high ceilings, where huge black-and-white photographic prints hung, showing hearty early-20th-century bikers engaging in rugged adventure that would make even the most ardent contemporary yearn for simpler times.

In stark contrast to those images, a huge high-definition television screen burned brightly with footage of a rock band singing about rebellion and freedom, the beat thumping through the dealership's sound system. I watched as the citizen began to nod his head to the music, gradually becoming more comfortable in his new environment. The rumble of throaty V-Twins out back and the sound of laughter coming from a trio of bikers standing by the coffeepot rounded out this scene's symphony. The citizen smiled, acknowledging that he had not walked into some dangerous outlaw biker lair, and his caution turned to curiosity.

I have watched scenes like this play out *hundreds* of times in my career. I've worked all sides—in stores, at corporate, and as a consultant. This time, it was during a brief consulting visit with a Harley-Davidson dealership.

My acc*sell*erated salesperson—"my guy," as I call him— approached the customer. In a flash, the citizen's disposition turned defensive again. He planted his feet and squared his shoulders, ready to head off the dreaded, high-pressure sales attack.

"Day off?" my guy asked innocently, hands comfortably in his pockets.

"No, well—um, sort of," the citizen stammered, surprised by this low-key approach. "I didn't take the whole day off, just the afternoon. I work down at the medical center, but I cut out early to stop by and check out the new Softail. I've been driving by here for a month, thinking about coming in but never actually stopping."

"Well, then, the first thing you'll need is a brochure. Tom Stevens," said my guy as he stuck out his hand.

"Bill Thompson," said the citizen, returning to his more relaxed state. (I've changed the names to protect the guilty!)

"Welcome, Bill Thompson," my guy smiled sincerely. "I'll be right back with your brochure."

He spun and headed back to his office to get the promised brochure (and to quickly capture all of this vital new information in the dealership's CRM system). On his way, my guy shot me a smile so large you'd have thought he just hit a walk-off home run in Game Seven of the World Series.

It worked exactly as we planned.

Using only two words, my guy—in a matter of seconds—differentiated himself from the "may-I-help-you" crowd, engaged the wary customer in pleasant conversation, discovered his buyer's primary interest (Harley-Davidson Softail motorcycles), exchanged first *and* last names, and, most importantly found out that, yes, this potential buyer is employed! Perhaps even *well* employed.

This acc*sell*erated salesperson also was leveraging the psychological principle of reciprocity with his use of the brochure—using this marketing tool, first and foremost, to help his potential buyer make a more informed decision, but also as a device that engineers time for our hero to capture this information in his CRM system (or, at the very least, jot a few quick notes at his desk so he can enter the details later).

Just like that, he created sales torque.

Sales Torque

Have you ever been pinned to the back of your seat in a high-performance sports car? Or clung for dear life as a motorcycle's handlebars felt as if they were being ripped from your hands as a result of your engine's thrust?

If so, you've felt the g-force created as a result of massive torque. It's what gets you moving down the road. Fast. Many people incorrectly believe that horsepower is the most important rating used to evaluate the performance of a motor. Actually, a higher torque rating is what results in faster starts.

Loosely defined for nonengineering types, torque is simply "force causing rotation"; it is what you *feel*. So, let's focus on output rather than input.

Most engineers will tell you that if you want to apply the idea of torque (or Newton meters, for European readers), you must address three critical variables: force, time, and work. Sales torque works much the same way:

» *Force* describes the expertise and credibility you bring to the exchange.
» *Time* is the efficient manner in which you bring that credibility to the table: not too fast, not too slow.
» *Work* describes your ability to provide the right information to the right person in the right manner.

When you do all this well, you create the "power curve" shown in the sales torque illustration in Figure 7.1. This means you are maxi-

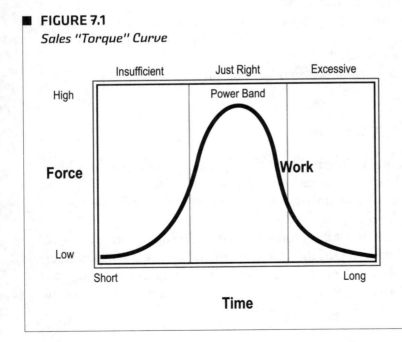

■ FIGURE 7.1
Sales "Torque" Curve

mizing the output of your sales engine. With actual motors, this is an exact science; with sales, it's more of an art form.

Two Words, Powerful Results

The questioning technique my guy demonstrated in the example with the citizen is what I call a "two-for" question: Two words, fol-

Economy of Words

In November 2010, the Associated Press reported that the United States Postal Service lost $8.5 billion the previous year, despite cutting more than 100,000 jobs. No doubt many reasons exist for this, but one certainly could be the lackluster service often provided by local postal workers. (I know, I know, some offices are better than others.) My wife and I couldn't help but notice an abundance of service options and point-of-sale items available now, offered in an effort to stimulate postal sales and revenue.

But the attempts by behind-the-counter employees to sell those services or items usually border on the feeble, if they're talked about at all. "Would you like your package to be sent overnight, Priority, First Class, or regular mail?" they often ask halfheartedly, usually sparking discussions about the differences in service and costs. And so it goes: "Would you like delivery confirmation?" "Do you need any stamps today?" "Are you interested in renting a post office box?" This all takes time, and most people want to get in and out of the post office as quickly as possible. Not to mention, when you are 15th in line, you've heard these phrases so much that they lose meaning.

If the U.S. Postal Service wants more business, their transactions should be more efficient! What's my solution? Why, two-for questions, of course: "Need stamps?" "P.O. box?" "First Class?"

lowed by a pregnant pause (absolutely crucial), and asked for three reasons: to differentiate the sales professional from others the prospective buyer has met, to begin a rapport by establishing a dialogue, and to discover essential information about the prospect.

That's a lot of work accomplished in very little time. And that's why I refer to the use of the two-for questions as sales torque. In my workshops and consulting practice, I've worked with thousands of salespeople over the past two decades, and this technique *never* fails to generate results. I taught this approach to one small-business owner who used it to garner a $20,000 sale just minutes after learning it. He enthusiastically reported back to me, "You said it. I used it. They bought it!"

Now, don't misinterpret this point. I'm not saying the two-for approach is the *only* reason why this small-business owner and others have enjoyed great sales success. There are far too many variables in the average sales exchange to make that kind of statement with any amount of authority. However, I am saying that it's a significant contributor to getting sales started.

Whether you are in a B2C or B2B selling environment, the possibilities for the two-for method are almost limitless.

B2C face-to-face exchanges might include: "Day off?" "Come far?" "Nice outside?" "Half day?" "Lunch break?"

B2B exchanges could be one of these: "Big project?" "Good meeting?" "Tough sell?" "Long day?" "Good call?" Or my personal favorite: "Got budget?"

The only boundary is your creativity—and perhaps good taste.

Not Just for "Opens" Anymore

Keep in mind that the two-for technique isn't limited to the opening moments of a conversation; it can be used anytime during your interactions. Then, listen as the other person provides vital information you can use to your advantage and his.

On many occasions in my consulting practice, I've used this "two for" approach in the middle of meetings with clients, during lunch breaks, or in discussions about other projects. One conversation went like this:

"Well, of course, we've got some tight deadlines on the ABC software integration," a client organization staff member said to another.

"Yeah, we sure do," his coworker commiserated.

Now, I was in the room, an invited guest sitting at the same table where this conversation took place. In no way was I wildly overstepping my boundaries when I piped in with "Big project?" (I then took a bite of my turkey sandwich, so I *couldn't* say anything else; over time, you'll develop similar techniques.)

"Oh, you have no idea!" the first employee exclaimed. "We've spent so much on this, it's incredible. Two years, lots of budget, and the problem is that the retail channel isn't on board."

"Plus, don't forget all the time and dollars spent on the big outside computer company before that," chimed in the other. "I don't know if we'll ever get full integration."

By this time, I had masticated enough of my sandwich bite to ask another two-for question.

"Tough sell?" (Then I took another bite, a sophisticated strategy.)

"You have no idea!" the first one started up again. "The retail channel is screaming bloody murder about the change, the field sales guys don't know what to think, and expectations are enormous. We could be in for a rough road getting this thing adopted."

"You know . . . ," the other snapped his fingers, looking at me as if he'd just discovered fire, "you might be *just* the person to help us."

To which I replied with one of my favorite two-for lines: "Happy to."

Not only did I enjoy a delicious turkey sandwich, I also found another piece of business that I used to leverage my talents and expertise by helping this client reach its objectives. That's the ultimate value exchange.

Determining quickly and effectively how you can help your buyers achieve their objectives leads to sales-career success. The old adage is true: If you help enough other people get what *they* want, you ultimately will get what *you* want.

If you take away just one nugget of information from this book (and there are dozens of nuggets), make it this technique. Use the two-for approach as I've described it, and you'll have the other person talking and sharing plenty of information. Guaranteed. And when they're talking, *you're* selling.

Create Peak Prospect Attraction

Two-for questions are just one of several ways you can create sales torque. In sales seminars, I used to ask people if they'd like to know the secret to doubling sales. Considering the room was usually full of commissioned salespeople, this was a bit like asking a hiker who spent the past two weeks climbing Mount Shasta if he'd like to come in to warm himself by the fire.

I'd go through this big routine of making seminar participants promise they'd keep this secret and not share it with others. Then, in a profound voice, I'd ask everyone to get out a pen and pad of paper and write down this: "The secret to doubling sales is . . . (big pause for dramatic effect) . . . to see . . . (another pause) . . . twice as many people."

At that point, most of my audience would groan, some would laugh, and others would scribble this secret down quickly so they wouldn't forget it. Regardless of how people responded, I know that I was speaking nothing but the truth. *The secret to doubling sales is to see twice as many people.*

If you want to sell more, you need to interact with more potential customers. But if you want to sell more, more quickly, you must attract buyers to interact with you. That's an important distinction. As a salesperson, when you approach someone about your offer, it's not necessarily a strong enough move. But when a buyer approaches you, that's a totally different situation.

Many salespeople don't do enough to attract prospects. Call it brand building; call it establishing your credibility; call it getting your name out. I call it peak prospect attraction. However you'd like to think of it, you need to engage in activities that will result in buyers coming to you.

How do you do this? Get out and about. Become a known figure in your buying community and within your greater industry. Establish yourself as the go-to person in your field by building your expertise and moving that expertise in front of the people who can buy from you.

If you build homes, become known as the company that builds quality homes, on time and on budget. If you sell building supplies, become known as the leader in your market, the one that understands costs and sourcing and possesses a variety of contacts that can always deliver. And if you sell real estate, your firm should become recognized as the most knowledgeable in the area.

Organizations become that way by first building their expertise, and then building their reputation. Then, after all of that assembling, you must get the word out—and two great ways are writing and speaking.

Write About It

Thanks to technology, there are numerous ways for you to use the written word to attract buyers, from posting on your LinkedIn page to writing a commercially published book. I know one motorcycle salesperson who, on his own initiative, keeps a running list of all his customers and prospects and regularly sends them a meaningful how-to paragraph every month. Another client uses the marketing department to publish a newsletter branded and personalized by the regional sales manager. And a local small-business owner publishes books on home repair and home maintenance to feed his primary business, which is home inspection.

Why should you engage in these activities, too? First, when buyers see your name in print, it positions you as an authority on the subject. People, especially consumers, often defer to the advice and guidance of experts. Second, you can reach many people with a meaningful yet nonpromotional message, enabling your readers to become more familiar with you to the point they feel they know you. In terms of creating sales torque, participating in these sorts of approaches is terrific. Look at all the great work you're getting done in a short period of time.

As a sales professional, you can take a variety of approaches with your writing strategies:

» Your organization's internal hard-copy or electronic newsletter
» Your organization's external hard-copy or electronic newsletter
» An article for an industry trade publication
» A piece for your local newspaper's op-ed section
» Social-media networks, via your own pages and those of your organization

Keep in mind—and this is crucial—that you're not writing promotional copy. You don't want to proclaim, "You won't believe the price we can get you on aluminum roof trusses!" Rather, these should be informative pieces that help your readers (your buyers, really) do, think, or feel differently about something: "The problem with northwest hardwood and how it will affect homebuilders in Iowa."

Include your name, with a current photo and contact information, and watch people seek you out for more information. Do this with some regularity, and you'll become a known entity. That's the idea behind peak prospect attraction; buyers come to you.

Use social-media platforms to burnish your image and reputation by posting a comment about something you heard in a keynote presentation at a cool seminar. This will start a conversation. Or simply post a question in one of the forums you frequent, such as, "What was the best marketing idea you saw this year?"

On the other hand, photographs of you passed out after Friday night's revelry might not be the best thing to post on your Facebook page if you're actually trying to drum up business. That profane and political rant about how the United States needs a third political party dedicated solely to the legalization of marijuana, about which you tweet incessantly? Stop.

Speak About It

Another way to create peak prospect attraction is to talk to groups of people in which there may be buyers or buyer recommenders. This follows the same approach as writing, just using different communication skills.

Who should you talk to?

» Local business clubs and associations
» Better Business Bureaus
» Area trade associations
» Audiences at specific industry events
» Attendees of off-site business functions
» Listeners to call-in radio talk shows

Anyplace you can position yourself as an expert will work. Remember, the message needs to be as nonpromotional as possible. If you sell computer consulting services, provide advance information on computing solutions that will be available in the coming year. If you sell cars, explain the resurgence of American muscle cars or the impact of hybrid vehicles. If you sell real estate, expound on the "new normal" and how it relates to property values. Do this enough, and you're talking real sales torque.

Few salespeople also double as professional public speakers, so it's wise to learn how to create an engaging "open"—an interesting way to start your talk. My favorite involves asking a rhetorical question. For example, "Have you ever wanted an automated solution that could make your job easier and your commissions higher?" Then make three to five brief points about your topic—each supported by a fact, statistic, or anecdote. Finally, summarize what you talked about and what you'd like your audience to do or feel as a result of spending time with you. (Go to www.AcceleratetheSale .com for a short video tutorial on speaking for sales professionals.)

Whether you're leading a talk at a local business association, writing op-ed pieces for newspapers on relevant topics, or starting meaningful discussions among your colleagues on LinkedIn, you mustn't be afraid to put yourself out there by engaging in activities that will attract more buyers.

To create even greater sales torque, find more of the *right* people.

Focus on the Buyer

"The number-one mistake most salespeople make," says Chuck West, program director for the University of Wisconsin's Executive

Education sales programs and a former sales executive for 3M, "is that they are not working high enough in the organization." He's talking about working with buyers. Not influencers. Not recommenders. *Buyers.*

A buyer is someone who is interested in your offering and who has the means and authority to pay for it. You need to quickly identify whether a person can buy what you are selling. Way too much time is squandered by salespeople spending time with people who can't buy. Oh, yes, there are always exceptions. For example, I know someone who once spent time with a prospect only to discover he had filed for bankruptcy; although he couldn't buy, he brought his friends who could. Things like that happen on rare occasions. Keep in mind that you should never be rude to someone; you just need to make good choices about how you spend your time.

If you're involved in B2C sales, spending time with people who can buy is a natural. Otherwise, why would they be talking to you? If you are involved in B2B sales, though, choose your clients wisely, targeting successful operations over low performers.

Professionals who create sales torque spend time with *buyers*; those who spend time with others just spin their wheels. When you work effectively with buyers, you also can dramatically reduce the time it takes to close a deal. But many salespeople, for a variety of reasons, don't spend time with the people who can say, "yes." This may be due to lack of access to high-powered decision makers. Or, more likely, those salespeople don't have the skills to comport themselves effectively when they are in front of the right people. As a result, they shy away from spending time with the very individuals who can dramatically acc*sell*erate their sales success.

Whether you are selling to large corporations, small-business principals, or the head of the family, here are some things to keep in mind.

Increase Your Business Acumen

Sales executives speak the language of balance sheets and income statements. It is fundamental to most of what they do, as these are among the tools used to measure their organizations' performance. The fastest way to build your business acumen is to learn the various components of an income statement. (See Figure 7.2.) This way, you'll be able to talk about what you offer and how it might positively impact your buyer's situation. What is the fastest way to do this? Be able to sketch an income statement by hand, from memory. When you can do this, you'll remember the various components and be able to ask questions based on these categories. This will genuinely and significantly improve your business acumen and your ability to relate to those higher in the organization. If, on the other hand, you're selling in a B2C environment and working with people buying big-ticket items, learn the basics of family budgeting.

Pick Two Thought-Provoking Questions

One reason more salespeople don't sell more, faster, is that they try to do too much. For example, many don't make great first impressions because they don't create that big "aha moment." Instead of trying to wrap your mind around the 57 different ways you can impress a prospect, pick two questions that will really make that person think.

■ **FIGURE 7.2**
Income Statement

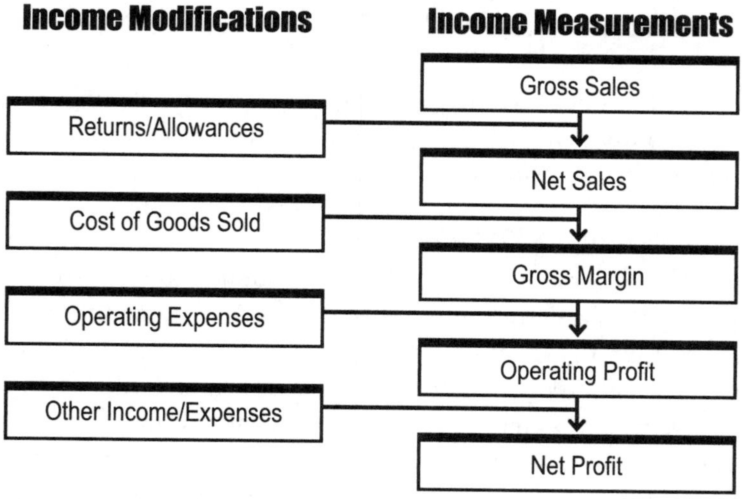

Income Modifications	Income Measurements
	Gross Sales
Returns/Allowances	Net Sales
Cost of Goods Sold	Gross Margin
Operating Expenses	Operating Profit
Other Income/Expenses	Net Profit

For example: "What's the one aspect of your business that's holding you back right now?"

Then follow up with: "If I may, what are the barriers preventing you from working through it?"

Those two questions always seem to get corporate buyers thinking. When working with consumers, two questions that typically work are, "What's the most compelling aspect of this offering to you?" and "If you could change just one thing about what you're currently doing, what would it be?" You may feel more comfortable asking different questions, but always have two good ones ready to go to get you off to a fast start.

Become a Person of Interest

Not in the criminal investigation kind of way, of course. Just be energizing to be around. Be interested in others, contribute to a conversation, and provide valuable insights. Conversation is a lost art these days, but don't let it become so with you.

Learn to read national and local newspapers quickly. One way to do this is to download smartphone apps for *USA Today* and *The New York Times*, and then practice what I call "4/3/2/1": Read the top four news stories of the day, the top three business stories, the top two sports stories, and, finally, the top book or movie review. If you do this, you'll be able to speak with just about anyone on just about anything—at least for a little while.

When you travel, learn something about the locale and the people who live and work there. Ask questions, then ask follow-up questions. When you are interested in others, they will be interested in you. It's that simple.

Find Something in Common

We spend more time with—and have a tendency to feel stronger bonds with—those with whom we have something in common. So, if you're looking to get off to a fast start with a prospect, find some common ground. Keep in mind that you should match the tone and tenor of your buyer's lead. If he wants to chat and find out about your background, chat. If she wants to start talking details right away, dissect the details. At the same time, always be looking for similarities you can draw. Military service, business philosophies, a fondness for Europe—whatever it is, find it and use it.

Understand the Import of Comport

When it comes to professional relationships, you can contribute to your sales torque by understanding the import of comport. By that, I mean behaving appropriately when interacting with buyers.

You can't go wrong being pleasant and polite. Smiling and congenial? Fantastic. Sullen and moody? No way. It should go without saying, but you also need to understand the basics of good manners and etiquette. Talking with your mouth full or stirring your drink with your finger should be avoided at all times. Know the basics of table settings and utensil use. Be yourself, by all means, but realize that executives you don't know will be forming opinions of you instantly.

Expensive, but Worth It

This chapter opened with a quick and easy technique to help sales professionals get off to fast starts with prospects, which led to a discussion of strategies and supporting tactics. Now, I'd like to end this chapter with a very fast, very effective way to create additional sales torque. It's not for the faint of heart, but if you can muster up the courage, you'll notice significant sales accselleration.

I learned this technique by reading Robert Cialdini's seminal book *Influence: The Psychology of Persuasion,* and I've since used it with great success. The idea is simply this: If you need to establish credibility quickly with someone, lead with your weakness.

This is antithetical to most salespeople's DNA. We're all about what we can do for buyers, not how we can fail them. But, as Cialdini explains so well, every offering has strengths and weaknesses. If you need to establish credibility fast, and you don't have days or weeks to build rapport, starting out by mentioning your greatest weakness proves to the prospect that you're knowledgeable enough about a particular issue to know both the pros and cons—and that you're honest enough to mention the negatives up front. Then, when you use a turnabout phrase—"However, our strengths overpower any shortcomings"—those strengths stand even taller. Cialdini cites many examples of advertising messages that adhere to this approach, one of the most famous being L'Oreal's "Expensive, but worth it" tagline (one, I might add, that I have unashamedly used during fee conversations with clients).

In the initial moments of your first conversation with a potential buyer, try a line like this: "We may not be the biggest consultancy, but the strengths of our highly skilled team overpower that shortcoming." On the phone with an interested consumer, give this a shot: "We're not the closest store, but you'll find we're worth the trip."

Remember, while engine torque will always be a very scientific and exact measurement, sales torque is an art form. Experiment and practice with these ideas, and you'll be off to the races.

CHAPTER 7 Accsellerators

>> Create appropriate two-word questions to help you garner important information from your buyers that will help you help them.

>> To create sales torque, make sure you leverage the variables of force, work, and time. Your force is your credibility and expertise; work is the information you gain; and time is how efficiently you perform your work.

>> "The number-one mistake most salespeople make," says Chuck West, program director for the University of Wisconsin's Executive Education sales programs and a former sales executive for 3M, "is that they are not working high enough in the organization." He's talking about working with buyers. Not influencers. Not recommenders. *Buyers.*

>> Target buyers who can pay for your offering—people who are employed, companies that are successful. Sound like common sense? You'd be shocked by how many salespeople forget this.

>> Speak the language of executives. Be able to sketch the categories of an income statement from memory and relate it to your client's situation.

■ **CHAPTER 8**

Accelerating Through the Curves

REBUTTING THE TOUGHEST OBJECTIONS

E   *arly one August morning, I boarded a bus with a* sleepy-eyed group of Canadian Harley-Davidson dealers. We were headed to a road-racing track in what to me, at least, appeared to be a remote region of the country. This was part of the annual Canadian Harley-Davidson New Model Announcement dealer meeting. We were preparing for some track time on the new motorcycles so we could experience their extraordinary design and engineering for ourselves.

Upon our arrival, but before strapping on our helmets and hitting the course, we received instructions from a diminutive Quebec road-racing instructor. For 10 minutes, he lectured us on the ins and outs of this particular track, and only the most attentive seemed to be giving him their full attention. He wrapped up his comments with a bit of dry humor when he informed us in a French-Canadian accent, "So, as you can see, the whole point of this is so you don't—hmm, how do I say it?—don't lose your ass!"

If he didn't have our attention earlier, he did now.

As this was my first time around a racetrack, I thought I needed to find out what I missed. As members of our group dispersed and headed for their motorcycles, I sought out our fearless leader and asked him what one thing I most needed to know about riding safely that day. His response? "Be careful taking the curves."

Very helpful.

Negotiating curves on a racetrack is an art. Riders need to read the curve and then position themselves to "take a line," meaning to set a direction through the curve that minimizes time in the curve and maximizes speed. Then, when they're in the right part of the curve, they twist the throttle and use the blend of speed, centrifugal force, and traction to shoot them out the other side. If you've ever worked the corners on a machine built for speed, you know this experience can be intoxicating.

Moving through the curves on a racetrack is not only a way to go faster, but as my wry racing instructor implied, it's also a safety precaution. You know the curves are coming, so you better handle them correctly. Doing so will keep you from losing any valuable body parts.

Same thing goes for sales objections. You know you're going to get them, so prepare to handle them accordingly, and make your sales ride faster and smoother. Remember, sales objections are a normal and necessary part of the sales process. Have you ever heard someone come back from a sales appointment and proclaim, "It was a great meeting; nobody raised a single objection!" only to discover that person rarely closes deals? His potential buyers don't have any objections because they're not interested in what he's selling!

Objections prove your buyer is listening—and interested. Plus, they indicate that the prospect considers you worthy of interaction—meaning that the two of you are, at minimum, equals in this transaction. Your sales acc*sell*eration depends on either a peer-to-peer relationship with the buyer or an expert-to-buyer relationship.

To excel at acc*sell*erating through sales curves, keep in mind that you can never be underhanded or manipulative. Those so-called techniques may get you the first sale, but odds are you won't see a second. You must always have the best interests of your buyer in mind. This applies to your entire sales career; it is your *raison d'être*. When you focus on helping your buyer achieve what he wants, sales will happen. When you focus on your commission, they won't.

It's also important to have realistic expectations of your ability to rebut, refute, drive through, or go around objections. You won't come out on top all the time, but there are plenty of things you can say and do to dramatically increase your chances. You also have to be willing to walk away. Yes, you read that right. In your mind, realize that this single piece of business is not going to make your week, your month, or your sales career. You must be so firmly confident of the abundance of business available to you—and in your own skills—that you don't come across as obsequious in your exchanges. Buyers can sense when you're desperate. (Research suggests that a body, when stressed, undergoes chemical changes that translate into physical manifestations that other people can detect.) And buyers want to do business with confident, yet not arrogant, sellers.

Here are some common sales objections:

» "I don't want it."
» "I don't need it."
» "I've never heard of you."
» "It's way too expensive."
» "We're going to wait and see what happens with the economy."
» "I'll have to talk it over with our executive leadership."
» "We just underwent a major reorganization, so the timing's not great."
» "We've been doing business with the other guys for years."

However they are phrased, objections typically come in four different categories. And once you categorize objections, you can

■ TABLE 8.1

Personality/Objection Matrix

	Socializer	Driver	Relator	Analyzer
No Need	Show how other people they know have used offering in a unique way.	Raise the performance bar; e.g., raised sales 10%? Who says it shouldn't have been 12%?	Show how others in their peer group have used offering to their advantage.	Let them do the math behind the performance improvement; they believe it if they do it.
No Hurry	Show why going ahead now will keep them with their social group.	Indicate how acting now will enable them to accomplish their goal faster.	Point out how acting now will keep them at "par" with their peers.	Don't rush unnecessarily: they need time to process; at the same time, point out what's lost if decision takes too long.
No Money	Show how not going ahead will cause them to lose their status or market position.	Prove how they can quickly source the funds or pay down the obligation.	Prove how this will protect their investment; e.g., their resale value or yearly return.	Help them break down costs into monthly or yearly figures; avoid daily breakdowns, because analyzers resist those.
No Trust	Show how others they respect have done what you're suggesting.	Show how other people in similar businesses have used offering to their advantage.	Personal interaction with a trusted and known peer here is crucial.	Use a well-known, objective, and respected third-party media source.

begin to develop strategies for resolving them. Following are the four categories and their respective solution strategies:

- » No need: Show your buyer alternate uses for the product or service.
- » No hurry: Prove to your buyer why buying now benefits him.
- » No money: Justify the investment; explain alternate forms of payment; break down costs.
- » No trust: Keep your promises; don't rush; prove your capabilities; use third-party endorsements.

Add to these four types of objections the four dominant personality traits you'll encounter when dealing with those who raise them:

- » Socializers: gregarious and outgoing; normative pressure is important
- » Drivers: hard-charging, get-it-done-yesterday people

» Relators: rely on interaction with peer groups
» Analyzers: want to know how (not just if) something works

Analyzing these in tandem provides you with a valuable perspective on interpreting and combating objections (see Table 8.1). Most salespeople have one or two specific objection types and one or two personality groups they are comfortable dealing with, but a prerequisite for acc*sell*erated sales is the ability to handle all four objections and all four personality types.

The Art of Communication

The basic communication model includes a sender, a receiver, a message, and a situation. But things are really much more compli-

You've Got to Believe

Doug Slotkin, sales vice president for real-estate website Zillow.com, believes success begins at the top:

It starts with the sales team believing that they have that rep's best interest at heart, and our customer's best interest at heart, when they're giving them advice. So, in terms of getting the troops fired up, the reps have to believe that the manager is giving them advice that's going to help, advice that is not theoretical but practical. My philosophy is that a manager has to have sold the product before they can become a manager.

To spur on my team, it means getting them excited about the opportunity that is out there, about the dollars that are on the table, and what the opportunity is for us to succeed and hit our numbers. They have to feel the passion from me. They have to feel that I care deeply in them being successful and their reps being successful.

cated than that. Every sender has a particular background, specific values, abilities, and all sorts of other influencers on the message they send. And sometimes that message comes out wrong. Likewise, the receiver's various components influence how the sender's message is interpreted. None of this even takes into consideration the environmental noise that complicates text-messaging and tweeting. It's no small wonder that people communicate effectively with each other at all; that a seller can successfully rebut a potential buyer's objections is even more difficult to fathom. (See Figure 8.1.)

The good news is that acc*sell*erating your sales doesn't mean you have to mire yourself in communication complexities. The following ideas are intended to help you better communicate with buyers.

To Be Convincing, You Must Be Convinced

While speaking with one motorcycle dealership sales manager, I asked him which motorcycle he rode. "Oh, I don't ride motorcycles," he replied. "They're overpriced and dangerous."

■ FIGURE 8.1

The "Communications Loop"

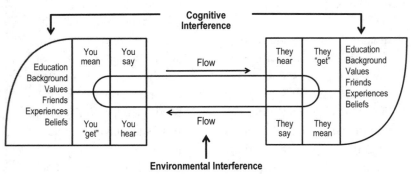

© 2000 Alan Weiss. Reprinted with permission from his book *The Great Big Book of Process Visuals*.

One of the bedrock principles of successfully countering a buyer's objection is to be firmly convinced of the value you bring to the table. If you don't believe in that value, how will you ever convince your buyer?

Understand the Power of Persuasive Psychology

Ellen Langer, a tenured professor of psychology at Harvard, has accomplished decades of fascinating work studying why people act as they do (often without thinking). In one of her most-cited studies, called "The Copy Machine," Langer asked people either to cut in line at a copy machine on campus or to interrupt a person who already was making copies. Philips Hilts, in his *New York Times* article "Scientist at Work: Ellen J. Langer: A Scholar of the Absent Mind," describes the experiment.

When an individual would attempt to make copies, one of Langer's research assistants would approach the person and ask something such as, "May I use the copy machine, because I'm in a major rush?" Ninety-five percent of the time, the person allowed the research assistant to make copies.

In the next phase of the experiment, the research assistants who interrupted asked only, "May I use the copy machine?" This resulted in only a 60 percent successful interruption rate. In the experiment's third and final phase, members of Langer's staff approached the unwitting copy-machine user and inquired, "May I use the copy machine, because I have to make some copies?" What was the result of this couldn't-be-less-compelling reason? Well, 93 percent of the intruding research assistants were allowed to cut and make their copies.

To convince someone to acquiesce to your request, simply give them a reason. And, as evidenced by the third phase of Langer's copy-machine research, that reason doesn't even have to be a good one. You, on the other hand, have great reasons why buyers should take your advice. So tell them! The other compelling piece of Langer's research is use of the word *because*. What does a four-year-old child incessantly ask? "Why?" After entertaining hundreds of these inquiries and trying to reasonably answer them to the best of their ability, frustrated parents almost always resort to a one-word answer: "Because." Psychologists suggest that the use of this single term is so powerfully engrained in our psyche that, even as adults, when we hear that word, whatever reason follows it is a satisfactory one. So when you're explaining to your buyer why acting now will benefit him, be sure to incorporate the word *because*. Why? Because it will improve your chances.

Ask Permission

Another language suggestion useful for rebutting objections is the incorporation of permission questions. These can be rhetorical or actual questions; either way, they soften your response, give you time to think, and usually are greeted in the affirmative. These types of questions include: "May I ask you a question?" "May I speak candidly?" "May I make a recommendation?" "May I offer another perspective?" "May I recommend another option?"

Compare "That's exactly why you should do business with us!" with "If I may, that's exactly why you should do business with us!" Or "I'll call you on the 12th" with "Is it OK to call you on the 12th?"

Use Provocative Questions

The real work of negotiating a curve is done prior to taking the curve. As the driver, you must position your vehicle, mentally establish the "line" you are going to take, and then decide when to make your move into the turn. Rebutting objections requires a similar process. The more information you have and the more positive image the buyer has of you, the better. So, how do you acquire more information and become more interesting? Try asking provocative questions: "What's different about your business now than it was five years ago?" "Do you consider this to be a positive or a negative trend?" "What is the one aspect outside of your control that may have the largest impact on your production effort?" "If your business were to double overnight, what segment of it would break down first?" "What's different about your financial perspective now compared to five years ago?" (Note the use of *perspective* over *condition*).

Questions like these will furnish you with insights other sales professionals won't have. And because they aren't the typical

"What's keeping you up at night?" inquiries, they will make you more compelling to your buyer. Differentiation is crucial.

Understand and Use Echoing

One of my favorite techniques is called echoing. This is when you take the final or last couple of words your buyer says and repeat them with an up inflection to form a question. Then, the power of a pregnant pause elicits more information from the buyer. If your prospect says something like, "I want to make sure I get a good deal," you respond with, "Good deal?"

Pause.

"Well, yeah, I want to be treated well."

"Treated well?"

Pause.

"Sure. I know cheapest isn't always the best; I just know we don't want to overpay. But I also know you guys bring a lot to the table. We have to be taken care of; that's what is most important."

See? You said four words and this buyer is talking himself right out of a price objection! Often listening is the best tactic when it comes to handling objections, and the echo effect can help.

Reduce Your Use of Absolutes

When you use such terms as *every*, *all*, and *most*, you are making an absolute statement: "Every credit union requires you to have a checking account and a savings account." "All consulting firms bill in six-minute increments." "Most politicians are unethical."

As you read those statements, you probably squawked, "That's not true!" That's exactly how your prospective customer will respond, too.

Given the different types of buyers out there, it's entirely possible that you might encounter an analytical type waiting to trip you up with a misstatement, often caused by the inaccurate use of an absolute. So avoid this trap by incorporating fewer absolutes into your presentation style. Don't stop speaking with authority and conviction; just start using more words like *many*, *often*, and *some*: "Many credit unions require you to have a checking account and a savings account." "Often, law firms bill in six-minute increments."

"Some politicians are unethical." Now your positions are on much less tenuous ground.

Leverage Emotion Through Ingratiation

Remember, logic makes you think, but emotion makes you act. The trick is making your prospective buyer feel emotion. The clichéd example involves a waiter in a fine restaurant. A guest orders the salmon, to which the waiter immediately confirms that guest's good judgment with an "excellent selection" comment. Now, you and I both know that the waiter is more than likely saying the same thing to every person in the restaurant that evening, regardless of what each individual orders. Yet, the waiter's behavior elicits a very human response. The moment he says, "Excellent selection," somewhere deep inside, that dinner guest smiles, as her inner voice confirms, *It* is *a great selection.*

As humans, we love to receive compliments, an act psychologists often refer to as ingratiation. Because we like to be complimented, we can't help but feel warmly about the person who is paying the compliment, so when your buyer raises an objection based on price, need, or timing, you can now leverage the principle of ingratiation by responding, "Great point!" or "Terrific question!" or "Now, that is a first-rate insight." This accomplishes two things for you: First, your buyer will agree with you (either inwardly or outwardly) and feel good about the compliment. Second, such comments will enable you to stay in control of the conversation and give you time to think ahead. Neurons in your brain travel at an estimated 250 miles per hour, so while you're complimenting your buyer, you're also allowing yourself time to build a better sales response.

Learn Conversational Aikido

Although the following events happened some time ago, they make this point perfectly. Several years ago, my wife, Amy, and I were in the market for a new television. We went to a store that shall remain nameless, where we selected a new television. Amy looked on encouragingly as a blue-shirted employee and I wrestled the monstrous set onto a large industrial cart.

Before we'd finished, a gaggle of salespeople surrounded us like stealthy Ninja fighters, and the leader began touting the benefits of protecting our purchase with an extended service contract, while the others nodded, apparently as some sort of backups.

Amy and I know a thing or two about extended service contracts. We've helped Harley-Davidson Financial Services increase service contract penetration for years, so we believe in service contract benefits and always buy them for our Harley-Davidson motorcycles. We also often get them for our cars, computers, and iPods. So, we are likely prospects.

By now, it may not surprise you that I treat interactions with other salespeople as ethnographic research, and I approach the task with the zeal of an archeologist on the verge of discovering the Ark of the Covenant. Some colleagues suggest I'm more like the sales Marquis de Sade, reveling in others people's discomfort. Regardless, I wasn't about to let this opportunity pass.

"I thought I just selected a fantastic TV. Why would I need a service plan?" I asked the sales team. The leader of the blue shirts stammered something about how the TV is not a divine creation and that things break. Another added a very convincing, "Yeah."

I hit them with another objection, then another. Finally, as I watched the team sputter, struggle, and shift back and forth trying to find answers they didn't know (even I eventually felt bad for them), I quickly revealed my background. "Guys, do you know what I do for a living?" I asked. All four, probably each under the age of 22, shook their heads back and forth in unison. "I help show people how to sell extended service plans."

It was as if I had suddenly flipped on a light switch, and the cockroaches scrambled. Almost immediately, Amy and I found ourselves alone with that gigantic TV. As you may have guessed, we passed on that particular extended service plan. If they didn't believe in it, why should we?

Now compare that exchange with the one we had days after the one above. Because of our busy travel schedules, Amy and I were in the market for a portable DVD player. At the time, portable DVD players were fairly expensive.

When we selected the model we wanted, the young salesperson we were working with suggested we should consider the extended service plan. You could almost hear Amy's eyes rolling as she realized what was coming next. With all the confidence of David

Ortiz approaching the plate in a T-ball game, I began steering the conversation.

"Well, I thought we just purchased a great DVD player," I began, using my familiar refrain. "Why would we need an extended service plan?"

Then I hit him with objection after objection, building up to my big reveal: "Young man," I said in my Homer Simpson pontificating voice, "do you know what I do for a living?"

Of course not, his expression conveyed.

"I show people how to sell extended service plans."

Without missing a beat, he exclaimed, "Perfect! Then you're going to want the four-year plan!"

We bought the four-year plan.

Why? Because with a masterful bit of conversational aikido— a Japanese form of self-defense—the young salesperson was able to grab the momentum of my objection and use it to prove that he believed in what he was selling. He was convincing because he himself was convinced that the extended service plan was a solid one that would suit our needs.

Isolate to Eradicate

Another strategy for negotiating the curves when handling objections is what I call "isolate to eradicate." When your buyer raises multiple objections, it's desirable to identify the exact barrier to purchase by asking a clarifying question: "So, is it really that you don't see the value in the offering, or is it that you don't have it in the budget? Those sound like two different challenges. If I may ask, is it one or the other—or both?"

"No, we see the value in the offer," might come the response. "We just don't have it in the budget."

"OK. So the budget issue is the main stumbling block at this point?"

"Yes."

"Putting that aside for the moment, what do you *like* about the offer?"

"Well, what's perfect for us about this is . . ."

Whenever someone makes a thoughtful decision, he or she has to first weigh the pros and cons. What's about to happen in the above situation is the buyer and his organization will load the value side of this equation with all the aspects of your offering they find appealing. Crucially, they are going through this publicly by admitting they like your offering and explaining why. This puts you on much more solid ground to solve the buyer's dilemma.

Often in a B2B situation, if the value is compelling, money can be sourced. If you're in a B2C situation, payment alternatives often exist (such as financing the purchase or paying in phases; even the layaway plan has made a comeback in some industries). The key here is to use language that isolates what's holding the buyer back. Mentally put that aside for a moment, review what's attractive about the offer, and then find solutions to remove the specific roadblock. Isolate, then eradicate.

Understand the ART of Objection Rebuttals

So far in this chapter, I've covered a collection of communication approaches that can help you overcome sales objections. Now, I'll show you the specific communication model to enable you to quickly and easily speed through those objection curves. The ART of objection rebuttals is simply this:

>> *Acknowledge* your buyer's objection by psychologically preparing him for what you are about to say.
>> *Respond* openly, honestly, and substantively in a compelling manner that will likely overcome whatever hesitancy the buyer displays.
>> *Transition* the conversation to other, more valuable and meaningful topics or phases of the sale.

Remember, no sales conversation is complete without employing the age-old "feel-felt-found" approach. If the customer balks at an expensive price, you might respond with something like this: "I know how you *feel*. At one time, I *felt* it was pricey, too. But I *found* out some things that changed my mind. And they might change yours, too."

Notice that when you tell the buyer you know how he *feels*, it puts the two of you in sync with each other; you've both experienced the same emotions. (And, let's be honest, how many of you have looked at your product offering at some point and not wondered whether it cost too much?)

Felt is past tense. By using it here, you imply that at some point, you underwent a change of heart. To make this turn of phrase even more persuasive, add specifically what you are referring to regarding the "felt" component: "I know how you feel. At one time, I felt *the three-month option* was expensive, too. But I found out some things that changed my mind. And they might change yours, too."

When you use the word *but,* you psycholinguistically cancel out what has come before it, which is exactly what you are trying to do in this case. And use of the term *found* is nothing short of the perfect segue to overcoming objection.

You can use other acknowledgment statements, too. As a matter of fact, you should have three to five in your sales arsenal at all times, for use in various situations. Here are some universal ones:

» "That's *exactly* why you should take us up on this offer . . ."
» "I hear you. At one time, I thought the same thing—until I found . . ."
» "Great point! I used to think that was crucial, too! And then I discovered . . ."

Like any tool, you want to use the right one for the job. Don't rely on the same acknowledgment statement all the time or you'll be like the guy who plays guitar and knows just one song; it's fun at first, but the excitement quickly wears off after the 701st time of hearing the opening chords to "Stairway to Heaven."

Now, let's put some of these ideas into practice and review responses to each of the four common objection areas using the ART of objection handling. We'll begin with a "no money" objection because that is a common one. Remember, the ART model consists of Acknowledge—Respond—Transition.

The "No Money" Objection: "These Name Brand Components Are Just Too Expensive."

Acknowledge: "I know how you feel. At one time, I thought name brand components were pricey, too. But I found out some things that changed my mind, and they might change yours. There are really three reasons why these components are worth the extra cost."

Respond: "First, these components are tested not only in a lab, but in actual user conditions. For example, these items were originally made out of 6061-T6 billet aluminum, just like the cheaper components that are readily available. What happened is the components broke down during testing, so now these items actually use a 2014-T6 alloy, which makes them stronger and more durable. Second, these items are not batch-plated with just any components. The plating here is done with new items, so the solution is never tainted. And the result is a brighter, more durable piece. And third, these components are covered under a two-year warranty—so you've got nothing to worry about."

Transition: "What do you think?"

As pointed out earlier, people love to think in triads; that's why it's best to harness the power of three. In fact, not only should you have three points, but you should *tell* prospects you have three points. People love lists. That's why magazine covers boldly proclaim "Seven ways to be friends with your boss" and "12 ideas for getting the most out of your job." Conveying three key points about you and your business also further establishes credibility. Your buyer will think, *This is somebody who knows what she's doing, has considered all sides of the issue, and is serious about what she does.*

In this example, the seller used substantive reasons to overcome the price or value hesitancy. The seller actually listed his points—first, second, and third—to help both buyer and seller stay on track. This kind of insider information about testing and plating processes (plus a terrific warranty) should be a salesperson's dream. It's easy to see how you can overcome a price objection with this sort of powerful response. But how can you acquire all those compelling facts about your offering?

Welcome to the game. As discussed in Chapter 3, "Crawling Under the Hood: *Really* Understanding Your Offering," which covered offering expertise, to be on top of your game, you must possess the mind-set of an investigative reporter. Do your research. Talk to the experts. Use the product. All of these things help make you more persuasive.

The transition statement—"What do you think?"—will help you determine in which direction the transaction is headed. A negative response—or anything less than a decision—will indicate that more work needs to be done to close the deal. If, however, the buyer responds in the affirmative, you now have permission to ask for his or her business.

The "No Trust" Objection: "Why Should I Do Business with You?"

Many sales professionals—regardless of whether they're selling cars or consulting services—*think* they can answer this question. But when somebody actually *asks* it, a salesperson usually hems, haws, and ultimately recites some fragmented element of his or her résumé or corporate mission statement. You need to provide a proper response, one that clearly conveys your competitive superiority in the marketplace and articulates your value proposition. Unfortunately, far too many salespeople and sales organizations can't do that.

Why not? Because they haven't actually done the difficult intellectual work of delineating what positively sets them apart from the competition. They haven't asked and answered such important questions as: "Do I/we save customers time, energy, and effort?" "Can I/we teach customers something about their business?" "Do I/we possess standout characteristics and personnel?" "Have I/we created a 'no-stress' business environment?" "Do I/we provide professional improvement opportunities for staff?" "Have I/we created new ways to acknowledge and appreciate customers?" "Do I/we provide legendary customer service?"

Once you have answered these questions, you will be much better prepared to satisfactorily answer the question of why someone

Warding Off Low-Price Competition

Low-price competition is always a challenge, admits Wayne Glowac, CEO of Glowac + Harris + Madison, a marketing and advertising firm in Madison, Wisconsin, that services companies in sectors as diverse as health care, food and beverage, and real estate and construction.

I think it begins with having the integrity to walk away from a low-price prospect. There are always going to be bottom-feeders in any particular category, and those are people who are just shopping for price. I think sometimes we fall prey to pursuing sales when we know this person is just shopping for price, and I think it's a huge mistake. Low-price buyers also tend to be high maintenance.

Secondly, you're never going to build loyalty with these buyers. As soon as someone comes along with something cheaper—and someone always will—you're going to lose that client. We're not in the business of churning business relationships; we're in the business of finding them, keeping them, nurturing them. That's where the real long-term profit comes in.

Different customers use different methods to justify expenditures, especially capital expenditures, adds Ken Bowman, vice president of industrial business unit Spacesaver Corporation, the storage-solutions company. He suggests that many buyers consider their internal rate of return—something that sales professionals can use to their advantage. "If you've done your job understanding and communicating the value you're bringing your client, the price issue goes away," he says. "If spending $500,000 with us helps your company from having to build a $10-million expansion to your facility, it just makes sense."

should conduct business with you. (And if you don't have programs, policies, and practices in place to support the above ideas, develop them!)

At this point, you are prepared to handle the ART of this objection: "Why should I do business with you?"

Acknowledge: "Great question! There are really three reasons why many people decide to do business with the Peak Performance Business Group."

Here, you've informed the prospect that you have a list to share, signaling to the individual that he or she better pay attention. You've also reinforced the name of your organization. Next, share your three points, clearly and concisely communicating your competitive superiority. Methodically walk through your list of competitive advantages, citing what's in it for your prospect.

Respond: "The first reason people choose to do business with us is because we get results, fast. Most of our clients experience significant business improvement within the first weeks of our involvement. Second, many of our client relationships last for decades, meaning we grow with our clients and continuously add value. We create partnerships for long-term client success. Third, we're an award-winning firm. You can be confident knowing you're working with recognized professionals who deliver world-class results."

Transition: "So now, if I may ask, what do you think I should know about *your* organization?"

This is a polite way of turning the conversation back to the buyer in an attempt to uncover additional information. Presenting this question effectively and compellingly is one of the surest ways of remaining in control of the buyer and the sale.

The "No Need" Objection: "I Don't Need a Harley-Davidson Motorcycle."

Acknowledge: "Well, of course, you don't." (This should be greeted with a moment of stupefied silence.) "No one *needs* a Harley-Davidson. But there are three reasons why a special, elite group of people *want* to own one."

Note the admission that the product is not for everyone. The underlying question for the buyer to answer is: Are you part of this unparalleled group?

Respond: "First, it links you forever to a rough-and-tumble, no-nonsense group of people for whom playing it straight comes naturally. Second, when you own a Harley-Davidson, you own a piece of Americana—a link to who we were as Americans, who we are today, and where we are going. And finally, you'll possess one of the finest manufactured products on the market. The fit, finish, and quality of today's Harley-Davidson motorcycles are unequaled. This is something you'll be able to pass down to your grandkids."

Transition: "Here's what I'm going to suggest. Let's find a motorcycle that fits you, physically and aesthetically. And if you like, we'll take it out for a ride. Which do you prefer, the Softail or the Super Glide?"

Focusing on emotional content, rather than product features or specifications, correlates to the idea that logic makes people think, but emotions make them act. The sales professional in this example linked owning a Harley-Davidson to a particular character trait, invoked American history, and acknowledged its incomparable quality by hinting at the potential buyer's personal legacy. And in the transition, expert language moved the conversation away from talking about the product to actually test-riding the product.

We used a Harley-Davidson motorcycle as an example here to make our example more understandable. Of course this "no need" response example can be tailored to any product or service, tangible or intangible item. It just takes a bit of intellectual effort.

The "Why Now" Objection: "Now Isn't a Good Time."

This objection can be verbalized in many different ways:

» "We're going to wait and see what happens with the economy."
» "Our industry is facing huge regulatory pressures right now. We need to deal with those first."
» "We've just had a complete reorganization and are going to wait until the dust settles."

The problem is that far too many salespeople, when slapped with this kind of response, are mentally relieved. They quickly reply, "I completely understand. I'll put it on my calendar to follow up with you next quarter."

Why are they relieved? Well, the buyer didn't say "no"; he or she said something that implied "later." Many salespeople can mentally sustain themselves for weeks knowing they have a "later" in the so-called pipeline. This is a delusionary state of mind I call "Objection Oz." Somewhere over the rainbow, there *might* be a sale. If that sounds like you, you may be able to sustain yourself mentally. But you certainly won't be able to sustain yourself (or your organization) financially. The objective here is to move on to the next phase of your sales progression, not to have a polite conversation and then walk away with nothing.

Whether your buyer cites the economy, the industry, or the organization, he or she has erected a speed bump in the middle of your road to acc*sell*erated sales. If your objective is to earn business fast, a buyer's stalling tactics obviously can be deadly. The key to staying in control here is to prove to the buyer that moving forward *right now* is the best course of action he or she can take.

Stress that by taking advantage of your offer now, your prospect won't lose out on a market opportunity. Speculate that competitors may already be ahead of him. Share any exclusive information you possess about the industry or the marketplace with which your prospect might not be familiar. Inform him or her that while your offer or product is available now, you're unable to guarantee it will be next quarter. And reinforce the fact that the price of your product or service will only increase as time goes by.

It is imperative for you to enter into buyer exchanges armed with several of these countertactics (peers appropriately and professionally push back on prospective buyers). As I've stressed throughout this book, the words and phrases you use pack clout with buyers, so consider dropping some of them into your conversations:

- » "You may want to *consider* . . ."
- » "It might be *advantageous* to move forward now . . ."
- » "It is *advisable* to consider all of the possibilities . . ."
- » The *appropriate* thing to look at is market opportunity . . ."
- » "It might be *beneficial* to speculate about what competitors are doing . . ."

» "There are some *practical* reasons to . . ."
» "A *rational* approach might be to . . ."
» "Sometimes it makes *good sense* to . . ."
» "I'd *urge* you to consider the future implications . . ."
» "While we're here, it's *reasonable* to think about . . ."

Note that while these words and phrases encourage positive actions, they must be carefully chosen and appropriate to a given situation. Pick ones that best suit your personality, and put them into your rebuttal repertoire. They may enable a potential customer to view his or her situation in another light, subsequently and dramatically improving your chances of sales success.

Here is how to handle the "why now" objection:

Acknowledge: "I hear you. And I certainly don't want to rush you into anything. But at the same time, your hesitation to buy might be *exactly* why now is the perfect time to seriously consider taking action."

Respond: "Some of your competitors are already moving in this direction. So the longer you wait, the more ground you may be losing to your competitors." (People are driven to act more by what they stand to lose than what they might gain.) "If you act now, we can work together to build a program that fits your timing and your budget. We currently have space on the calendar to help now. I can't promise that we will in three months."

Transition: "Here's what I'd like to recommend: Let's spend a few more minutes talking about your objectives and how much better off you'll be once you reach them. Within 48 hours, I'll send you a proposal with options to reach those objectives. Then you can choose how you'd like to move forward. Now, may I ask you a question? What is your top priority, right this minute?"

This example is obviously a B2B one, but with some minor adjustments, the strategy works just as effectively in B2C situations: Replace *competitors* with *friends*, replace *program* with *promotion*, and replace *space on the calendar* with *a product*. With only minimal effort, this approach can be applied to just about any selling situation in which the potential buyer is dragging his or her proverbial feet.

Stifle the Sycophant

I have experienced sales situations in which the salesperson seems to be hat in hand when facing an objection. For example, the customer might say, "I'm just going to pay cash instead of using your financing." To which the salesperson responds, "Wow, it sure must be nice to have that much cash available. I sure wish I did." Or the customer says, "It just doesn't make sense," and the salesperson responds, "Well, you're a savvy businessperson; how could we ever tell *you* what to do?"

Whenever I hear exchanges like these, I think, *Who would buy from this person?* I'm a reasonably simple guy. I don't take fitness suggestions from a doctor who smokes, and I don't seek financial advice from someone who doesn't have as much money as I do. So while you as a sales professional will occasionally encounter people who have greater financial resources or stronger business acumen than you do, don't allow these differences to shine through in your discussions with clients.

It's imperative for your buyer to see you as an expert, or at least an equal, in your field and with your offering. In that context, you bring tremendous value to the exchange. This certainly doesn't require arrogance; simply enter into the exchange confidently, knowing you can add value to the discussion. Stifle the sycophant, and take on objections with confidence.

Six More Ways to Acc*selle*rate Through the Curves

» **Drop your -er.** Watch out for the language tic that uses the comparative *-er* when referring to new products or services—as in "nicer," "sleeker," or "faster" than another product or service you sell. Just drop the *-er.* Try "nice," or "sleek," or "fast."

» **Work your way through unreasonable demands.** Sometimes (although, thankfully, not as often as most salespeople fear), buyers' positions will become intractable: "If you don't give me a 50 percent price reduction, I'm going to your competitor!" One of my favorite phrases to use in these situations is *unrea-*

sonable demands—as in, "I'm sorry, but you are really making unreasonable demands." Most people don't want to have their motives or actions characterized in that manner, so when you have to, do so.

» **Ask for help.** When you're looking for clarification, don't be afraid to ask. For example, when you're trying to isolate an objection, say something like, "Help me understand why you feel that way." It's a great step toward easily transitioning into your fact-finding missions.

» **Be careful how you acknowledge the point.** I chuckle when a salesperson responds to an objection with an honest "Actually, you make a good point"—as if the customer was able to somehow come up with something smart and relevant to say. Avoid it, and acknowledge the point without faux flattery.

» **Don't settle for little solutions.** No one wants a "little" solution. They want a powerful solution, a unique solution, a significant solution. Don't belittle your own contribution.

» **Don't accept "no" for an answer.** When a potential customer delivers a flat-out "no," ask very politely if, were you to tell him something about the pending sale that he has yet to consider, he would be willing to change his mind. If the answer is "yes," that "no" just got upgraded to a "maybe." And then . . .

Take Two Shots, Then Salute

I'm often asked in my seminars and workshops how hard a salesperson should push when handling objections. I love it when someone repeats the hackneyed ABC mantra ("Always Be Closing"), or suggests following the "make 'em say 'no' six times before you quit" model. I learned how to sell seven miles outside of Philadelphia, where that sort of advice would get you punched in the face.

Salespeople need to be assertive, but they also should know how to stop just short of becoming aggressive. How do you make that distinction? Take two shots, then salute. Let the customer raise an objection, then rebut it using the ideas presented here. Let them reraise the objection or phrase it in a slightly different manner, and take one more shot at a rebuttal. After that, if there is still no agreement, salute. Either you acquiesce to their requests, or you move on to other aspects of the transaction or to other buyers.

Keep in mind that no approach works every time. If you are unable to overcome a particular objection, don't sweat it. Learn from the exchange, and live to fight (and sell) another day. But this I can assure you with absolute certainty: Apply the concepts in this chapter, and you will be able to acc*sell*erate through more sales-objection curves than ever before.

CHAPTER 8 Acc*sell*erators

» Handling objections is much like negotiating curves on a racetrack. Anticipate them, then figure out the best way to minimize the time you spend on them while maximizing your speed to get to your next agreement in the conversation.

» Be glad you're hearing objections. They prove your buyer is listening and interested and finds you worthy of spending time with. We don't always want to hear it, but objections are a positive indicator of business success.

» You must have a mind-set that says you're willing to walk away. Buyers can sense desperation, and it will scuttle your efforts. Buyers want to do business with someone who confidently possesses the skills and solutions to help.

» Learn and use conversational aikido. When you hear, "We don't have the budget right now," respond with, "That's *exactly* why you need me."

» Understand the ART of objection handling: acknowledge the objection; respond in an open, honest, and substantive manner; and then transition on to your next agreement.

CHAPTER 9

The Power of Referrals

NITROUS OXIDE FOR YOUR SALES ENGINE

t goes by different names: Juice. Giggle gas. Some people even refer to it as "having a bottle in the trunk." Whatever you call it, nitrous oxide is a favorite additive for go-fast types everywhere. (*Giggle gas* is a fairly obvious reference to its role as a dental anesthesia; *bottle in the trunk* describes, well, literally a bottle of nitrous oxide in the back of your vehicle.) As mentioned previously, a vehicle's internal combustion engine uses gas, oxygen, compression, and an ignition spark to create combustion that powers the vehicle and gets you where you want to go. When you need to get there faster, adding a nitrous oxide system to the fuel injection can be just the ticket. Please note one very important disclaimer: Do not try this at home or anywhere but on a racetrack!

Foregoing complicated, scientific descriptions, I'll explain how nitrous oxide works as simply as possible: When nitrous oxide is injected into the combustion chamber, it allows more oxygen into the fuel/air mixture, making for a better, more complete combustion event. The more thorough the combustion, the more power your vehicle boasts.

The key here is how to get more oxygen into your sales efforts. Sales professionals often focus on the wrong aspects of their business. I can't tell you how many times I've been asked how to maximize profit margins, handle price objections, and sell against low-price competition. Worthy endeavors all, but these are the wrong aspects on which to concentrate.

Far too many salespeople get stuck in the mud working with intractable, unreasonable, or apathetic prospects. What if, instead, you focused your efforts on the nitrous oxide of your sales engine: high-potential referrals? Doing so eliminates several other concerns that ultimately result in wasted time. Let's start by clarifying what I mean by referrals.

Referral business is business acquired though direct reference by an existing buyer. (See Figure 9.1.) Buyer A recommends you contact prospective Buyer B, or Buyer A contacts prospective Buyer B on your behalf. (The former is preferable, because you are more in control.) The best option is when Buyer A actually introduces you to Buyer B, either face-to-face or via phone or e-mail.

■ **FIGURE 9.1**
Referral Business

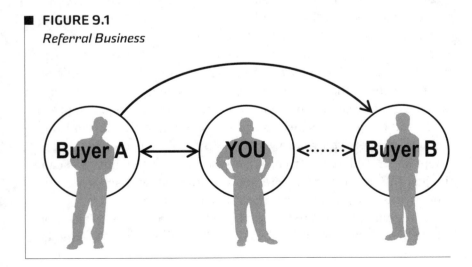

Be they friends, family members, colleagues, or coworkers, these contacts are the oxygen for your sales combustion.

Please don't confuse referral efforts with cold-call prospecting, networking, direct-mail marketing, or advertising. And, for heaven's sake, we're not talking about the "viral" approach. All of these actions may have a place in your marketing toolbox, but right now, we're concentrating on interpersonal referral business as defined above: An existing buyer gives you the name of someone he or she knows and for whom that individual thinks you and your offerings may be a good fit.

Referral business, in my mind, is the strongest way to boost sales for many reasons. First, the existing buyer has already taken action and purchased your product or service. This person didn't just talk about it; he or she actually took you up on your offer. There is a big difference between the two, so this is significant. Second, if you're talented and focused enough on your business to be reading this book, presumably you've performed admirably for your clients. After all, no amount of marketing wizardry is going to build a business or a career if your offerings are substandard. That's why those clients are willing to recommend you to others.

When you put these two elements together, your chances for obtaining a high-potential referral increase dramatically. Here are some other reasons referrals make sense:

» **Referrals minimize your advertising and marketing expenses.** I know that sounds like a line lifted from a Visa commercial, but it's true. Traditional advertising can be expensive. For a 12-week, black-and-white, quarter-page newspaper ad, some estimates place the average cost at $1,300 per week. Direct-mail postcards can run $1,500 for 10,000; an aggressive online campaign might set you back $1,800 or more per month; and billboards can cost tens of thousands of dollars. The actual cash required to ask existing customers for referrals? $0. Realize, however, that what referrals lack in monetary expense they make up for with the effort and energy they require.

» **Referrals provide "warm" contact with prospects.** Consumers and businesspeople are inundated with sales offers and advertising messages. The trick is to cut through the noise and get those individuals to spend their precious time thinking about you and your offer. (Do you know most people spend less than 10 seconds on any given website?) But how do you cut through the noise? By providing a "warm" contact, which includes the name of someone familiar to the prospect. For example, if you receive a midevening phone call from a cold-calling telemarketer trying to sell you Iraqi oil futures, you'll more than likely say, "No, thank you" (or perhaps something stronger). But the next night, say, you receive a call around the same time from someone who begins the conversation like this: "Hi, Sean. This is Mark Rodgers from Merrill Lynch. Our mutual friend, Janak Venu, suggested I give you a call." Now, I have Sean's attention.

» **Referrals dramatically improve the likelihood of success.** They instantly give you what's known as third-party credibility. This is the belief that you can be trusted. People want to do business with those they feel will keep their promises and remain honest throughout the transaction. Third-party credibility is often the best kind, because it is considered more objective than first-person claims. (If someone else tells me you are a good salesperson, I'm more inclined to believe it than if you tell me you are a good salesperson.) Referrals also leverage the element of "social proof." If someone's friends are doing something— such as buying and riding the Harley-Davidson motorcycles you sell—that particular person is more likely going to engage in similar behavior, too.

» **Referrals give your customers an opportunity to contribute.** Often, buyers want to feel as if they are on the inside— privy to a piece of unpublished information about a new product or a bit of important industry news. Buyers want to be part of something, and referring a colleague, a friend, or a family member who ultimately decides to do business with you makes them feel accomplished, sharing in your success. We've all seen the buyer who boasts at a cocktail party, "I brought Mark and this company together!" The motivation doesn't come from the goodness of their hearts (at least not most of the time). Rather, it's a confirmation of their choice: *I ride a Harley-Davidson motorcycle, and you should, too!* Or *I do business with Mark; you should, as* *well*. They are letting others know they've made an informed decision.

Referral Barriers

The problem isn't that sales professionals don't realize that referral business is a good thing. If you get a group of sales practitioners or sales managers together and bring up the topic of referral business, most will unanimously agree that referrals are the keys that unlock the door to sales success. And the barrier certainly isn't the nature of referrals. None of the points just mentioned are so complicated that you had to reread them. Rather, the problem is creating the mind-set, the skills, and the system that consistently produces referral business. The following are some of the barriers that get in the way of even the best referral intentions:

Referral Barrier #1

The prospect is unsure of your offerings. To be referred, you have to have something worth referring. Your product, your service, and your professionalism must all be of high quality and consistent with your claims. You simply have to ask yourself: Are you good, better, or the best? Fortunately (and unfortunately), this is not industry specific—meaning buyers will compare their experiences with you to their experiences with others, like FedEx and The Walt Disney Company, who are known for great customer experiences. And that means you must be "memorably referable." One of my favorite examples of a memorably referable sales professional is Tom Bradford, sales manager at a motorcycle dealership just outside of Milwaukee, Wisconsin. When I met Bradford, he stuck out his hand and said, "Tom Bradford, your six-second salesperson."

I was taken aback. "You're my *what?*"

"I'm your six-second salesperson." (Straightaway, I interpreted this to mean he was going to sell me a motorcycle in six seconds, at which I immediately started calculating in my head what must be his enormous commissions.)

He quickly responded. "I am the fourth guy in the world to break the seven-second barrier on a NHRA pro-stock motorcycle, running a 6.98 at 192 mph." When people interested in motorcycling hear something like that, they instinctively gasp, "Wow!" You can almost hear Bradford's customers saying to their buddies, "Hey, you've got to meet this dude, Tom. He can be your six-second salesman." (To listen to my interview with Bradford and hear how fast he goes with his sales today, visit www.AcceleratetheSale.com.)

If your organization's people or services are not memorably referable, people may still do business with you. But they won't be *driven* to do business with you.

Referral Barrier #2

If there is so much evidence proving why referrals are important— and enough consensus among sales professionals regarding the positive nature of referrals—why are referrals still underutilized? It comes down to what I call referral reluctance, the overwhelming

---

STREET SMARTS

Worst Sales Mistakes

Chuck West, program director of sales, sales management, and advanced management programs for executive education at the University of Wisconsin–Madison's School of Business, shares the worst sales mistake he knows: poor call preparation:

> Salespeople seem to create what I would call relatively vague call targets, in terms of what they're trying to

accomplish. I'm going to steal a page from Stephen Covey and suggest to begin with the end in mind. Look at the desired result of the call. If it goes exceptionally well, where will you end up? I think if people would think that way, they would organize their calls differently, and better, and they'd be more directed at future behaviors. Call prep sets us up to succeed or fail.

psychological state that paralyzes salespeople and prevents them from cultivating referral business. To work through this requires more than a rousing pep talk or dress-down, as you'll soon see. Here are some of the reasons why many sales professionals don't do more with referrals:

» **They don't want to ruin a new, positive relationship.** Sometimes people will say to me, "But, Mark, I've just closed the deal, and now I have to ask for more business?" Been there and have the ticket stub. This reluctance is understandable. The early stages of a new relationship between a salesperson and a customer can seem especially fragile. In fact, this is often why salespeople are reluctant to have colleagues interact with their own clients or customers. Take another look at the language used above. The term *closed* represents that the relationship is so tenuous that it took everything the seller had to get the buyer to commit, and now the seller doesn't want to jeopardize that delicate condition. So what's the solution? Make sure you're on firmer footing with your buyer. Your relationship needs to be based on mutual trust and respect. Go out of your way to impress with your willingness to work hard, and be honest and forthright. Keep your promises—early, often, and always. It's essential that this relationship be a strong one. In essence, be like your favorite leather jacket: comfortable and relaxed. (Then ask yourself if maybe, just maybe, the fragility of this new relationship exists largely in your own mind, not that of the buyer.)

» **They don't want to sound like they're selling encyclopedias.** You've probably noticed there aren't too many of those peddlers around anymore. There's a reason for that, and never mind the Internet: Customers don't want to interact with stereotypical, high-pressure salespeople. (Read this in your best Rocky Balboa voice: "So, you know anyone else who might want to buy from me?") To counteract buyers' fears of high-pressure attacks, acquire the strategies, tactics, and skills to prove you possess the confidence to make any sale.

» **They don't want to put the customer in an awkward position.** And they shouldn't. If you can't ask for referrals properly, don't do it.

» **They don't really know how to ask.** I'm dumbfounded by sales managers who growl, "Everyone knows how to ask for referrals." I don't think so. Asking for referrals is a specialized skill, and it's unlike any other aspect of selling. Generating referrals broadens the scope of the interaction between buyer and seller, boasts a social component, and boosts your own credibility. This is actually complicated stuff. Developing formal instructions for requesting and acting on referrals is a dynamite idea. The notion that someone should just naturally know how to get referrals is ridiculous.

Referral Barrier #3

Stagnant or nonexistent referral-request systems are in place. Some of my sales workshop participants tell me they don't ask for referrals "because our computer program doesn't capture personal referral information."

Excuse me?

You don't need a computer program to do this. If you have a sophisticated customer relationship management system, fantastic; if you don't, get referrals some other way. Don't let the absence of a CRM system bring your pursuit of referral business—and your sales career—to a screeching halt. Capture referrals using a simple spreadsheet, word processor, or even just a notebook! I can't imagine reflecting on my career 20 years from now and thinking, *Yep, I could have been much more successful as a salesman, but I just didn't have the right computer program.*

Either you purchase the program you need, or you find another way to do it. Some of the most effective salespeople I've known use nothing more complicated than a pocket-size spiral-bound notebook. There's always a way. Don't play the victim and quit.

The other component to this barrier is a stagnant referral system. Simply handing out referral cards isn't enough. A high-quality referral program needs to be integrated into your sales process, not implemented as some stand-alone, short-term initiative. It needs to be like healthy eating and exercise; it should become part of the selling lifestyle.

Referral Barrier #4

The referral process lacks accountability. Referral business tends to get fantastic lip service from management; in reality, it receives little action or accountability. It's up to sales managers to ensure referral business is actively and professionally sought and that the confirmation of such activities is easily verified. Call records, name submissions, and sales records are all ways this can be achieved.

Here is the greatest management two-for statement ever: "Show me." Show me how you're tracking referrals. Show me how you ask for referrals. Show me how you follow up.

Then, if any of the above show-me actions is unsatisfactory, it's up to the sales manager to determine whether the obstacle is a skill or a will issue, then rectify it. This can be determined by posing the question, "Could this salesperson accomplish a particular task if a gun were pointed at his head?" If the answer is "no," the problem is skill-related, and training will likely help. If, on the other hand, the answer is "yes," the problem stems from something else, usually having to do with the salesperson's *will* to do the job. (Remember, the gun reference is a metaphor, not an actual management technique.)

Referral Deferral

Guess who else may be apprehensive when it comes to giving you referrals? That's right, your buyers. There are several explanations for why even your best clients might be reluctant. Here are a few:

» They don't want their friends to think they've joined some sort of cult-like business movement. Seriously.
» They don't want their friends to think they are now multilevel marketers. Again, seriously.
» They don't know what to say to their friends after they refer them to you.
» They had a bad experience in the past after giving a referral, and they don't want to repeat it.

Look at this issue from your customers' perspective, and help them work through it. Model the language you use, remove the risk, and always ask—but never force—them to suggest referrals. The following are questions *not* to pose during this process. (I have heard each of these used at some point in my sales travels, and I still cringe when I repeat them.)

» "Do you have any friends?" (Presumed response: "No, I live alone in a cabin in the wilderness.")
» "Are any of your family members employed and willing to do business with us?" (Presumed response: "No, we were hoping perhaps *you* could support us.")
» "Can you help us out here? Do you know anyone who might buy from us? (Presumed response: "Wow, you really are self-centered and pathetically begging for business.")

Seven Best Practices for Referral Success

Instead of making a costly mistake like the ones just listed, follow these seven best practices for referral success:

1. Set the Stage Early in the Process

Referrals should be part of the natural reciprocal sales exchange. Getting them shouldn't be an ambush—and they won't be, if you properly prepare your buyer. After you've verified you have an honest-to-goodness prospect, not someone you tackled at a cocktail reception and held hostage while the hors d'oeuvres were being replenished, you must pass the rapport-building stage and move confidently toward exploring a real working relationship. Consider asking this: "At some point down the road, how will you determine whether we've done a good job for you?"

Then let the customer talk. Prompt him for more with a strategically placed "What else?" Take mental or actual notes; your customer is telling you what you need to do to win, retain, and extend the sale. After that, add something like this to the conversation: "We're on a campaign to reinvigorate the economy. But we can't do it alone. Our promise is to strive to make you so deliriously happy with your experience that you'll *want* to refer others to us."

Here's what I like about this approach:

» "We're on a campaign" employs very active language and suggests you and your organization are action oriented and unified.

» ". . . to reinvigorate the economy" makes the referral exchange about a worthy cause—not just about furthering your own professional gain. (We *all* should be on a campaign to reinvigorate the economy, by the way.)

» "But we can't do it alone" suggests you'd like the customer to become your partner. This results in collaborative thinking between buyer and seller.

» "Our promise is to strive to make you so deliriously happy with your experience that you'll *want* to refer others to us" is a bold, compelling statement that piques the customer's interest (think Babe Ruth calling his shot), creates a social contract between buyer and seller, and forces you to keep striving to do better. It also kick-starts the proverbial cycle of reciprocity.

Such an approach also can be shortened: "We want to do such a great job for you that you'll tell others about your experience here." "Our plan is to make you so happy you'll invite your friends to talk with us." "We hope to do so well for you that you'll tell others." Use whatever words best fit your situation and selling style, and communicate your promise to perform phenomenally now and ask for referrals later. You don't have to elicit a referral commitment right away; just plant the seed.

But if you'd like to strengthen this approach, ask for a verbal commitment from your buyer up-front. All you have to add is a casual "Sound good to you?" to any of the above statements, and the race is on to greater sales: "We want to do such a great job for you that you'll want to tell others. Sound good to you?"

Feel free to experiment with other commitment questions, as well as the upward inflection in your voice, which turns just about any statement into a question: "Fair enough?" "Cool?" "That work for you?"

Be careful you don't get too crazy with vocal inflections. The last thing you need are customers misinterpreting your sales style as one continuous Tiny Tim impression. (Never heard of Tiny Tim? Time for a YouTube search!) Just a little goes a long way in these situations. More than likely, your buyer will say something like "OK," "Sure," "No problem," or "I'd be happy to."

You now have your verbal commitment, which dramatically increases the likelihood you'll be successful beyond this sale. When customers actually confirm they will provide you with a referral or two, they feel compelled to keep their promise and follow through. Nobody wants to be a hypocrite.

If this seems hard to do, the results will be easy to accept. I realize it takes courage to ask these questions and make these statements up-front. But doing so makes it easier for you to ask for the referral (you already said you would) and for customers to make the referral (they said they would, too). Then get back to work for your buyer by using a transition statement such as "Now, let's pick up where we left off." You'll be guiding the conversation while keeping the transaction moving.

2. Pick the Right Time

There isn't a comedian alive who at one point or other in their career who hasn't heard the admonition: "It's all about the timing, kid."

That's as true in the referral game as it is in comedy. Some moments are better than others when asking for referrals. The initial moments upon meeting someone are not the best time. Imagine going on a blind date, and that individual's opening line is, "Would you like to get married?" That's a surefire way to see a door slammed in your face. And so it goes with sales and referrals. Pick the right time to pop the question.

After you set the stage as described earlier, there will be plenty of other opportunities to make a referral request. One might be when you hear a positive trigger phrase during the sales process: "Wow, I really like doing business with you and your firm!" "You're doing a great job handling our portfolio." "Your team really knows your stuff." The buyer has acknowledged that you've provided value, so now is an ideal time to bring up referrals.

How you respond to such a compliment could determine the future of your relationship with that particular buyer. Here is one way to respond to a compliment in which the customer reveals he likes you and your company: "Well, we like you, too. And we're always trying to spread the good news, so if you know of others we could help, by all means, don't keep that information to yourself." Let's break down this casual, soft-sell approach:

» "Well, we like you, too." In life, people tend to gravitate toward others with the same interests, preferences, or ideologies. They like each other, and often say so. Joe Girard, hailed as the "world's greatest salesman" by Guinness World Records, distributed cards and buttons that read simply, "I like you." And he sold an average of six cars every day!

» "And we're always trying to spread the good news . . ." Who can fault you for trying to spread good news?

» ". . . so if you know of others we could help, by all means, don't keep that information to yourself." Notice this puts the emphasis on what you can do for others, rather than on what they can do for you. And in a friendly, good-natured, almost chiding manner, you're encouraging customers to share with others their experiences with you. Typically, buyers chuckle when I make this request. That is good.

If your buyer doesn't comment about you specifically but focuses instead on the value you've provided, try this approach: "Happy to help. You know, we're always trying to spread the good news . . ." or "Glad you like it. You know, . . ."

Planting that referral seed early reaps other benefits, too. Something inevitably will go a little sideways with any given sale. A part won't be in, a form has to be redone, or a wait time is longer than expected; few sales go off absolutely flawlessly. But by asking for referrals early, proving your value, and promising to keep the buyer deliriously happy, you've more than likely already gained the buyer's trust to work through any of the transaction's unexpected and unwanted developments.

By awaiting that trigger phrase, you're guarding against being "red-lighted" or jumping the gun on the drag strip of your sales relationship. Once you hear it, you'll know you have the go-ahead to pursue referrals.

3. Use Your Agreement

If you incorporate written agreements, contracts, or proposals in your sales efforts, consider adding referral language to it. A "right of referral" could read like this:

> Mark Rodgers's Peak Performance Business Group has built its business and its reputation on providing dramatic improvement for clients. As such, when we've done the same for you, we respectfully request the personal introduction to two other firms that may benefit by knowing us.

No risk, no referrals.

Some advice givers will tell you not to put anything in a proposal that will flag your agreement or give a potential client any reason to delay or unfairly scrutinize your arrangement. (Keep in mind that larger companies often have confidentiality agreements with clients that prohibit this sort of request.) I say go ahead and include it. Don't try to "sneak" it in, rather just be up-front, mention it in your conversations early, and recap in your agreement. You'll find more organizations willing to do this than you imagine. So move forward confidently and ask for the referral.

4. After the Sale, Follow Up

A postsale phone call or e-mail is *always* appropriate. Most salespeople skip this step, fearing the customer will have something negative to say. But it's important to overcome this fear. Researchers estimate that follow-up calls end up being positive experiences approximately 87 percent of the time. Plus, these calls provide a golden opportunity to request referrals. As for that remaining 13 percent, don't you want to turn those negatives into positives? *Then* you can ask for referrals.

Don't just rely on recent customers, either. You can always go back to your client list and follow up with them about their buying experience with you. Ask them this: "What one thing would have made your experience with us better?" or "We want to understand how we are serving our clients. On a scale of 1 to 10, with 1 being abysmal and 10 being outstanding, where would you rank your experience with us?" Then, after you receive a positive response, ask for referrals.

5. Obtain the Right Information

Here's what you want in terms of information: the bare minimum. Make this process fast and easy. A name and a phone number (or e-mail address) are the only pieces of information you require. Anything else is superfluous. Start with quantity, then shift to quality. Soon, you'll quickly be able to identify whether the referral has high or low potential by asking the current buyer these questions: "How do you know this person?" "What made you think of him so quickly?" "When is the best time to call?" "Does she prefer to be contacted by phone or e-mail?" "Does he have any particular interests I should know about?" "How would you describe her personality?" Such inquiries will help tailor your approach and strengthen your footing when contacting these referrals and determining their potential.

One more thing to ask: "Has what you've told me become public knowledge?" In other words, "Is it OK for me to know this information?" The client's referral might have just moved as a result of foreclosure. Or that person could recently have been laid off in a nasty round of budget cuts at a local manufacturing plant. What you know and what you can share about what you know are two completely different things.

I learned my "Is it OK for me to know?" lesson early in my career. In the Harley-Davidson world, individuals value nicknames. So I wasn't too surprised when I received a referral from one customer who told me his friend's name was Steve, "but he goes by 'Curly.'" So I gave him a call.

"Hey, Curly," I exclaimed. "Mark Rodgers, from the Harley dealership in town!"

Dead silence.

Back at me growled the deep, threatening voice of a person obviously not amused by my casual approach. "You can't call me 'Curly,'" he warned. "You haven't earned the right. Only my *friends* call me 'Curly.'"

Not a lesson I had to learn twice.

6. Use the Right Words

You've set the stage, picked the right time to make the request, and been clear about the information you need. Now, exactly *how* do you ask for that referral? Choose your language carefully, using words such as *recommend, suggest, advise,* or *propose*—as in, "Do you know someone you could recommend I call?" or "Is there someone you could suggest I call?"

What I like about these terms is that they give a psychological nod to your customers. The words defer to customers' knowledge and expertise. Earlier, I suggested ways in which you can leverage your authority by using powerful words. Here, you can achieve your objectives by deferring your authority to your customers. You're putting them in charge (which, of course, they really are). Here's an example of how this works:

You: "I mentioned earlier that our company is on a campaign to reinvigorate the economy in our area. Do you know someone else we can help, someone you could recommend I call?"

Customer: "Hmm. I would suggest you call Stephanie Whitford. She's been talking about doing just the sort of things you guys do for years. Let me look on my cell for her number; here it is . . . ."

Terrific! You are now doing good things for your business, your economy, and a future customer by the name of Stephanie Whitford!

Want more? When your current customer gives you the name of a potential future customer, follow up with a casual, "Great! Who else?"

Pause.

Chances are, you'll get another name. But if not, move on. If a buyer seems stumped trying to come up with referrals, use prompts to stimulate his thinking: "Family?" Pause. "Friends?" Pause. "Coworkers?"

Pause.

You could also "paint the perfect picture," as I like to call it. Describe to your current buyer your ideal buyer: "Do you know anyone who is _____?" If I'm digging for Harley-Davidson referrals, I might fill in the blank with such adjectives as *adventurous, bold, fun-loving,* or some combination thereof. (One of my favorites was the Harley-Davidson dealer who announced,

THE POWER OF REFERRALS

"We're starting a motorcycle gang. Know anyone who wants join our club?" Although abandoning adjectives to paint a different kind of picture, he still managed to make his point and get a laugh.)

For consulting clients, I might ask one of the following questions: "Do you know anyone else looking to become a leader in the industry?" "Do you know anyone else who'd like to improve his sales and profitability?" "Do you know anyone else who would like to accelerate his sales results?" "Do you know anyone else who is doing well in his business but might want to do even better?" (The best clients are those who already are successful.)

7. Use the Right Tools

On the spectrum of referral technology, a pad of paper and a pencil reside at one end, advancing through spreadsheets, contact lists, databases, and CRM systems. At the extreme opposite end, you'll find such sophisticated referral technology as the iPhone app used by U.S. President Barack Obama during his 2008 campaign, with enabled peer-to-peer referrals. This app sorted contacts by battleground states, enabling supporters to call friends quickly and easily, encouraging them to vote. Once the call was completed, the call stats were updated and that person would be crossed off the call list. It also provided alerts to local election happenings and a fast way to make donations. (Regardless of your politics, you have to admit that's pretty cool.)

I'm a fan of technology, and as a sales professional, I use it to my advantage. To reiterate a statement I made previously in this book, I have little tolerance for those who use their lack of technology as a crutch. Regardless of the technology available to you, one referral tool that every salesperson can use is a postcard or data document (whichever is more appropriate for your business). This sheet will include details about what you and your company can do for customers and reiterate reasons why their referral business is so valuable. Then, at some point during a productive sales conversation, present this postcard or document to your buyer with these words: "Well, you're going to be a terrific addition to our client family. As I mentioned when we first met, we are always trying to reinvigorate our local economy and spread the good news of local businesses."

Then walk them through the message printed on your sample referral sheet:

Every year, more than 90 percent of our customers come to us because someone they trusted suggested they should. Our existing customers are so excited about their experience here that they send their colleagues, coworkers, family members, and friends to us. We hope you'll do the same. Please jot down the name and phone number (or e-mail address) of a person you think we might be able to help, and we'll give that individual the same first-class experience we provided for you. We'll even mention your name!

NAME	PHONE NUMBER	E-MAIL
1. _____		
2. _____		
3. _____		

Then hand your current customer the card and say something like this: "If you'd like, you can either fill that out now or wait until later, if that's easier for you." Offering options puts your buyer at ease and provides him with additional choices. Force him, and he'll resist; give him options, and he'll pick one.

If the customer opts to complete the form on the spot, turn and allow time and space to do so. Chances are good that he'll check his cell phone to look up numbers and provide you with the necessary contact info. After all, you asked so politely. Upon receiving the referrals, remember to ask if there is anything else you need to know about those names. After the customer leaves, retain the data sheet for accountability purposes. And, of course, add the names into the database type of your choice.

If a customer prefers to fill out the referral sheet later, indicate that you're fine with that arrangement and that you will follow up in a few days. A hesitation here might indicate resistance, or the client might suspect a high-pressure pitch. You certainly don't want to make customers do anything they are uncomfortable doing. If someone doesn't want to participate, he or she will probably inform you of that with a terse, "I don't give referrals." To which you should go back to the tried-and-true two-for questioning technique: "Bad experience?" Pause.

Buyer: "Yeah, I gave a referral to one sales guy, and he hounded my friend for weeks. I'll never do that again!"

You: "Let me assure you, we don't have a low-pressure approach; we have a no-pressure approach. Here's how we typically approach referrals . . . ."

Put the customer at ease by explaining what you will say to the prospects your buyer recommends. But remember, two shots and salute. Avoid being overly aggressive.

When discussing tools used to garner referrals, it would be impossible to have a complete conversation without mentioning incentives for your existing clients. Here are some of my favorites:

» **Cash, or at least credit, toward another project or purchase:** Few things move short-term actions more than money—within the limits of state and federal laws, of course.
» **Trade:** Barter your products or services for referral contacts.
» **Service:** Perhaps you can provide faster turnarounds for referring clients.
» **Experiential:** In the motorcycle business, we call this "letting them lead the parade." Maybe you can provide your referring buyers an "experience"—such as inviting them to be among the first riders at a motorcycle rally and, well, lead an actual parade; hooking them up with concert tickets or club seats at a local

sporting event; or treating them to a round of golf. (That one always seems to work.)

» **Recognition:** Include referrers' names in company publications, and mention them in staff meetings.

Eight More Ways to Add Nitrous Oxide to Your Sales Efforts

Here are final takeaways for your referral efforts. Review these and then add them to your efforts. You'll be glad you did.

» **Practice the "every time, every buyer" rule.** Ask for referrals from 100 percent of your clients, on 100 percent of your projects, and watch referrals soar.

» **Spend a significant amount of time each day managing referrals.** Five minutes a day isn't enough, and this practice is too easy to skip. Set aside an hour every day to ask for referrals, contact referrals, improve referral skills, or develop new referral processes. Your commissions will reflect it.

» **Know when less is best.** When gathering referral information, just stick to the basics. You can always call your buyer back and say, "I was getting ready to contact your friend and wanted to ask a few more questions."

» **Update the referring party.** If a customer gives you a referral name or two, update him or her on your progress. It's the professional (and polite) thing to do. This proves to the customer that his or her input is valuable, and may even convince him or her to give you another name.

» **Give referrals; get referrals.** If you're aware that one of your clients is looking to purchase a new roof for his or her home, and you're also familiar with a reputable roofing company, put them together. If you know an executive recruiter who is looking for a senior vice president of sales, and you know someone who fits the bill and also is looking for a new job, introduce them to each other. Karma will bring those gestures back around to you.

» **Use the power of the postscript.** Two letters, *P.S.*, can emerge as a powerful piece of written communication, because they feel (and are!) part of a special message separate from the rest of a document. Use this to your referral advantage when writing letters or e-mails to clients: "P.S. We're working to grow the local economy. If you know someone we can help, give me a shout."

» **Honor thy customer.** If it fits within the context of your business, create a "customer salesperson of the year contest," highlighted by a coveted reward for the existing customer who sends the most new business your way.

» **Perform an annual checkup.** At least once a year, review your current client/customer list to determine how much of it came from referrals, who referred that business, and what one thing you could do better to garner more referral business.

You won't get referrals from everyone. But I guarantee that if you use the ideas presented here, you'll walk away with more than you expect. And you'll be imminently more successful than most of your selling counterparts. However, here's where our nitrous oxide analogy stops short. As mentioned earlier, nitrous oxide provides a powerful boost to your combustion performance. But typically, it's only used for a short-term boost; your referral efforts should never stop.

CHAPTER 9 Acc*sell*erators

» Nitrous oxide boosts engine performance by allowing more oxygen into your combustion chamber. Referrals increase your sales performance by adding more prospects into your sales pipeline.

» Use the seven steps of referral success: Set the stage early, pick the right time, use your agreements, ask after the sale, obtain the right information, use the right language, and use the right tools.

» Use the "every time, every buyer" rule. Ask for referrals from 100 percent of your buyers, on 100 percent of your projects or purchases, and watch referrals soar.

» You have to spend a significant amount of time on referrals. Five minutes a day doesn't cut it.

» Less is best. Unless your referrer is chatty, you don't need his mother's maiden name. Just get the first and last name and contact info. Then stop. You can always obtain more later.

CHAPTER 10

Shift into High Gear

KICKING YOUR CAREER INTO OVERDRIVE

*L*ooming like an oncoming semitrailer in my rearview mirror—who am I kidding? It *was* a semitrailer—certain death roared toward me. Glancing at the reflection, I watched as the image grew even closer than it appeared and showed no signs of slowing down. I rolled on the throttle, kicked the transmission into gear, and felt the reserve power of my Harley-Davidson Dyna Glide come to life. As the bike gained RPMs and speed, I easily passed three cars and returned safely to the right lane. Just in time, too. As the truck blew past, its wake turbulence grabbed me like an invisible giant, shaking my motorcycle and me as a child might shake a rattle.

What happened to me out on that open road can happen in your own sales career, too. Which is why, sometimes, you need to kick into high gear to avoid getting run over.

Shifting a manual transmission requires you to increase the RPMs of your current gear and "top out" in its power band. Then, at the top of that curve, you must pull the clutch lever (or press the clutch pedal) to disengage the clutch plates, shift into the next gear, and smoothly reengage the clutch by releasing the clutch lever.

That's how it works in your sales career as well. Shifting into high gear requires the ability to master change, identify and rectify performance discrepancies, acquire new skills, and set goals. It also mandates a conscious examination of why you should even bother to shift in the first place.

External and Internal Reasons to Shift

Just as in the dangerous-traffic situation above, an extrinsic motivator sometimes is required to spur higher performance. Fear helps. And for many people, that is, indeed, the motivation. When your company wants to implement that new CRM system with an integrated SFA system ASAP, you're going to need new skills fast, or you'll be SOL PDQ. Other extrinsic motivators can occur when you are given a new territory, directed to report to a new manager, or assigned a new product line.

But seeking higher performance isn't just relegated to outside influences; in fact, those may pale in comparison to intrinsic forces. Sometimes, you just desire to do better *for yourself.* You *want* to go after that higher-paying sales job, you *want* to increase your commissions, you *want* to earn a new territory. Or you may find yourself in an unsustainable position: too much travel, too much stress, too much political maneuvering. Broadly and basically put, shift catalysts are either external or internal.

Material Gain vs. Loss Aversion

Further understanding of your reasons for seeking change can be found by exploring the concepts of material (meaning substantial, not necessarily physical) gain and loss aversion. People do things because they think it will significantly improve themselves in some manner; exercising regularly, for example, results in a healthier lifestyle. But if we, as humans, do not look to substantially improve our own condition, we have a tendency toward what some social psychologists refer to as "status quo bias," or a preference for the current situation.

The Why Behind the What

Eric Dorobiala, sales director for Harley-Davidson Financial Services, suggests that full disclosure is critical when convincing a sales team to shift performance gears:

We prepare our sales team to shift their performance by getting them to understand what it is that we're trying to accomplish. If they understand what we are trying to accomplish as an organization, it allows them to buy into the process. To just ask them to do something without providing the information, the input, you won't be as successful.

If we're able to, as an organization, put forth a plan or strategy that allows us to tell them why we're doing what we're doing, the sales team is much more apt to participate and go along willingly to try to accomplish those objectives. It's setting the stage for what it is that we're trying to do.

The greatest cause of action in human beings is what psychologist Daniel Kahneman, Ph.D., and his late research collaborator Amos Tversky, Ph.D., called "loss aversion." Simply put, this means we're much more driven by what we stand to lose than by what we stand to gain. Whether profit, power, or prestige, these are the things that compel us to shift. Rest assured, however, this internal shift catalyst doesn't have to be a selfish pursuit. In fact, it shouldn't be.

Enlightened vs. Unenlightened Self-Interest

The concept of enlightened self-interest was likely first described by the 19th-century French economist and social observer Alexis de Tocqueville in his landmark work, *Democracy in America*. He observed that Americans work together to further the interests of a group, which thereby further the interests of individuals to do what is right.

This fundamentally American idea was wrapped up in Benjamin Franklin's belief that a person could "do well by doing good." Today, it can be argued that navigating away from this tenet contributed to the meltdown of the United States economy in 2008. As a matter of fact, that is *exactly* what public-opinion analyst and social scientist Daniel Yankelovich argues in his work, *Profit with Honor: The New Stage of Market Capitalism.* In it, he states that "traditional enlightened self-interest led business executives to search for strategies that benefited others, as well as themselves." Yankelovich further proffers that *unenlightened* self-interest—winning just for oneself—has resulted in business executives "gaming the system."

It's also important to distinguish between a scarcity mentality and abundance thinking. A scarcity mentality states that if you get something, I lose something; in other words, if you take a piece of pie, there will be less pie for me. Abundance thinking presumes that there is enough for all, so let's make a bigger pie.

Drivers for Change

You are a part of an integrated whole. You, your buyers, and your company are cogs in the system. If your sales motives are pure for you, your buyers, and your organization, then it makes perfect business sense to proceed in that direction. I believe it is this interconnectedness that drives meaningful change.

The idea here is to do things that are positive and right (meaning both ethical and profitable) for your organization, positive for you (leading to increased income and professional status), and positive for the larger whole in which you operate (your industry and your community). (See Figure 10.1.) Self-interest can be good; enlightened self-interest is great.

To recap, your motivation for change can be external or internal, driven by a desire to increase material gain or to minimize a loss.

■ FIGURE 10.1

Enlightened Self-Interest

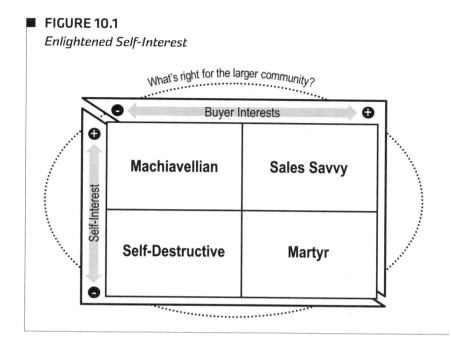

And deep and meaningful shifts are prompted when you can openly and honestly say that such shifts make your world and the world of those around you brighter and better.

But you can't just be well intentioned. For you to truly be successful, you need to know how to shift effectively and adapt to significant (dare I say it?) paradigm shifts. The following ideas will help you speed your way to higher performance.

Understand the Conundrum of Constant Mesh

When things slow down, I'm going to get that MBA. How many times has that thought raced through your mind? Or how about these?

» I just need to make it past this busy period, then I'm going to learn that new software program.

> » When we get through the fourth quarter, I'm going to start eating right and get in shape.
> » Someday, I just need to take a long vacation to recharge.

Enhancing your education, learning new skills, and taking good care of yourself are all actions that can provide you with the horsepower needed to propel you to a higher level of performance.

But I've got news for you: It's never going to happen.

All of those good thoughts are never going to become reality if you continue to wait for the perfect time. Don't get me wrong. It's a fun fantasy, dreaming about uninterrupted time for you to hone, polish, and work on all those self-improvement ideas—it's one I indulge in myself. But the only people who can really make those things happen seem to be the ones who take professional sabbaticals—something I've *heard* about but never known anyone outside of academia who has actually *taken* one.

Here's a recent epiphany I had: Life is like a Harley-Davidson transmission; it's constant mesh. This is a mechanical term that describes when all of the gears are in constant engagement with one another. So, if you're spending time dreaming about when you can actually unplug and carefully study and focus on the ideas that can launch you toward greater success, I'm here to suggest you need another plan. You're going to have to focus while you're currently engaged.

Here are four ways you can create change while surviving the "constant mesh" of your career and life:

1. Embrace the Concept of Balance. To successfully ride a motorcycle, you obviously must keep it upright. But there are other dynamics at play, such as centrifugal force, gyroscopic effects, and—not unimportantly—a sense of balance in the rider.

Compare riding a motorcycle to creating change in a busy career. How do you balance the constant demands placed on you? First, identify your highest 2 or 3 priorities. Not 57, but 2 or 3. Then, be reasonable and balanced in your approach to meeting those priorities. Spend one hour a day reading material in your field, for example, or listening to an informative audio book or podcast. There's no need to try to do everything all at once. Gradual change is good and even desired. Most people can find 60 minutes each day to make this happen.

Balance is a subjective objective. It can't be created by spending equal amounts of time performing equal tasks. Rather, it is accomplished by spending the right amount of time on the right activities. Just 20 minutes a day can make a huge impact on your career—if you're spending it on important, powerful activities such as acquiring skills, creating intellectual horsepower, improving your physical or mental health, and expanding your professional network.

Shifting to a higher level of performance while engaged in the constant mesh of your day-to-day existence requires a balanced, sustained effort over time. Zealotry doesn't help; it's actually counterproductive.

But focus isn't. Intense focus enables that balanced approach to work effectively. It's also what, in my opinion, most sales professionals lack. A focused effort involves identifying your highest priorities and working toward meeting them with the concentration of a neurosurgeon.

Say you need to read a competitive analysis to better understand your market, or you must update your CRM/SFA system, or you just want to make those prospecting calls you've been putting off. Set aside the necessary time to *really* focus on accomplishing the task. But how many sales professionals can't string together three prospecting calls without checking Facebook, sending a text message, or updating their e-mail inbox? Log off, at least while you are focusing intensely. You'll find your productivity will skyrocket—even if you aren't multitasking.

I suggest a 50/10 split, meaning put forth a concentrated effort for approximately 50 minutes and then getting up to grab a beverage, take a walk, or simply clear your mind for 10 minutes. The average adult reportedly can channel his or her mental abilities for no longer than 50 minutes straight.

2. Realize That Energy Makes the Difference. If you're reading this book, you're more than likely a successful sales professional. Most successful sales professionals I know are well organized, with daily planners, to-do lists, and a strong grasp of time management. Perhaps they don't execute perfectly all the time, but they understand the importance of heading into a day, a workweek, or a sales call with a solid plan. For them, that's nothing more than standard operating procedure. They just need to channel the proper energy to get them through the required tasks.

Think back to a customer-service problem in which you played no role but that affected you, nonetheless. You know that sale you worked so hard to attain but then someone in the home office messed up the delivery? Remember how getting upset and fuming about the circumstances did nothing to alleviate them? That was because you, no doubt, were channeling the wrong kind of energy. In times like that, you need calm, cool, and intelligent problem-solving approaches that will enable you to rectify the situation at hand and create a process to help minimize the chances of it occurring again. Otherwise, you may cause irrevocable damage. Remember, you need to use the right kind of energy to accomplish the right tasks.

3. Forget About Perfection. Do you know anyone who figuratively uses a five-pound sledgehammer to drive a carpet tack? The sledgehammer gets the job done, but it takes more energy than using a tack hammer—and probably damages something in the process.

Think about how much energy you are putting into a special project or an everyday task. One of the greatest energy drains is perfectionism. Take a tip from my friend and mentor, consultant Alan Weiss: "Go for success, not perfection." The energy you spend trying to achieve perfection is usually wasted. The difference between 80 percent and 100 percent is often negligible and not significant enough to be appreciated by your buyer. Achieve success, then use the remaining energy to work toward your other areas of development.

4. Harness the Power of Circadian Rhythms. The term *circadian rhythm* was coined by Dr. Franz Halberg of Germany in 1959. Loosely interpreted, it means to find what you do best—and when—and then use that information to maximize your performance.

For example, some people do their best thinking late at night; for others, it's first thing in the morning. Some like physical activity before the sun comes up; others prefer afternoon workouts. Identify when you function optimally, and try to capture those moments. If you're at your best in the morning, consider making those prospecting calls after you've had your first cup of joe. Are you usually flat at the end of the day? Then choose that time to accomplish mundane tasks that require little thought.

Harnessing the power of your circadian rhythms typically makes your work easier. Plus, you'll notice that you're performing better and feeling more energized about your work. You more than likely won't be able to structure every day based on your circadian rhythms—after all, you do need to work within your buyers' schedules. But do it when you can. You'll maximize your energy.

Know What Gear You Are In

Shifting yourself or your sales team to a higher level of performance requires significant forethought, effort, and analysis. One way to begin is by breaking the competencies required for sales success into reasonably sized chunks. Using the competency model categories unveiled in Chapter 2, "Fuel-Injection Connection: The Parameters for Sales Success," it's important to understand your current abilities in the following seven areas:

» Offering expertise
» Language skills
» Process proficiency
» Knowing yourself
» Knowing your buyer
» Knowing your market
» Knowing your competition

Much like shifting gears on a motorcycle or in a car, doing so correctly requires you to maximize the gear you're in by monitoring your tachometer, listening to your engine, and *feeling* the right time to shift. It doesn't mean just blindly accelerating. You must understand the need to "top out" at a current gear before you shift to the next. Likewise, you must have acquired and demonstrated reasonable levels of competency in one skill area before you move to a higher one.

On a scale of 1 to 10, with 1 being the lowest and 10 the highest, where do your abilities fall in your current professional situation? Can you manage your sales territory or your sales team with your eyes closed? Do you know every conceivable angle of your current offerings? Can you answer objections to your offerings in a conversational yet compelling manner? (To determine whether you are ready to shift into higher gear, complete the assessments in the Appendix.)

If you marked "yes" to these questions, it may be time for you to go after the larger accounts, jockey for a position with more responsibility, and engage more sophisticated buyers. You're ready to shift into a higher gear.

Disengage First

When you activate the clutch lever on a motorcycle or press the clutch pedal in a motor vehicle, you're really disengaging your clutch plates. These help transfer power from your engine to your transmission. When you operate your clutch lever or pedal, you enable the plates to momentarily disengage from the power train and move to a higher gear. Similarly, you must momentarily disengage from your sales efforts.

You know how experts are always telling you that there's "danger in the comfort zone?" How you should always be pushing yourself higher and harder? Well, there is some truth to that. But not in this case.

When you are pursuing the acquisition of new skills, new credentials, or new contacts, there might also be a time when you want to hang out in the pocket of your comfort zone to keep other aspects of your life and career in check. Much like the advice to young couples to not get married and buy a house at the same time because it results in too much stress on inchoate relationships, you should not go back to school for your MBA two months after you've been assigned a new sales territory, along with a new sales manager and a new SFA system. It's just too much.

If you can currently handle your workload with relative ease, don't hesitate to make your move. (For me, writing this book was an important development project; my speaking and consulting schedule remained busy, but I made sure the programs I delivered and the client work I took on was well within my competency areas. I did not court new clients, sample new programs, or explore new business models; I had a book to write.)

Move the Shifter

Do you remember when you first learned to drive a manual transmission? You no doubt were unsure of how it really worked or where exactly the shift pattern was, and you ended up (at least a few times) creating noises worse than a dining utensil caught in a whirling industrial garbage disposal. Your driving teacher probably winced more than once.

Moving a shift lever on your manual transmission takes only a moment; rectifying your performance discrepancies and acquiring next-level skills take significantly longer. Here are the three basic sequences of shifting to a higher performance level:

» Be certain of what skill you are trying to attain.
» Understand clearly where the performance gaps exist.
» Acquire the necessary information, ideas, and processes to close that gap.

One reason for the gap might be language skills. Say you sell construction materials and have no problem speaking with construction crews. But the moment a crew supervisor, the project developer, or financial guys join the conversation, you get nervous and tongue-tied. You need to shift some of your language skills to a higher gear. You might, for example, need to acquire the mental references to ensure you communicate with individuals of authority as an equal, as well as the vocabulary and the conversational skills to do so.

Another example of a performance gap could be your offering expertise. You may be able to discuss the basics of the product or service you're selling, but when it comes to explaining how your offering fits into the competitive landscape, you fall short.

There are countless performance discrepancies. But if you want to close more business, close the gaps.

Closing the Gap

Having the competency to acquire the skills necessary to shift your career into a higher gear is the secret to long-term success. During my career, when I've been able to shift my own performance and the performance of others, it was the result of my continuous aptitude in analyzing my performance, identifying the discrepancy, and closing the gap quickly and efficiently. I internalized that skill and moved on to the next business challenge. The following are some of my favorite ways to accomplish that.

Self-Guided Efforts

With the preponderance of information available these days, anyone can teach themselves just about anything. The challenge now is to make sure you are obtaining accurate information. Consider downloading free university podcasts, researching scientific journals, enrolling in online learning courses, or using that old standby known as the local library (one of today's most vastly underutilized resources). Acclimate yourself to a routine of being a lifelong learner, because becoming a situational learner is crucial to acc-*sell*erating your sales success.

Formal Training and Education

On-the-job training usually happens faster than education, but arguments can be made for considering both. Few things can give you the skills you need like participating in a well-run, high-quality, appropriately targeted skills workshop. (If you think you've found one, ask others who have attended how their performance improved as a result. If they're unable to mention specific skills transferred and performance improvements made, keep looking.) Formal education, such as obtaining your M.B.A. or another degree, also can provide a terrific shift for your sales career. But it takes a ton of time and money, so make sure you're able to dedicate both of those prior to going for it.

Mastermind Groups

There's nothing quite like the organized yet flexible coming together of like-minded salespeople who all want to improve their performance. You can meet face-to-face or remotely by teleconference, videoconference, or Internet chat rooms to exchange best practices. Sometimes organized by leaders of a workshop you've attended or by a company, association, or community, mastermind groups can be fantastic ways to help shift performance gears and close skill gaps. Imperative in these groups is the ability to participate fully, knowing other members have your best interests at heart and realizing that—at least when your group gathers—you are not competitors with one another.

The challenge is keeping participation in these groups alive for more than a few months. The good news is that if one in which you're involved dissolves, you can easily find others, or even start one of your own. Or join ours on LinkedIn, called "Mark Rodgers— Accelerate the Sale." (For information on how to form and run sales mastermind groups, visit www.AcceleratetheSale.com.)

Mentors

A mentor is a wise and trusted counselor or teacher. He or she can either be a formal, paid relationship or an informal, unpaid one. The critical component is finding someone who already has accomplished whatever it is you're trying to accomplish. This was made crystal clear to me when participating in Alan Weiss's mentor program. I asked him for guidance on a particular business matter and shared with him the guidance I received from someone else. He simply responded, "There are three of us having this conversation, and only one of us has done it." Point made. I took his advice and never looked back.

Keep in mind that mentorship is not about having a coffee buddy or someone to commiserate with you. There may be some of that, of course, but coffee time should really constitute a fraction of 1 percent of the relationship. As Weiss often says: "If you want a friend, get a dog." He's never rude or impolite—to the contrary—but you also better have your act together. When I interact with him these days, I make sure it's regarding a significant issue, one I've tried to work through on my own first. I go to him because I can't get his kind of insight or perspective anywhere else.

Unfortunately, a regrettable lack of informal or formal mentoring happens in sales organizations these days. But if you seek out and develop mentor relationships with the right people, you'll rectify your skill discrepancies and shift to a higher gear almost immediately.

Chuck West, program director of sales, sales management, and advanced management programs for executive education at the University of Wisconsin–Madison's School of Business, has this to say about mentors:

> The state of mentoring sales professionals today is sadly lacking. If you remember back to the '90s, when we were right-sizing and downsizing organizations like crazy, one of the areas that I think was downsized too much was sales management. The result is that today we have a lot of sales administrators with a span of control way greater than what they can actually mentor. Salespeople are left to figure out for themselves many times what the new sales call should look like, and they don't have as much management coaching. So, they're seeking outside resources to get that done. A whole new industry is outsourcing sales management as a function, and companies are developed in that area. I think that's a sad commentary on the fact that, as companies, we haven't made mentoring a sales-management priority.

Reengage Your Clutch

Once you've started acquiring new skills, you need to internalize them by moving from conscious to unconscious use of them. In sales-exchange moments of opportunity, you want to perform, not just think.

I once watched an interview with musician James Taylor, who was asked what he thought about while performing one of his most-enduring hits, "Fire and Rain." Specifically, the interviewer wanted to know if Taylor summons his personal commitment to the lyrics when he sings them or if he focuses on the chord changes. Taylor sort of chuckled and responded that he used to think about those types of things when he was younger. But now he focuses on a specific person in the third row or even considers what he might do after the show. The point is, James Taylor doesn't have to think about his performance anymore. He's that good, and he's performed "Fire and Rain" so many times that he's now unconsciously competent. When it comes to selling, you should be that good, too.

Here are a few ways to get that good:

» **Choose low-risk environments first.** The first time you try a new prospecting approach, questioning sequence, or objection rebuttal, choose an environment in which you feel comfortable. It's also a good idea to test it out in a relatively low-risk situation. The best circumstances would involve a tried-and-true buyer—not a million-dollar prospect.

» **Get rich feedback.** The other reason to use a trusted, long-term buyer in this situation is because he or she likely will be willing to provide useful feedback about your new skills. For example, ask your client this: "We have a new method of showing prospective buyers what it is we do. May I run it by you to find out what you would think as a potential user of our services?"

» **Keep trying.** I always chuckle when, after spending time with a salesperson who has usually sought *me* out for advice, I make a suggestion and then he responds with, "I tried that; it didn't work." Well, first of all, this particular person may have tried it when MC Hammer was getting airplay; maybe he should give it another shot. Second, it takes many repetitions of a new skill to make it successful. This is why practice opportunities are so important. I've found that working with an accountability partner—someone with whom you touch base regularly to review your professional and personal improvements—can help in achieving new levels of success. That person also can serve as a sanity barometer just when you need it most!

My accountability partner is my friend and colleague, John Carroll, a talented consultant (www.uperform.com) based in Charleston, South Carolina. We touch base via phone every week or two, spending between 30 and 60 minutes reviewing each other's accomplishments, action plans, and objectives. We also share advice about sales challenges, marketing ideas, and skills coaching. I learn from John and he learns from me in what has become a wonderful reciprocity.

You can find accountability partners in trusted colleagues or through professional associations and university affiliations. Keep your accountability partners intact as long as it makes sense to do so, and stop the relationships when they no longer work. For example, John and I have stopped and started on several occasions, as befits our situations. That's key; the relationship between accountability partners must be honest, open, flexible, and mutually beneficial.

Shifting Your Career into Overdrive

We've covered the everyday kind of shifting required to rectify performance discrepancies on a small scale. Now, we'll explore ways to shift your entire career into overdrive.

What must you do to create dramatic shifts in your performance? For one, aim higher in your buyer organizations. Many sales professionals would greatly improve their own conditions if they learned how to effectively execute higher-level executive selling. Five minutes spent in the company of a vice president who can buy is better than five weeks spent with an underling who can't.

Focus on Successful Prospects

Guess which prospects make the best prospects: Ones who can buy! Focus your attention on those. Well-employed individuals or thriving companies are typically your best bets.

Seek to compete with the best, too. One way to shift your performance into overdrive is to make sure you are interacting with ever more skilled individuals—both buyers and fellow sales professionals.

John Duffy, CEO of mobile-applications company 3Cinteractive, says, "As a collegiate wrestler, I relate things back to sports. If

Shifting Up

Chuck West makes the following distinction between high-performing sales organizations and mediocre ones:

The high-performing ones call higher in their client's organizational structure; they call on the decision maker—from the vice president of operations to CFOs, CEOs, and up through the executive suite. Companies that have learned to call higher are the ones that are the most successful today and best positioned for the future.

How do you call higher? Is your message even worthy of that level? The first step is to develop a message about your products or services that resonates at a higher level within the client organization. That takes a lot of work. Second, figure out how to score an initial meeting without burning bridges.

Finally, of course, you must have enough financial savvy, business acumen, and overall strategic understanding to call at a higher level, remain relevant, and conduct a discussion worthy of executives' time.

Another step is be perceived as an outside expert, a peer. *I will call higher,* high-performing salespeople tell themselves. *I will increase my business acumen. I will increase my financial acumen.*

One more piece of advice: Don't hire salespeople; hire really good businesspeople, those who understand how businesses make money. That's the mantra among personnel managers today. Sales professionals these days must be trained in a wide variety of areas in order to succeed in higher-level situations and provide well-rounded knowledge to their organizations.

you want to make your team great, throw an All-American into the workouts. This will show others what it takes to be great. They will learn from him, follow his example, or end up getting beat up a lot. Want to get really great? Throw two All-Americans into the mix."

Shifting into overdrive means dramatically improving your business or career results. How do you attain a broader understanding of business in general? How do you more deeply understand your own organization? How can you create a network of contacts to boost your performance? How do you acquire the credentials necessary to open more doors to buyers?

Keep Shifting

Once you've worked your way through the metaphorical gears of your current position, you'll want to seek out a new "vehicle" to propel you toward the next level of your sales career. (See Figure 10.2.)

Whether engaging in a new type of sales (technology solutions rather than traditional products, for example) or selling to different types of buyers, for a different company, or in a new industry, these types of challenges will keep you growing and provide you with a whole new set of gears to shift through.

■ **FIGURE 10.2**
Shift into High Gear

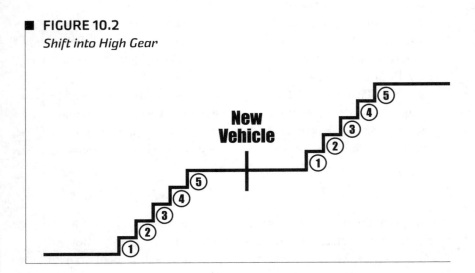

CHAPTER 10 Acc*sell*erators

» Shifting into high gear is a metaphor for progressing through your career. This requires you to be adept at mastering change, rectifying performance discrepancies, and acquiring skills.

» Enlightened self-interest is the closest to true motivation. When your sales methods are good for you, good for your organization, and good for the larger community in which you operate, that's the essence of savvy selling.

» To work through constant mesh, balance your life, increase focus, apply your energy, and forget about perfection.

» Before you shift, you must "top out" in your current gear. Make sure you're competent in one area before you move to the next. You don't have be an expert; just competent.

» To shift into high gear, you've got to sell higher in the organization. Five positive minutes with a vice president who can buy is better than five weeks with an underling who can't.

CHAPTER 11

Trouble at High Speed

HOW NOT TO LOSE CONTROL OF YOUR BUYER

Staring straight ahead, firmly gripping the wheel, the driver fixated on the snowy road in front of him. His jaw clenched, he steadily—subconsciously, perhaps—pressed harder on the gas pedal as he and his vehicle pushed onward through the driving snow. But he wasn't thinking about the road; instead, the driver's mind was on everything else: his job, his finances, tomorrow's schedule.

Then, like a toy car at the mercy of a child's hands, his vehicle began to hydroplane, sending it into three terrifying 360-degree spins before finally smashing into the snow-covered median. Heart pounding, eyes wide open, and still gripping the steering wheel, the driver quickly and repeatedly thanked his Creator and vowed from that moment forward to be more in control behind the wheel.

I should know; that driver was me.

If you've ever lost control while driving, as I did that frightful winter night, you know how harrowing the experience can be.

Losing control can happen so fast and for so many reasons: driver inattention, road conditions, other motorists' actions. But to arrive safely at a given destination, you must either be able to retain your focus or be skilled enough to drive through any type of conditions.

And so it goes with navigating your sales. Hopefully, your selling situations don't involve live-or-die scenarios (even though at times they may feel that way). Remember, each sales encounter can be a valuable one, even if it doesn't result in an actual sale.

The concept of acc*sell*erating the sale revolves around closing more deals faster. The quickest route to this destination is not always tearing down the highway; if you're not careful, you can encounter trouble at high speed. Just as you want to maintain control of your vehicle, you also want to maintain control of your buyer.

What do I mean by that? Well, I certainly *don't* mean using underhanded tactics to unduly leverage buyers in such a way that they ultimately resent the exchange. Rather, you should know where you're headed with the transaction and maintain control of the sales relationship and its progression at all times.

In the sales success model, I have shown how you must possess intellectual horsepower, which includes understanding your offering, possessing powerful verbal skills, and knowledge of "what's next" in the sales process. You also must know how to respond to the hairpin turns that can sneak up on you in any sales exchange. The following ideas can help keep you in control when that happens.

Possess Business Acumen

First and foremost, the person sitting across the desk (or standing across the product) from you should know that you are an equal. You're not some subservient vendor to be dispatched; you're an individual with whom spending time can genuinely be to the advantage of a prospective buyer. To enhance your credibility, you must understand basic business acumen as well as know some of the specifics about your potential customer's business.

Earlier, I discussed the importance of being familiar with and understanding basic business tools like income statements. Now, think about adding to your knowledge basics regarding balance sheets and cash-flow statements. You can't help your buyers if you don't understand their business. Be conversant with terms like *asset, liability, revenue, expense, equity, accounts receivable, accounts payable,* and, of course, *return on investment* and *return on equity.* Then apply your general knowledge of those terms to your potential buyer's organization. If that organization is a publicly held company, you can find plenty of details on the Internet. Once you're aware of the gross revenue, gross profit margin, and net profit of your prospect's firm, you'll likely be more knowledgeable than 85 percent of that company's rank-and-file employees! You needn't be

STREET SMARTS

Not-So-Easy Rider

Forget the media image of Harley-Davidson riders as fun-loving weekend warriors. Some of them are tougher than they look, as are many Harley-Davidson dealers. Leading the field-sales team responsible for interacting with these rough-riding dealer principals is John Early, vice president of sales for Harley-Davidson Financial Services. Here, he offers sage advice for how his team maintains control at high speeds:

You have to be well researched. You've got to go into a dealer call knowing what this person's business is like, what their pain points are, and what their current performance is. You need to be able to diffuse any tense situation and any misperceptions about facts.

But even more important than that, you have to bring something to the table, something no one else does. You have to be able to impart best practices that can improve this person's business. Although Harley-Davidson dealers can be a tough, smart, demanding bunch, if you can improve their situation, you can develop a mutually beneficial and trusting relationship. That's what helps us keep things under control.

a certified accountant, but accounting terms have been referred to as the "language of business." If you want to stay in control of your buyer, you'd better be able to discuss the basics and speak the language.

How does this apply to you if you're selling in a B2C situation? For large-ticket items, you'll want to discuss impacts to your prospect's monthly budgets, insurance parameters, and depreciation and taxes. For starters, simply apply the business concept to personal finances, and your buyer will be hooked.

Grasp of Your Buyer's Issues

Let's say you're selling consulting services to the financial-services sector. Your potential buyer mentions his "book," and you ask if it's a "good read." Bid farewell to that sale, my friend, because you'll be as welcome as Elton John in the opening-act slot at a Metallica concert (a "book" is an individual's or company's business portfolio, which includes loans or insurance contracts).

Retail sales are full of similar pitfalls. If you're not familiar with the latest advertisements, celebrity endorsements, or news about the products you represent—as well as those of your competitors—you're not going to succeed. To remain in control you must understand the market and its current conditions. Here's how:

Listen to the Conversation

If you're selling in a B2B environment, read at least three back issues of each trade magazine that covers your prospect's industry. The time you spend doing so will speed your ability to establish credibility and communicate effectively by speaking the prospect's language. Look for supply-chain relationships, political and regulatory issues, and consumer-related concerns. If you're involved in B2C selling, obtain copies of at least three consumer magazines that spotlight your products or services. Look for competitive comparisons, reliability reports, and consumer feedback.

Once you've opened those magazines, the fastest way to get to the heart of a particular industry's conversation is by reading the letters to the editor. This section spotlights individuals who were driven enough—*passionate* enough—to write to the publication and share their thoughts with the rest of the industry. Such letters can be a goldmine of consumer (and, thus, buyer) sentiment.

In addition, consider spending some time browsing online forums, where people share what matters most to them regarding a seemingly infinite number of topics. Keep in mind that individuals who frequent such forums often are part of a vocal minority, so don't let their comments sway your sales actions too much. Despite this caveat, online forums can serve as a sales barometer for practically any product or service available.

"Shop" Your Prospect's Business

If you really want to understand a business, shop it just like any other customer. Peruse the company's website, identifying things about it that you like and noting things that can be improved. Don't be shy. Call the company with a basic buyer's inquiry, and evaluate employee promptness, politeness, and helpfulness. Was a "next step"—such as an invitation to visit the store—offered by the person with whom you spoke? Or did the conversation terminate after your questions were answered?

Few things are as powerful as objectively pointing out disparities between policy and practice. So when your potential buyer describes his or her business operations—and you can say, "That's not what happened when I shopped your business"—you instantly place the burden of proof on the prospect. You'll also likely be greeted with a second or two of stupefying speechlessness. That's when you'll know you're in control.

Buyers spend precious little time looking at their businesses from the perspective of a consumer or client. (At the time of this writing, a popular television program called "Undercover Boss" invited CEOs of well-known companies to work with their employees as the "new person" on the job, uncovering all sorts of deficiencies in the way these companies conduct business. The highlight of each episode is when the CEO experiences an epiphany about the disparities between management's strategy and employee execution. Shocking.) When you can provide insight about how something really works—or doesn't work—you're offering your prospect valuable information.

The surest route to acc*sell*erating the sale is engaging your prospect during those early verbal exchanges. Come into the conversation knowing the pertinent issues, and you and your prospect will both be well served.

Gain "Insider's Prestige"

We mentioned this in Chapter 3, "Crawling Under the Hood: *Really Understanding Your Offering*"; it's so important, I want to raise the issue again. When you can speak the language of a particular business, your potential buyer will interpret your perceptive insights as one or both of the following:

1. You already possess a high degree of understanding about his or her business.
2. You are willing to learn more about that business.

Your ability to quickly convey to your buyer that you know something about how his or her operation works—and maybe can even offer new perspectives on current market conditions—helps you build rapport quickly and close the deal faster.

STREET SMARTS

Make It Fun

Enjoyment is an important component of the sales transaction, according to Chuck West of the University of Wisconsin–Madison's School of Business. "Make it fun for your client and fun for yourself," he suggests. "Fun may be an over-statement, but at least make it enjoyable for both parties. That way, there's relationship-building and a real tight kind of honesty as you move forward on a business agenda. If it's enjoyable, both parties can participate freely and openly."

210

For example, insurance salespeople need to be familiar with terms like *ACV* ("actual cash value"), *captive* (not a hostage, but an affiliate or subsidiary), and *tails* (claims not yet reported). In a banking scenario, understanding *cross-collateralization, the right of offset*, and *debt-to-income ratio* is critical. If you're talking computers, know the meaning of such terms as *client, kernel*, and *WAN*.

If you travel to a country in which your primary language is not spoken, you'll rapidly discover that if you attempt to learn and speak a few words and phrases in the native language, most of the natives will admire your effort (even if your usage is poor), because you have shown an attempt to embrace the culture. By spending time learning the language and culture of your buyer, you will ingratiate yourself in a similar fashion.

Don't misunderstand me: You won't become an industry expert overnight, and I'm not suggesting that you portray yourself as someone you're not. But by demonstrating that you have done your homework, have a firm grasp of industry-specific issues, and can provide sound direction to ultimately help improve your prospect's image and performance in that industry, you've proven that you're serious about making this sale.

Provide an "Aha" Moment

At the risk of infuriating trademark attorneys at Oprah Winfrey's Harpo Productions, I dare to use this colloquial phrase because it communicates my point so well. One of the surest ways to remain in control as you speed toward closing a sale is to provide a moment during which your buyer scratches his or her head and says, "That's an intriguing idea. I've never thought of it like that."

Aha.

Now, you've once again established yourself as different from all of the other salespeople this prospect has encountered over the years. Now, you're adding value. Now, you're enabling the potential buyer to learn something he or she didn't know before speaking with you. This is a major component of sales success. So practice engineering those aha moments with a series of "what if" questions. This type of inquiry allows you and your buyer to suspend reality and consider the possibilities.

B2B questions might include: What if you expanded internationally? What if you had lower volume, but higher profitability? What if your salespeople were relieved of their administrative duties? What if you reduced your advertising budget and increased your sales force?

B2C questions might include: What if you could have the new model and not see any increase in your monthly payment? What if we came to you, and you never had to leave your home or office to do business with us? What if we could assure you that you would always have someone to call—and that you would always speak to a knowledgeable person on the other end?

It's easy to come up with "what if" questions based on the circumstances surrounding your client. Such thought-provoking inquiries challenge a buyer's conventional wisdom. If you can identify sacred cows and change the way the prospect thinks about them, both of you may be leading those cows to the slaughter. And that's a good thing. There's no need to be rude or unreasonably abrupt, but don't be afraid to take a risk and challenge convention.

After the "what if" questions, the next-best way to challenge convention is to simply ask, "Why?" Why does your client distribute products the way it does? Why is customer feedback considered so important—or, conversely, so unimportant? Why are sales efforts concentrated only in certain areas? Help provide moments of clarity.

Leverage Your Authority

As mentioned in our discussion of language, people defer to experts. If a doctor diagnoses it, we believe it. If the *New York Times* prints it, we accept it (most of the time). If a politician proclaims it . . . OK, bad example.

The fact is, if a person who has a high degree of credibility says something, the human tendency is to believe it. The trick to acc-*sell*erating your sales is to subtly display your authority so you can rapidly move forward without your buyer thinking you're overbearing and arrogant. The key word here is *subtly*.

Robert Cialdini, a social psychologist at Arizona State University and an expert in the study of human persuasion, compared patients' compliance with the prescribed behavior dispensed by both physicians and physical therapists. As things turned out, patients followed their doctors' orders, but not those of their physical therapists.

Next, Cialdini evaluated the environment in which both sets of medical professionals were dispensing their diagnoses to patients. The physicians, naturally, wore white coats and spoke to patients against the backdrop of a wall filled with credentials and diplomas. The physical therapists, on the other hand, were surrounded by generic artwork and motivational posters (at least one of which probably featured a kitten clinging for life, spouting such nonsense as "Hang in there"). Cialdini then asked the physical therapists in the study—all highly trained, educated, and accomplished—to display their credentials in the area in which they were making their diagnoses. The result? Physical-therapist patient compliance increased 34 percent!

Meaningful credentials speak volumes. Display diplomas, awards, and other documents denoting serious achievement in your sales space so clients can clearly see them. My wife, Amy, and I recently spent time in the office of a local "wealth manager" who displayed a blue ribbon (like one you might have received in elementary school for holding open a classroom door for the teacher) for "Best Speech" from a Toastmasters International meeting. I'm all for self-development, and Toastmasters International does important work. But when I'm interviewing a wealth manager, I want to see an M.B.A. from The Wharton School hanging on that person's wall, not a blue ribbon.

I know what you're thinking: *But, Mark, I'm often on the buyers' turf. I go to them. It's not like I'm going to drag my diplomas with me.*

Of course you're not. But here are a few ways you can make yourself and your credentials stand out while not making a spectacle of yourself:

» Use credentials in your e-mail signature. If you have a Ph.D., M.B.A., or other specific credential, such as an executive education certificate, use it.
» If you or your company won an award, that also should be noted in your e-mail signature. For example: "Rated No. 1 in Customer Satisfaction by J.D. Power and Associates."
» In conversation, casually reference your relevant experiences, special projects, and relationships: "We had a similar situation occur while working on the Apple project." You don't want a reputation as a name-dropper, so do this sparingly and strategically. But do it. People don't know your experiences or triumphs unless you tell them.

The credentials issue recently became a fascinating topic of discussion during one of the executive education programs I teach for the University of Wisconsin. After several minutes spent talking about these techniques, the director of one company somewhat sheepishly raised his hand—exceptional, in and of itself, because I like these conversations to be more of a free-for-all. The participant, a frequent attendee, explained that he recently purchased a university-logoed travel coffee mug. Now, he takes it to all of his meetings, both internally and on-site with clients. Sometimes people comment on it, he said, and since he started carrying it with him, his credibility had increased, and people seemed more willing to take his advice.

Simple. Subtle. Brilliant.

I mentioned this earlier, but it bears repeating: You can subtly demonstrate your authority and thereby maintain control of your buyer by using the language of experts. Such terms as *recommend*, *suggest*, and *advise* all reinforce your credibility and guide your buyer to what is best for him or her. When you say to your buyer, "Here's what I recommend we do . . ." or "I'd like to suggest . . . ," chances are dramatically higher that your prospect will follow your lead.

Understand Why Machiavelli Was Right

Niccolò Machiavelli, an Italian philosopher from the end of the 15th century and the first part of the 16th, is considered one of the founders of modern political science (some say *The Prince* was the first self-help book). Because of his views on winning, losing, and manipulation, Machiavelli has been painted with a very black brush. I won't try to change history's take on the man, but I will suggest that you not disregard what he had to say. Take this piece of advice from *The Prince*: "Whosoever desires constant success must change his conduct with the times." In other words, to have a long and peaceful reign, one must behave in accordance with the conventional and ethical standards of the day.

The modern sales professional can take away some solid lessons from this idea. For example, if you are selling to or for Nike, you'd better be physically fit and work out regularly. If you're selling to or for Harley-Davidson, you're not doing yourself any favors if you ride a Honda Gold Wing. And if you sell Microsoft products, keep that iPhone in your pocket.

When operating in a B2B environment, understand that your buyer's company has a culture. It's important for you to have a sense of that culture so you can work within it. Let's discuss appropriate wardrobe, for example. Is the dress code at your client's office business or business casual? If it's the latter, get an accurate description, especially because there are varying interpretations of the term *business casual* these days. Then, when meeting with representatives from that organization, dress one notch above the acceptable attire. Literally suit your manner to the situation.

Multiple studies have proven that people are much more prone to comply with a request from someone ("Pick up that bag"; "Stand on the other side of that sign"), or follow the lead of someone (a jaywalker, for instance), who is smartly dressed. Contrary to those who say you should try to match the wardrobe decisions of other employees, in a sales situation you should always err on the side of caution. Gary Ramey of Beretta U.S.A. comments about his company's approach to wardrobe: "We wear Beretta apparel to our meetings. We'll have on tweed jackets and slacks, and we'll have on Beretta shirts. You won't see us show up in jeans and a T-shirt that says 'Got guns?' We're going to show up dressed well."

But be careful: If you dress two notches above everybody else, you'll stand out—and not in a good way. If you are in a B2C situation, you want the way you're perceived to be similar to that of the average buyer of that particular product. If you're selling Harley-Davidson motorcycles, for example, dress somewhere in between what you'd wear to a Hell's Angels rally and what you'd wear walking into the Goldman Sachs headquarters.

Watch your meeting behavior, too. What is acceptable in terms of using humor? In some organizations, if you don't have a sense of humor, you're about as welcome as an IRS agent; in others, if you do attempt to be funny, you're viewed with disdain as a corporate Carrot Top. Be smart. If you opt for wit with clients, make sure that wit is appropriate and never off-color.

Similarly, can you calibrate yourself to the current language of your buyer? In many organizations (as in society), phrases come in and out of vogue. Metaphors like *burning platform*, *low-hanging fruit*, or *win-win* are overused and abused. Some have more staying power than others, but you must get a grip on the vernacular. If your client favors variations of the term *reach out*, as in "I reached out to Sahana in marketing to get her take," then you should "reach out," too. As Thomas Jefferson said, "In matters of style, swim with the current."

Although altering your conduct to keep pace with the situation may seem antithetical, as if you are relinquishing power rather than maintaining control, it is not. Imagine yourself in a kayak, navigating the mighty Mississippi River; you harness the power of the current to accomplish the task at hand.

Get Your Buyer Involved

Another great way of speeding toward closing while still harnessing your power is to involve your buyer as much as possible in the discussion. This is just plain common sense; conventional wisdom holds that while people hate to be sold, they love to buy. Ask your client questions to make him or her enjoy the act of buying:

» "So, in terms of a fix for your situation, are you looking for a good, better, or best solution?"
» "On a scale of 1 to 10—1 being the lowest and 10 being the highest—how would you rate your situation (or your problem, your urgency, your whatever)?"
» "If you were to describe your current perspective on your situation (or that of your coworkers, your spouse, or any other purchase influencer), would you describe it as positive, neutral, or negative?"
» "In terms of your current performance (or that of your organization, your department, or your service), would you describe it as acceptable, above average, or the ultimate?"
» "What within your organization is working? How do you know?"
» "What isn't working? What evidence have you seen of that?"
» "From your perspective, what is the one thing that, if changed, would yield the most dramatic improvements in your organization?"
» "What's the main stumbling block preventing you from making that improvement a reality?"

As with most methods presented in this book, these questions work in most B2B sales settings and can readily be applied to B2C situations. For example, a car salesperson can ask a would-be car buyer something like this: "If you were to describe your wife's reaction to your decision to purchase a new Corvette, would you describe it as positive, neutral, or negative?" Soliciting the buyer's perspective helps you maintain control by better understanding buying motivations and influences, enabling you to tailor your next steps based on the feedback you receive.

Leverage the Psychology of Opinions

Most sales go unconsummated because the salesperson fails to do one simple thing: Ask for the prospect's business. Most professionals know they *need* to "close," but they run into a mental roadblock—fear—that keeps many of them in the slow lane.

Imagine you've established a strong relationship with your prospect and flawlessly executed your sales progression. You are now speeding down the road toward sales success, and your mind is racing, too. *Should I try to close now?* you wonder. The origins of this mental spinout are coming from you, not the buyer! So what should you do? How do you proceed? Although revisiting the steps to the sale is not my intent here, you do need to check yourself to ensure that you've done all the requisite preparatory work. It's important to move though all of the steps of the sales process and not take shortcuts. (As discussed previously, there are possibly more available sales models today than there are flavors of Ben & Jerry's ice cream. So, whether you decide to use five steps, seven steps, the magical mystery model, or invent one on your own, you must make sure it works consistently; otherwise, find a new model.)

Consider putting in place safeguards to make sure you're not getting ahead of yourself and hydroplaning your way out of a deal. For starters, arm yourself with a comprehension of basic psychology. When you ask someone if he or she would like to buy something, you are asking for a commitment. And commitment, for many people, can be threatening. The natural inclination is to resist and respond negatively. So what's a sales professional to do?

Instead of asking whether the buyer is ready to seal the deal, ask not for a commitment but for an opinion. As discussed in Chapter 5, "One Down, Four Up: The Power of Process," this is often referred to as a trial close because you are testing the waters. Plus, it offers a great opportunity to use your language skills. To speed up a sale that's slowing down, simply ask the prospect: "What do you think?"

This innocuous question will provide you with the feedback you need to determine whether you can—or even should—proceed. When you ask, "What do you think?" you're directly involving the buyer and conveying that you care about his or her opinion. Everyone has one, and most people are prepared to share that opinion at the slightest provocation. So provoke—I mean, inquire.

At this point, the buyer typically will go in one of two directions: The affirmative ("I like it!") or the negative ("I'm not sure," or worse). Regardless of that opinion, you now have the necessary directions to your destination. If your buyer responds in the affirmative, close the deal. If he or she responds in the negative, you have more work to do.

Know What to Do When Buyers Say "No"

The opinion-question technique just described does wonders to assuage many sales professionals' fear of being turned down. But that alone is not enough. Acc*sell*erated salespeople know how to respond in a spinout, when the buyer flat-out says "no."

Any worthy salesperson should anticipate being turned down. Just as you avoid traffic jams by taking alternate routes, you can react to sales slowdowns with alternate offers. This is sometimes referred to as "rejection, then retreat." When rejected, you retreat to a smaller, less significant offer.

This technique has been proven effective time and again. My favorite examples, however, come once more from social psychologist Robert Cialdini. Walking in front of his university library one day, Dr. Cialdini was approached by a Boy Scout who asked him if he would like to purchase tickets to the Scouts' circus to be held that Saturday at the local coliseum. The tickets were $5 apiece. Cialdini declined. Without losing an ounce of composure, the boy replied, "Oh, well, then would you like to buy a couple of our chocolate bars? They are only $1 each." Cialdini bought two chocolate bars. Stunned, he knew something significant had just happened . . . because he doesn't like chocolate!

Analyzing this exchange Dr. Cialdini discovered what he calls "concessional reciprocity." The idea is that when you decline someone's offer and they come back with a smaller, less extreme offer, you want to say "yes" to reciprocate for the concession they have made to you.

Wanting to test this idea further, Cialdini took to the streets of Phoenix. Posing as representatives of a youth counseling program, Cialdini and his research assistants approached college students to see if they would be interested in chaperoning a bus trip to the zoo for a group of juvenile delinquents. Seriously! Not surprisingly, 83 percent of them turned him down. (I'd be interested in studying the 17 percent who *did* respond positively to Cialdini's request.)

Cialdini and his assistants then asked another group of passersby if they would consider something more outlandish. Would they consider dedicating two hours per week serving as counselors to juvenile delinquents for a minimum of two years? Not surprisingly 100 percent of the students turned down this request. When they did, the naysayers were immediately offered the smaller zoo trip request, to which 50 percent agreed to go. That's a tripling of the agreement rate!

Inherent in the "rejection, then retreat" sales strategy is making numerous pricing scenarios, commitment levels, and timing horizons available to buyers. That way, if a customer says "no" to one, you can retreat to your next offer. Here are some ways in which to leverage this concept:

» **Pricing and value:** Pricing is often the easiest way to organize alternatives, regardless of what you're selling. Consider the Mercedes-Benz S, E, and C Class offerings. Once a buyer has committed to the Mercedes-Benz brand, he or she can choose a $90,000, $50,000, or $35,000 price point, plus a vast array of options within each class.

» **Involvement and effort:** By applying price differentials to services, price points can be based on the involvement and effort required of the buyer or the organization. In my consulting practice, I provide options based on whether I handle all aspects of a given project, just handle some aspects of the project, or only provide advice and coaching while letting the client do the rest of the work.

» **Phases and timing:** Break your offer into phases or parts. One way to do this with a product is to ship it incrementally; for services, divide them into an "assessment phase" and an "implementation phase." Either approach creates additional options to help your buyer make the best decision.

How many different options should you offer? Barry Schwartz, in *The Paradox of Choice: Why More Is Less*, suggests that an overabundance of choices actually decreases customer satisfaction and, in many cases, customer action. In my work, I've found that three or four options are enough; fewer than that seem constrictive, while more tend to confuse. Present the options in one of two ways: Offer the largest and most complete option first, and then ask for the buyer's business; if he or she defers, retreat to your next option. Or simply lay out all of the options at once, and ask the buyer how he or she would like to proceed.

The first approach requires a bit more technique via a face-to-face meeting or phone conversation. The second, because it's less dicey, can be done in writing just as effectively as in person or over the phone. The key is making sure you can provide alternatives to "no."

Latin Isn't Dead

Another way sales practitioners can lose control of their buyer is when they hear the buyer ask, "What can you do for me?" Inherent in this question is the expectation of a discount. It is here, in the price-reduction request, that many salespeople skid wildly out of control.

As I mentioned in this book's Introduction, The Sales Board, Inc., which studied the behavior of more than 16,000 customers and 300 salespeople in 25 industries, concluded that 82 percent of salespeople rely on discount pricing in order to make the sale. I'm not a fan of price reductions, and it is not my intent to dispense advice regarding discounting philosophies. Suffice to say that your tendency toward price reductions should be filtered through many things, including your business's current cash flow and debt load as well as your team's skills.

Although we covered rebutting price objections in Chapter 8, "Accelerating Through the Curves: Rebutting the Toughest Objections," I want to suggest here an alternative response to price objections that will shift your transaction into maximum overdrive.

Typically, when you present a buyer with different options and different price points, one of those options will strike the discount seeker's fancy. To many salespeople, this nugget of knowledge comes as an epiphany. If the buyer specifically requests a price concession, leverage a bit of negotiating strategy known as *quid pro quo*—Latin for "something for something." Here are examples of valuable something-for-something exchanges:

» **Full up-front payment:** In B2B circumstances, you know that cash flow and capital are critical. You may be able to easily allow a reasonable price concession in exchange for full and immediate payment (pending approval of your senior managers, that is).
» **Faster payment:** You negotiate, say, 30 days instead of 90. This is a variation on the concept above. It's not as good, but it's still a perfectly acceptable exchange.
» **Written testimonial:** Testimonials are the oil that makes your sales engine run smoother. Obtain them at every opportunity, and this is an opportunity in which you can almost demand one.
» **Audio or video testimonial:** This format is even more compelling than a written testimonial.
» **Referrals:** Considered the platinum standard for obtaining new business (see Chapter 9, "The Power of Referrals: Nitrous Oxide for Your Sales Engine"), referrals are worthy of a reasonable price concession.
» **Feedback:** A client willing to sit down and provide meaningful feedback about a recently completed transaction helps tune your engine for the next race.

The idea here is that if you're going to give price concessions, do so smartly. How might you incorporate *quid pro quo* into your own sales transactions? Try something like this:

Customer: I like your offer, but I'm going to need you to come in 10 percent lower than your proposal price. I just can't afford the full fee.

Salesperson: I'm unable to reduce the proposal price alone, but what I *can* do is offer you a *quid pro quo*. Would you like to hear it?

Customer: Sure.

Salesperson: *Quid pro quo*—I'll meet your price reduction, but instead of adhering to the typical 90-day payment terms, I'll need to receive full payment immediately. *(Pause. Then stick out your hand.)* Deal?

Experiment with language and cadence to find what best fits your style—and what makes you most comfortable. It works. Why?

Because it capitalizes on what I call the "instant of opportunity," that window that opens for a split-second when people negotiate face to face. It keeps you in control of the deal and increases the likelihood that your customers will say "yes," because they will believe they have "traded" well.

Few things are more critical in successful selling than maintaining control of the buyer. This is not accomplished through underhanded or manipulative means but rather in a manner that allows sales professionals to expertly guide buyers through the twists and turns of a sales exchange.

Intellectual horsepower is crucial to being perceived as the buyer's peer, while superlative verbal and nonverbal communication helps position you as an authority. And knowing "what's next" in the process—and how to respond to any given moment of opportunity—is essential. When you act with your buyer's best interests in mind and can effectively employ some or all of the approaches presented here, you will not only retain control of your clients, but you'll keep your sales career on the fast track.

CHAPTER 11 Acc*sell*erators

» Intellectual sales horsepower means offering expertise, employing superb language skills, and demonstrating sales process proficiency.
» In addition to becoming familiar with income statements, also learn how to read a balance sheet and a cash-flow statement. You don't need to be a CPA, but you have to understand how these items can impact your B2B buyers.
» Machiavelli wasn't all bad; he taught us we need to work with the culture of an organization, not against it.
» Know what to do when your buyer says "no." Robert Cialdini's take on concessional reciprocity works wonders.
» *Quid pro quo* helps keep you in control. Give up something, get something in return—a referral, a testimonial, faster payment, something! Never give without getting something back.

Beyond Redline

WHEN YOU'VE PUSHED YOUR MOTOR PAST ITS LIMITS

et out!"

"What are you saying?" the salesperson retorted, not moving a muscle.

"I don't know how I can say this any more clearly," growled the small-business owner. "Get. Out. Of. My. Office. *Now!*"

This sales call was not going well.

Standing now, the emergency medical supplies salesperson reached into his coat. "Let me give you my card."

The business owner stared in disbelief.

Pulling a piece of tape from a nearby tabletop dispenser, the salesman slapped the card on the underside of the owner's desk and affixed it, credentials side out. "When you're lying on the floor, your chest in crushing pain from a massive coronary, and you don't have one of my company's defibrillators hanging on the wall to save your life, the last thing I want you to see is . . . *my name.*"

With that, he turned and walked out of the office amidst a flurry of profanity that would make a Hell's Angel blush.

True story.

Was this an awful salesperson? No. He was the top seller at his firm. He was, however, awful at that moment.

I've devoted a lot of space in this book to doing more—and doing it faster. Now, I'd like to acknowledge that every engine—and every person—has a capacity at which performance falters. Oh, you can find other ways to sell more: different channels, bigger clients, more creative distribution. But that's not what I mean. I mean that humans, just like high-performing engines, have limits. Call it physical or mental redlining.

Hopefully, neither you nor a member of your sales team has been involved in a contentious experience like the one with the medical supply salesperson in our example. But things like that do happen, and they usually occur when someone doesn't recognize the need to make a pit stop and refuel.

(If you have a sales stress experience you'd like to share, post it at www.AcceleratetheSale.com so others can learn from your experience. Note that I said "learn," not "laugh.")

How Do You Know You've Hit Redline?

Everyone has different methods of tolerating the stress related to the endeavor of selling. But when that stress keeps you from productivity, it can be catastrophic to your career and perhaps even to your life.

Having the ability and maturity to know when you're at capacity contributes significantly to your personal and professional success.

The following are warning signs that stress is taking over—and probably winning:

» You act with increased aggression or hostility, especially to those closest to you.
» You find it increasingly difficult to make business and personal decisions.
» You find it challenging to concentrate on what you are doing at any given moment.
» You find yourself spending, or wanting to spend, more time alone than usual.
» You become more forgetful about everything from household tasks to work responsibilities.

Shooting Straight

Gary Ramey, vice president of sales and marketing for Beretta U.S.A., says he and his team strive to set aggressive goals that are within reach:

> If we see some dealer struggling in terms of orders, we'll contact the salesperson and say, "Hey, what's going on? What can we do to help?" We never let them struggle on their own. If one of our guys is struggling, I promise you, the first thing we'll ask is, "Have we done enough to help this person? What more can we do?" If it requires a product manager to go down and spend a week with that salesperson and see some accounts, then we do it. If it means that I need to go jump on a plane, then I'll do it. It's all part of a team environment and making sure that everybody feels valued.

» You are anxious about the state of your commission check or your career.
» You lie awake at night fearing what *might* happen, not thinking about what actually *did* happen.
» Your mood pendulum swings back and forth between optimism and doom.
» Others describe you as difficult to work with.
» You use substances (alcohol, drugs, or food) to deal with stress.

Sales-Related Stressors

Selling creates its own set of stressors:

» Unattainable goals or objectives
» Inadequate tools or technology
» Insufficient management support

» Lack of high-quality training
» Poor economic conditions
» Product problems
» Improper service or execution

Eustress, I Stress, We All Stress

Not all stress is detrimental. (I'll spare you the fight-or-flight bit.) A little stress can spur you and your team to work harder, be more creative, and develop innovative solutions. The problem is when stress becomes overwhelming or unending.

As shown in Figure 12.1, too little stress makes us apathetic. But too much of it can shut us down. What we're really looking for is the ideal balance between no stress and "helpful" stress, often referred to as *eustress*.

■ **FIGURE 12.1**

Relationship Between Stress and Innovation

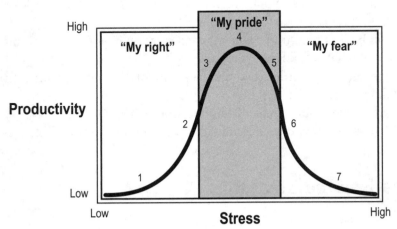

© 2000 Alan Weiss. Reprinted with permission from his book *Process Visuals*.

Channel the Pressure

Doug Slotkin, sales vice president for Zillow.com, makes sure he builds a little fear into each member of his sales team:

> For reps, obviously, the stress is to hit their number every month. If they're in sales, they understand very well what's expected of them. We make it very clear, in terms of their effort level and sales numbers. So can that be stressful? Yes.
>
> Sometimes, it ends up being positive stress, because at the end of the month, they hit the gas really hard and they hit their number. That means their stress is channeled properly. Otherwise, it's channeled negatively: salespeople start to get frustrated, reps get confrontational with clients. When they're not hitting their numbers, they shut down and don't do other activities that are important. That's when a manager must step in and say, "'You know what? I understand you're feeling the pressure. You've got to channel that pressure positively."
>
> Doing so involves researching, prospecting, presenting and following up. When you're able to channel all of that pressure positively, you separate yourself from the competition.

Stress and Buyers

Have you ever had one of *those* days? Nothing but unreturned voice-mail and e-mail messages, not to mention fruitless cold calls and frantic text messages from your boss about the numbers. Plus, your water heater conked out this morning, and your son has a hockey game tonight. After 12 hours on the job, you want nothing more than to leave the day behind and relax.

What if, a few minutes before you were heading home that day, a customer calls regarding some follow-up? There's no new business to be gained here, just wrapping up nagging details on a deal from which the commission has long since been spent. How should this buyer be treated?

If you have a trusting relationship with this particular customer, you might consider saying something like this: "Your issue is too important for me to be able to give you a thoughtful response right now. May I think about it, talk to some other people, and get back to you when I know more?" Or: "Will you allow me until the close of business tomorrow to get things sorted out?" That way, you can make sure your buyer knows he or she is valued while also giving yourself some breathing room. On the other hand, these are the moments when sales relationships have the opportunity to become irreparably damaged; if your buyer's issue is urgent, it's wise not to detain action.

Selling in today's environment could not be more competitive. Every experience that each buyer has with your business is of utmost importance. He or she won't get you at your best if you're laboring under undue stress.

Stress and Coworkers

Stress can have a big effect on how well you interact with others. As a sales professional, you need the cooperation of many people in your organization, and you're less likely to get it if you are abrupt or terse and snap at those you rely on. On top of that, mistakes resulting from stress can affect the workplace environment. A deal not approved on time could delay a sale and upset a big-spending client, or a pricey sale might be stalled because the paperwork wasn't ready on time, creating tension between you and the office staff.

These situations escalate into conflict among colleagues, which can lead to even more mistakes. Your business suffers when stress takes its toll, which is why you need to treat your coworkers with the same respect and gentility you would a buyer. Maybe even more.

Stress and Time

Have you ever been stumped by a decision that needs to be made? Nearly paralyzed by the complexity of a particular situation? Chances are the issue is stress. Stress increases the amount of time it takes to accomplish a task; in the process, it decreases decision-making capabilities. A great example can be found when trying to sort out complex buyer issues. If you're under a great deal of stress, your skills may not be sharp, leading to inconsistent problem solving and execution.

Two of the most potentially dangerous side effects of stress are worry and alcohol.

1. **Worry is a useless emotion.** Do you spend your nights worrying about meeting this month's sales projections? Do you need more projects in the pipeline, plus a couple of hot prospects to "pop"? Are you dwelling on the possibility that this month might not be successful? Don't worry about it, because worry only contributes to a significant degradation of quality of life. We're on this earth for just a short while; don't squander it with this futile emotion.

2. **Alcohol is a vicious cycle.** Far too many sales professionals tend to ease the stress of a long day, or a long week, with alcohol. Then the next day, they're tired, hung over, and not rested or recharged. Instead of addressing their stress-related issues, they've compounded them: These salespeople don't have the energy to problem solve or call on that next buyer. Their performance is lowered as the pressure intensifies to meet their objectives.

   Alcohol isn't the only vice that can create this sort of vicious cycle. Drugs, food, and Facebook (I'm being only slightly facetious with that one; some people do have social-media addictions) can be substituted in Figure 12.2.

■ FIGURE 12.2
Vicious Cycles

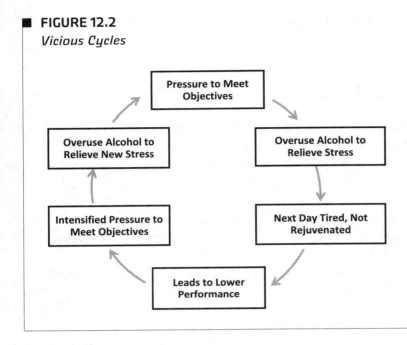

Three Types of Stress

To deal with stress, you first must understand where it comes from. The American Management Association identifies three basic types of stress:

» Individually oriented stress
» Interpersonally oriented stress
» Organizationally oriented stress

Let's break down each of these stress types and explore where and how they originate.

Individually Oriented Stress

Face it, most of us create our own stress. It is internal and very often one of the most challenging types of stress to overcome. Some symptoms of individually oriented stress include:

» Fear of failure
» Self-set deadlines
» Long hours
» Unrealistic expectations of self, career, or goals
» An overwhelming sense of personal responsibility
» A self-perceived lack of self-control, personal support, or feedback

You are your own toughest critic. As with most things, balance is a significant consideration. You need to take initiative and push yourself, but not to the detriment of your health or well-being.

Interpersonally Oriented Stress

This is the tension I referred to when discussing buyers and coworkers. When people feel unappreciated or misunderstood by superiors, peers, or subordinates, hard feelings take root. Stress also can occur when people believe their colleagues aren't performing up to par. Open communication works best when battling this type of stress.

I believe no one intentionally shows up at work and says, "I'm going to mess up today!" Most people really want to do a good job. If, for example, you have an employee who is constantly forgetting to provide the follow-up support necessary to close deals, take the time to show that individual what needs to be done and why. And then pull a maneuver from the *Jerry McGuire* playbook and ask him or her to "help me help you." Just don't berate your employee. Show them how doing what you're asking will make their world a bit brighter. As we've mentioned throughout, everyone is driven by enlightened self-interest. When you can appeal to that . . . you're in.

Organizationally Oriented Stress

Employers can create stress the following ways:

» Making unrealistic demands
» Placing too much emphasis on competition
» Creating unclear job requirements
» Giving too little credit for accomplishments
» Failing to give expected promotions

» Providing little information about career paths
» Aggravating workplace politics
» Failing to participate in decision making
» Providing poor work conditions

Managers can easily fall into what I call the "insatiable more" complex, meaning they always demand more and more in terms of business performance. This often can be an exercise in futility because of all the variables impacting your business. *Management must*, you cry out, *be reasonable*!

Seventeen Ways to Handle Sales-Related Stress

Psychologists report that stress, anxiety, and tension reduce many people to operating at only half of their abilities. Here is what you need to know to ensure that you and your employees run at full capacity, all the time.

1. Be Realistic About Your Goals

Don't try to conquer the world in one day. A career is a marathon, not a sprint. Don't beat yourself up if you can't double your prospect list within 24 hours. As the saying goes, the rewards don't always go to the fastest runners but to those who stay in the race.

2. Confront the Fear of Failure

Everyone experiences fear of failure. But instead of expending valuable energy worrying about what will go wrong, put that extra energy into planning and preparing for what can go right. It's called the Pygmalion effect, a form of self-fulfilling prophesy in which what you think will happen actually happens. Even if you aren't successful at that, here's a comforting thought: The best sales professionals experience failure regularly, but that means they are trying new things and constantly expanding their skill sets. So, go ahead and try that new prospect or approach. If it works, great! If not, no big deal. Move on.

3. Communicate, Communicate, Communicate

If you have a misunderstanding with someone at work, talk it out. Don't let something negative overwhelm your thoughts or activities. As soon as possible, pick up the phone or go see that person to explain your position. Somebody once told me, "If you have to go ugly, go ugly early." In other words, communicate your position as soon as possible. This allows you time to solve the problem and then to concentrate on the business of getting more people to say, "yes."

4. Don't Become a Victim of Unrealistic Demands

Buyers sometimes make requests that are impossible to fulfill: "We have no money, but we'd like to take you up on your offer." You're a sales professional, not a professional magician. If you think someone is making an unrealistic demand, take a few minutes to examine the request more closely. Sometimes the "impossible" really is possible, so do not use "unrealistic demands" as an easy way out. If, however, the demands truly are unrealistic, explain your position to the prospect. If he or she bolts, that's OK. You weren't going to be able to help that person anyway.

5. Get More Rest

You're not getting enough sleep, according to the National Sleep Foundation. Adults average 6.9 hours of sleep a night, even though many experts contend they need between 7 and 9 hours. The resulting sleep deprivation results in reduced productivity at work, irritability, diminished driving capacity, and a variety of health problems.

Although everyone's biological makeup is different, if you try to do more by sleeping less, you could be entering another type of vicious cycle. People are much more effective when they're mentally and physically alert. Get more sleep by allowing yourself time at the end of the day to wind down. Avoid television and computers before bedtime; the extra light has a tendency to signal your brain that you shouldn't be sleeping. Try reading instead. You can increase your intellectual horsepower while participating in an often-soporific activity. Dan Ciampa stated in the January 2005

Harvard Business Review that there are three keys to becoming a CEO of a company: management savvy, political intelligence, and personal style. A key to Ciampa's comments regarding the latter is the ability to stay on the "rested edge" and avoid the "ragged edge." Those professionals who ultimately move up in their businesses are those who can perform while making it all look effortless. There is no way to go 100 miles an hour all the time. Every once in awhile, you need to stop for gas and change the oil.

6. Get to Work Early

Employees who arrive early have a few spare minutes to better prepare for the day. Be one of them, and take that time to organize a daily to-do list or wrap up any loose ends from the previous day. You'll be amazed at how much better you'll feel when you can get a jump on the day.

7. Get in Shape

Being in good physical condition leads to more energy—thanks to improved blood flow to muscles and the brain, faster muscle recovery, and better use of oxygen. How do you determine if you are in good condition? Many experts consider the best indicator of health to be your resting heart rate. Physicians rank heart rate as the most important vital sign when evaluating patients. Most people have a resting heart rate between 70 and 90 beats per minute. A physically fit person will have a resting heart rate around 50 beats per minute. Dr. Kenneth Cooper, a pioneer in the world of aerobic conditioning (in fact, he coined the term), claims the lowest resting heart rate registered on one of his patients was 28 beats per minute by marathon runner Hal Higdon, who is nearing the age of 80.

The best time to evaluate your resting heart rate is first thing in the morning, before you even get out of bed. Apply two fingers (but not the thumb) to your wrist, and count the number of beats for 60 seconds. The lower the number, the better your health.

Scientific studies show a direct correlation between physical exercise and mental well-being, proving that aerobic exercise such as walking, running, and bicycling for 30 minutes three times a week actually works. Doing so creates natural endorphins that allow for stronger stress management. Exercise also gives you more energy to do more work, thus creating a virtuous cycle, not a vicious one.

8. Eat Right

Nutrition plays a major role in a person's ability to handle stress. Eating the right foods at the right time gives you more energy and the ability to accomplish more. Forget about that greasy fast-food burger; pack your lunch. It'll save you calories and dollars, and, after all, isn't that what a smart salesperson does? Better yet, take a qualified buyer out to lunch, and enjoy salmon and a salad. Get healthy while building relationships.

9. Add ALCAR and ALA to Your Daily Supplements

Think about adding acetyl L-carnitine and alpha lipoic acid to your vitamin regimen. (What's that? You *don't* have a vitamin regimen?) Researchers at the University of California, Berkeley, fed elderly rats both supplements for a couple of months. After measuring their mitochondrial activity, they found that the aged rats actually had the memory and overall energy of young to middle-age rats. Research reporters likened this to "a group of 80-year-old humans throwing away their walking sticks and acting 35 years younger." Always seek the advice of your physician before adding any supplements to your diet, but I've been taking ALA and ALCAR for years with no negative side effects. (I'll let you draw your own conclusions about the parallel between myself and the test subjects.)

10. Cut Back on the Caffeine

Caffeine does *not* give you energy; rather, it stimulates your nervous system and adrenals. That's not energy—that's stress! It's been reported that a single 250-milligram dose of caffeine (about 2.5 six-ounce cups of coffee) can increase levels of the stress hormone epinephrine (adrenaline) by more than 200 percent. If you cut back on your caffeine intake too quickly, though, you will likely suffer headaches. Stephen Cherniske, author of *Caffeine Blues: Wake Up to the Hidden Dangers of America's No. 1 Drug*, says the headaches occur as a result of an increase in blood flowing to the brain. Be reasonable with your caffeine consumption, and understand that it isn't a source of "real" energy.

11. Lose the Smokes

If reviewing the results of a Google image search of "smokers' lungs" isn't enough to make you stop smoking, perhaps the fact that cigarettes contain an estimated 4,000 known toxins with several known carcinogens will. Cigarette smoking also contributes to severe vitamin deficiencies and reduces your body's ability to oxygenate. How do you quit? Try interval sprinting every other day, which should at least make you think twice before lighting up.

12. Spend Time on Yourself

Go for a brisk walk early in the morning, or take the long way home in the evening. Everybody needs quiet time to recharge their mental batteries. Maybe the best thing you could do? Find a scenic route away from traffic, and go for a long motorcycle ride. Most of us got into the motorcycle business because we are enthusiasts first. We call it "cycle therapy."

13. Turn off Metallica, and Turn on Mozart

Bombarding your senses with electronic stimulation can be incredibly fatiguing. Music, talk radio, and the television all contribute to a general sense of tiredness. Try turning off the stuff a few extra minutes a day, and see if you don't feel calmer and more rested. While you're at it, put on some Mozart. Years ago, according to *The Virginian-Pilot* of Norfolk, then 16-year-old David Merrell worked with an Old Dominion University professor to study the effects of music on mice. The pair used three groups of mice: one listened to silence, another to Mozart, and the third to the thrash-metal band Anthrax. Then the mice were forced to navigate a maze.

After establishing a baseline navigation time of 10 minutes for all groups, Merrell exposed the mice to their predetermined playlists for 10 hours per day. You guessed it: The control group kept in silence reduced their maze-navigation time by 5 minutes, and the Mozart group by 8.5 minutes. But the dazed and confused mice listening to Anthrax took an average of 30 minutes longer to negotiate the same maze. (But they had much cooler T-shirts.)

The young Mr. Merrell kept the mice in this experiment in individual living quarters. Why? In a similar test conducted earlier, the mice listening to heavy music actually killed each other.

14. Get Input from Others

Talking to friends, family members, and coworkers about situations that cause stress can provide a different perspective. (Be sure to avoid whining to these people.) Constructive conversation can be a great tool for relieving stress. Often, it's that sense of community and companionship that can see you through tough situations.

15. Use Positive Mental Affirmations

Much research has been conducted on the rejuvenating powers of the mind. (For two of the best books on this topic, read *Learned Optimism: How to Change Your Mind and Your Life*, by Martin Seligman, and *Feeling Good: The New Mood Therapy*, by David Burns.) Look at the amazing feats of endurance and strength that humans have exhibited, from Sir Edmund Hillary and Tenzing Norgay reaching the summit of Mount Everest in 1953 to climber Aron Ralston, who, after being pinned under a 200-pound rock, was forced to cut off his own arm with a dull pocketknife in order to survive (Ralston's story was chronicled in the 2010 film, *127 Hours*). None of these feats could have been accomplished without extraordinary mental strength.

These people achieved a vision of success and continued to remind themselves repeatedly that they could survive. Hopefully, your job is not that stressful, but sales professionals can learn a thing or two from the likes of Hillary, Norgay, and Ralston.

Psychologists claim that most of an individual's "self-talk" is negative, which creates a defeatist attitude and low energy. When you feel your energy starting to ebb, and you're focusing on how tired you are, try passing a powerful, energizing thought through your head. For the spiritually inclined, I like Isaiah 40:31 in the King James Version (go ahead, look it up). For something more secular, try the affirmation made famous by late-19th-century French psychotherapist Émile Coué: "Every day, in every way, I'm getting better and better." I use both. A lot. They should see you through some stressful situations, too.

16. Understand Control and Influence

I was taught long ago that successful people spend the majority of their time on what they can control, some time on what they can influence, and precious little time on what they can't control or influence. Instead of agonizing over the possibility of failure, use your resources to think of ways to get more projects in the pipeline or to generate ideas to intensify the desire of your hot prospects. One huge contributor to being overwhelmed is feeling like you have no control. Work on what you can control, and don't worry about the rest. Not always easy to do, but it's well worth it.

17. Have High-Quality Options

That's great advice. For whatever reason, the times in my life when I've succumbed to stress and behaved in ways I wish I hadn't typically occurred because I felt I didn't have options. Build your skills, have financial reserves, establish scores of terrific professional partnerships, and you will always find that you have options.

Even the highest-performing engines have limits. The profession of selling can be a high-stakes, high-pressure ride. No matter how talented or skilled or connected you are, everyone has mental and physical limits. Knowing how to keep yourself at or below redline can help your career, your buyers, and your organization go more miles over the long haul.

CHAPTER 12 Accsellerators

» Sales-related stress can be the cause of some very contentious situations and could cause irreparable damage.

» Hostility toward loved ones, difficulty concentrating, sleeplessness, and anxiety are signs of stress.

» Anticipate stressful situations by thinking through how you might deal with such events. Prepare responses, buy time, and try not to overreact.

» Be afraid of not failing. If you don't fail, you're not trying. Sometimes I actually keep track of how many times I get turned down in a day. (My record is five, but I bet I can beat that!)

» Establish high-quality options to help dramatically reduce your stress. Save your money, acquire new skills, and build terrific partnerships. You'll do better, and you'll feel better, too.

CHAPTER 13

Peak Sales Performance

KEEPING YOUR COMPETITION IN THE REARVIEW MIRROR AND YOUR EYES ON THE ROAD AHEAD

H*ave you ever had one of* those *days?*
I don't mean one of those days in which everything goes wrong. I mean one of those in which everything goes *right.*

"I'm so on fire, if they don't nail down the lamps, I'm planning on selling the furniture!" one Harley-Davidson sales professional who was in selling nirvana on exactly one of those days proclaimed to me recently.

That's what I'm talking about here.

In the Selling Zone

Colloquially, we describe it as being *hot*, *in the zone*, *on target*, or *firing on all cylinders*. But what we're really experiencing—at least partially—is what Claremont Graduate University professor Mihaly Csikszentmihalyi (pronounced MEE-hye CHEEK-sent-mə-HYE-ee) calls "the state of flow."

In his groundbreaking 1990 book *Flow: The Psychology of Optimal Experience*, Csikszentmihalyi described *flow* as "the process of total involvement with life." Later, in a 1996 interview with *Wired* magazine, he defined *flow* as "being completely involved in an activity for its own sake. The ego falls away. Time flies. Every action, movement, and thought follows inevitably from the previous one, like playing jazz. Your whole being is involved, and you're using your skills to the utmost."

Unwittingly, Csikszentmihalyi also was describing peak performance, which occurs when you perform almost effortlessly at an incredibly high ability in challenging situations: The athlete who easily hits the ball over the center-field fence in the ninth inning of the big game. The composer who writes the perfect song connecting melody and emotion when the record company demands a hit. The salesperson who performs gracefully and comfortably in challenging and complex selling situations.

The Right Road

I've talked a lot in this book about sharpening your preparation, developing your skills, and creating the mind-set necessary to operate in today's competitive sales landscape, from threshold competencies to more sophisticated approaches, to working individually and within groups. Now, I'd like to spend some time analyzing where you're headed with this powerful new sales "machine."

For you to maximize acc*sell*eration, keep your eyes on the road ahead. In so doing, and by dint of clarity in your direction, you also will keep your competition in the rearview mirror. When on a motorcycle, riders "go where they look," meaning that if you find yourself concentrating on the shoulder of the road, you'll gravitate toward that dangerous segment of the road. If you look "through" the curve to the road ahead, you'll likely navigate that curve successfully and keep rolling smoothly to your destination.

In the introduction to *Flow*, Csikszentmihalyi notes that "twenty-three-hundred years ago, Aristotle concluded that, more than anything else, men and women seek happiness." Just about everything else we do is done primarily because we expect it to increase our happiness. And I think happiness begins with heading in the right direction. Even the highest-performing vehicle won't perform if it's not on the proper road. Put a Ferrari on a pothole-ridden dirt path in the middle of Indiana, and it won't perform nearly as well as it does on the Indianapolis Motor Speedway. Whether your aims are personal or professional, sales oriented or social, the question remains: Where are you headed? And are you on the right road?

The Sales Professional's Favorite Topic: Money

Ask most sales professionals about their goals and objectives, and you'll find one common denominator: money. Although certainly not your only objective, money can provide the necessary fuel for you to live the life you want. I always tell people that money certainly isn't everything, but I'd like to see you live without it. And I believe it is virtually impossible to have a conversation with sales professionals about goals and *not* bring up the topic of money. (In a hallway conversation with the then-Harley-Davidson president and CEO, Rich Teerlink told me to be careful of people who tell you they're not interested in money—because they'll lie to you about other things, too!)

I once asked a corporate vice president how much money he needed; not how much he earned, but how much he *needed*. He said he had no idea what I was talking about. Clarifying my question, I asked how much money he would personally need to feel financially independent, enabling him to not *have* to work.

"I have absolutely no clue," he admitted.

I was dumbfounded, because I know *exactly* how much I need.

Apparently, not knowing is common: According to the Employee Benefit Research Group, a Washington, D.C.–based organization "dedicated to the development of sound employee benefit programs and public policy through objective education and research," most respondents to the 2010 Retirement Confidence Survey reported they are clueless about savings goals. Many workers surveyed continue to be unaware of how much they need to save for retirement, and less than half (46 percent) report they and/or their spouse have attempted to calculate how much money they will need to enjoy a comfortable retirement. Even more frightening, the study indicates that many respondents have no personal savings at all. In fact, 54 percent report that the total value of their household's savings and investments, excluding the value of their primary home and any defined benefit plans, is less than $25,000.

The question I posed to that confused corporate vice president is the premise of a 2006 book called *The Number: What Do You Need for the Rest of Your Life and What Will It Cost?*, by Lee Eisenberg. It's also the basis for a series of television commercials by The Netherlands–based investment company ING, which show people walking around carrying various seven-digit numbers under their arm. The answer to this fundamental question—how much money do you need?—may not be exact and is subject to change. But it is monumental when considering where you're headed. High-performing sales professionals simply *must* know where they're going.

Most salespeople I know have as their ultimate financial goal the ability to comfortably retire (a word with dramatically different meanings to different people) or to be financially independent (sometimes referred to as having a "walking fund," meaning enough money to tell everyone else in the rat race to take a hike). Others simply talk about attaining a certain net worth, such as $1 million. (To listen to an interview with accomplished financial planner Art Rothschild on the ins and outs of establishing your own number, go to www.AcceleratetheSale.com.)

What Would You Do with It?

Sparing you the how-do-you-get-there-if-you-don't-know-where-you-want-to-go message, I'll also skip the can't-find-a-destination-in-

Los-Angeles-if-all-you-have-is-a-map-of-Detroit talk. But I will ask you this: If you made your dream sale or hit your personal financial targets, what would you do with the money? Would you spend more time with your family? Pay off personal debt? Solidify your kids' college funds? Buy a second home or pay off your first? Travel around the world? Something else entirely?

Thinking like this asks you to consider whether money is a means to an ends, the "ends" you are striving to achieve (after all, we really don't just want money; we want what money can provide). By determining those ends, you can make them more real, more meaningful, and perhaps even more attainable. What would you do with the money, and why would you do it?

A college professor once told me that money lets you *have* things, but wealth allows you to *do* things (for both yourself and others). That made a lot of sense to me, and it set me off to seek the latter. But what is wealth?

Alan Weiss, who holds a doctorate in psychology, has authored more than 30 books, and is a preeminent consultant, comments frequently that wealth isn't money but rather discretionary time. Now *that*, friends, is a provocative concept. In his world, money and time aren't mutually exclusive ideas on the mental plane of success. Money without discretionary time isn't useful, and discretionary time without adequate money can be painful. Weiss rounds out his theory of wealth as discretionary time by adding that money isn't a limited resource; you can always earn more, but you can't replace or replenish time.

Although I try to avoid clichés, the often-asked question "What would you do if you had six months to live?" crystallizes things for me—and it should for you, too. It speaks directly about your priorities. If you knew your time was perilously short, what might you do differently? Would you right wrongs, spend time with loved ones, contribute something meaningful to society? These are weighty issues that I'll leave you to ponder, but here's one more word to the wise from Weiss: "You don't have a personal life and a professional life. You have *a* life."

Keeping that in mind, let's turn our attention to how your professional sales intentions can fuel your personal journey through that life. (What would you do with just six months left to live? Share your ideas, and read what others want to accomplish, at www.Accel eratetheSale.com.)

SMART and FAST

If you're reading this book, you're more than likely experienced enough to be familiar with SMART (Specific, Measurable, Attainable, Realistic, and Timely) goals. For truly great goal setting, I believe your goals should be both SMART and FAST—my acronym for Factorial, Audacious, Sacrosanct, and Tenable.

Factorial

Factorial literally means the product of positive integers: $1 \times 2 \times 3 \times 4 = 24$. I use this metaphorically to apply to your ambitions, meaning that the dominant activities in which you engage dramatically increase the speed with which you succeed. To do this, they must pay off in numerous ways. If you're working out and eating right, you not only feel better about yourself, you'll present yourself more confidently to buyers, as well as have the strength and energy necessary to carry out your specific mission. Reading quality business books (much like this one) makes you a better resource for your clients and often increase your vocabulary, which in turn has been said to increases IQ and provide additional topics in which to engage prospects in conversation.

Audacious

At least some of your objectives should be bold and unrestrained. In some situations, to truly acc*sell*erate your sales, you must be willing to take those dangerous curves without fear. On my first day of work at a Harley-Davidson dealership near Philadelphia, I told my new colleagues that I would someday work for Harley-Davidson headquarters in Milwaukee. At the time, that was almost the equivalent of saying I was going to be an astronaut.

Three years later, I was packing my belongings to relocate to Milwaukee and start my new job at the downtown corporate offices of the Harley-Davidson Motor Company. As I packed, I told myself that I was going to become a millionaire by the time I turned 40. Back then, I was 24 years old and had $200 dollars to my name. But six months before my 40th birthday, I attained my objective, despite being told repeatedly that I never would. Since then I've set and achieved many other goals, financial and otherwise. My point is to give your objectives a second look and to make sure you are thinking big enough.

Sacrosanct

Also make sure some of your objectives are sacrosanct, meaning that you won't deviate from your path toward achieving them, regardless of what happens. Some objectives simply *have* to be that important. Education, family, self-development, renewal, and spirituality are examples of goal categories from which you won't want to veer. Just don't become insanely inflexible. I earned a master's degree in education from a private college in Wisconsin while working a corporate job that required a ton of travel. There were no online programs available then, and it took me more than five years. But it was a goal I was unwilling to let go of.

Tenable

Finally, your objectives must be tenable; that is, they need to be defendable. Why in the world do you want to do what you want to do? Can you mount an argument that defends your position and your intent, morally and ethically? Can you explain why it is important to you? If so, chances are you'll reach it. This goes back to our discussion of enlightened self-interest. Is it good for you, good for your organization, and good for the larger community in which you operate? If so, then it's a tenable position.

Six Steps to Goal-Setting Success

You may be able to think of other steps, but for me, these are the six essential steps that will send you on the road to peak sales performance. Follow these and I guarantee you will acc*sell*erate your performance. Again, it's like physical exercise—it's not enough to know these steps; you actually have to *do* these steps.

1. Write Down Your SMART and FAST Goal

Putting pen to paper is a great way to clarify your goal. For example, perhaps your goal is: "I will increase my March gross sales numbers by 12 percent over last year, while maintaining a profit margin of 30 percent." This meets the SMART goal criteria and passes through the FAST filter by stating specifically what you are trying to do (increase sales numbers) and providing a benchmark from which to measure your performance (last March's numbers), as well as a specific increase (12 percent). Most importantly, it provides a time frame (one month) to accomplish the task. And, of course, the fact that you are writing down the goal and perhaps sharing it with others helps to instantiate the goal and commit you to working toward it.

2. Write Down What's in It for You

To increase your chances of success, write down the reasons you are pursuing a specific goal, which serve to reaffirm your efforts and provide a constant reminder of "why" you are doing "what."

3. Identify Potential Challenges

What likely roadblocks might you encounter along the way to your stated goal? One common challenge is time. Ask yourself, *Will I be able to give this goal the attention it deserves?* You may need to delegate work to others, reprioritize other goals, or give your time-management skills a workout. Other considerations may be more tangible, such as inventory availability and market conditions. Each goal presents a different set of challenges, and identifying the tricky areas will simplify navigating toward those goals.

4. Identify and Interact with Needed Resources

Find individuals along the way who can help you expedite your goal success. Previously, I mentioned the importance of socialization via accountability partners, mentors, or other trusted people. Now, identify others whom you can help on their way, perhaps someone *you* can mentor. This sets off a powerful cycle of reciprocity. You'll learn more as the other individual learns more, and you'll be forging positive relationships that may evolve into powerful tools.

Which Is More Important: Qualitative vs. Quantitative?

Qualitative sales objectives are harder to measure than quantitative sales objectives, but they are no less important. Such objectives include building outstanding relationships, contributing to brand awareness, exemplifying organizational culture, demonstrating corporate values, and becoming a trusted advisor or valuable partner. A blended approach to sales objectives both quantitative and qualitative is one of the quickest ways to sales acc*sell*eration.

5. Identify and Acquire Needed Skills

You might set goals that are unattainable with your current set of skills, meaning that additional education and training could be required. This could include becoming proficient with a new computer program, learning another language, or developing better prospecting or objection-handling skills. Don't shy away from setting goals that require new skills. These goals may be tougher to reach, but they're well worth the extra effort.

6. Create and Execute Your Action Plan

Some experts contend that planning efforts pay off in a five-to-one ratio—that is, every hour you spend planning can eventually save you five! Write down the actions you will need to take to achieve each of your goals. Talk to someone about them, read a book about them, or obtain additional information about them from other outside sources. All of this input will help you develop an action plan, forcing you to look at goals in smaller, "bite-size" tasks and reducing the odds of feeling overwhelmed. It also makes getting started easier. Be flexible; conditions and situations change constantly, and there is more than one way to reach a goal. As you progress, don't hesitate to adjust your action plan.

Reaching the Peak

The following are additional actions you can take to ensure peak sales performance.

Monitor Your Time and Journal Your Work

One of the best exercises you can engage in is tracking your time usage over a long period and reflecting on your effectiveness. I first did this exercise as part of an Alan Weiss program about moving from earning six-figure salaries to seven-figure ones. As prep work for this workshop, I tracked my days in 15-minute intervals (yes, I did) for approximately one month.

Of course, I didn't frantically write down everything I did every 15 minutes, but I did get into the habit several times a day of stopping to jot down how I had spent the past several hours. I learned some very revealing truths about my time usage—primarily that my focus was often fragmented. E-mails, phone calls, and other distractions prevented me from accomplishing long bouts of concentrated effort.

Around the same time, I also read a book called *The 4-Hour Workweek: Escape 9-5, Live Anywhere, and Join the New Rich*. In this book, author Tim Ferris suggests not checking e-mail first thing in the morning. He claims checking your e-mail sends you on all sorts of diversionary paths that prevent you from accomplishing the high-leverage work of your day.

I followed Ferris's advice, and my productivity skyrocketed. I spent several of my best, freshest, most creative hours of the day on my most important projects. (I've spoken with people who say, "I could never do that. What if I receive an urgent e-mail?" These people are kidding themselves and just offering excuses not to give it a whirl. And they probably are still in the same position they were three years ago, earning the same amount of money!)

Another approach to rapid sales success is writing your thoughts in a journal. Don't consider it a diary; rather, this notebook should be dedicated to tracking time and sales efforts. In my journal, I ask myself the following questions:

» What was my biggest accomplishment of the day?
» What key thing did I learn?

» What was my biggest frustration?
» How can I correct this situation going forward?
» What surprised me the most today?

I've found that when I display the discipline necessary to perform daily tracking and self-reflection, I accomplish so much so fast that it's almost *too* much! I have *too* many client projects, *too* many proposals, *too* many cool new ideas. And that's almost *too* good to believe!

ID Successes: Small, Large, and Derivative

For you to win the long sales race ahead of you, it's imperative to get regular injections of fuel. For many, that fuel comes in the form of celebrating successes. As covered extensively in Chapter 1, "The Checkered Flag: Lessons from Your Victory Lap," identify as many facets of success as possible, then reflect on a job well done. I'm not saying you should take the afternoon off, but I am suggesting you pause and mentally pat yourself on the back for leveraging new skills gained.

Comb through each day to find as many things as possible that you did well. Build up your mental conditioning by thinking about success. The sales profession is a rejection game (remember, in baseball, three hits in every 10 at-bats can make you an All-Star), and you'll need vast reservoirs of positive reserves if you want to win.

Engage in Repetition, Not Superstition

It's been said that race-car drivers are second only to baseball players in terms of success superstitions. Avoiding the color green, not uttering or hearing the word *trophy*, and implementing a no-peanuts-near-the-car policy are all reportedly part of the competitive drivers' catalog of don'ts.

I'm not going to suggest you start practicing your own superstitions as they pertain to increasing sales. Rather, if you want to achieve success more quickly, consider engaging in repetition. What I mean by this is reflecting on your previous successes and repeating what you've done in the past. By beginning meetings the same way each time or closing deals at the coffee shop on the corner, you bring a level of comfort and familiarity to an otherwise potentially nerve-wracking situation. (I even have a favorite pair of Allen Edmonds shoes I wear for important business events!)

You Don't Have to Win by a Mile

Find a balance between understanding and exploiting what you do well and understanding and fixing what's holding you back. The trick is to use the perfect amount of resources necessary for success. No more, no less. Not every project, presentation, or prospect demands the same intensity.

The winner of the Indianapolis 500 doesn't win by five laps; he wins this 500-mile race by seconds—or even fractions of a second. In 1982, Gordon Johncock beat Rick Mears by just .16 of a second. But the winning driver typically earns three times the prize money as the second-place finisher.

Destroy Your "Pathological Critic"

Too many salespeople lack self-confidence. Oh, they talk a good game. But inside, they're a mess, telling themselves, *I should be better* . . . or *I can't* . . .

In their book *Self-Esteem: A Proven Program of Cognitive Techniques for Assessing, Improving, and Maintaining Your Self-Esteem*, Matthew McKay, Ph.D., and Patrick Fanning call this mental rumination an individual's "pathological critic"—that inner voice that is always reminding someone how he or she failed to live up to the task at hand. The pathological critic creates self-doubt, a killer in terms of creating peak sales performance.

McKay and Fanning suggest taking steps to squelch this negative inner voice by creating an honest self-assessment. List your strengths (how well you deal with people, perhaps, or your ability to solve problems) and your weaknesses (your dislike for conflict or disdain for details). Then, add either some piece of positive evidence or a potential solution. Some examples might look like this:

» "I keep my promises and am excellent at maintaining long-term relationships, as evidenced by my 10-year relationship with our firm's top client."
» "I am independent and can get myself out of most jams. Many people have contributed to my success, for which I am thankful.

Vertical and Horizontal

I think the number one mistake most sales people make is underestimating the value of long-term sustainable relationships and how to develop them over time," says Doug Albregts, vice president of sales and marketing for Samsung Electronics America for the Enter- prise Division. "The second biggest mistake is relying on one relationship and not working their clients in a vertical and horizontal fashion. Both mistakes go somewhat hand in hand and can be lethal in terms of account stability."

At the same time, I need to recognize and admire the nature of my accomplishments."

» "When meeting new clients, I get nervous and need to recognize this is a natural and normal reaction. (They're probably nervous, too!) I will go into these situations with some conversation items and questions ready. I will concentrate on being interested in the clients."

» "Although I am typically calm and relaxed in social situations, I have occasionally made a social blunder, said the wrong thing, or used a word incorrectly. But so has everyone else. Going forward, I'll just make a joke and say, 'Am I having a senior moment already?'"

Remember that nobody is either all right or all wrong. (Even Gandhi probably had a bad habit or two.) But with an honest review of what you do well, what you don't, and what actions you can take, you are on your way to destroying that pathological critic.

Frequently Review Your Assessment

After you've created your self-assessment, review it frequently—in the morning when you rise and right before bedtime are when most people are in the proper mental state to accept this type of self-evaluation. Then, as you memorize those honest assessments and corollary actions, monitor your mental conversations for any sign of your pathological critic. When it rears its self-defeating, sales-killing head, start reviewing again. Soon, your self-confidence will return, positioning you to handle practically any sales (or social) situation.

Enjoy Your Success, Then Get Back to Work

One warm Tuesday in February, I found myself in our family's special place, the summer resort town of Rehoboth Beach, Delaware, taking a stroll on the boardwalk. (I like to do things at odd times.) I was behind an octogenarian—that's right, he was walking faster than me—and when he reached the end of the one-mile boardwalk, he stomped his foot and proclaimed "Ha!"

Then he turned around and set off in the opposite direction.

At first, this startled me. But surprise turned to intrigue as I followed him—watching him stomp and hearing him bellow "Ha!" at each end of the boardwalk. At some point in this process, it occurred to me that the man was briefly but publicly celebrating his success.

"Ha!"

And then it was back to work.

This is my suggestion for you, too. If you want to acc*sell*erate your sales success, briefly bask in the winner's circle, then get back to work. It's that sort of dogged determination that leads to winning again and again.

We've traveled great distances together in this book, you and me. Hopefully, as you've read, you've considered lots of options, chuckled a little, and even started plotting your next sales success.

As we head toward the finish line, I want to share two final important ideas. Don't skip this; it's the big finish.

Whispered Wisdom

I love this phrase: *whispered wisdom*. It evokes images of the secrets of the ages being passed from generation to generation. In this book, I've endeavored to bring you diverse perspectives from successful sales practitioners in a wealth of industries—from motorcycles to marketing, from forensics to firearms.

During my interviews with these professionals, we covered a lot of ground. Some of my questions were developed specifically for that individual; others were consistent among all interviews. One question I asked everyone was, "What's the single greatest piece of sales advice you've ever been given? The following are a few gems from their collective whispered wisdom.

Compartmentalization

"I once had a manager who was great at giving me advice," says Doug Slotkin, inside sales vice president for the real-estate website Zillow.com. One of the most important lessons she taught Slotkin was the gift of compartmentalization. "If you're frustrated about something, you can't let it affect your overall demeanor," he says. "You've got to compartmentalize. You've got to understand that you're not going to sell every client. Don't let that negativity overwhelm your overall approach. Each call is its own entity, as opposed to being cumulative."

Would You Buy It?

"This goes back 25 years, when I was trying to sell tickets over the phone to individuals and corporations," says Mike Tatoian, executive vice president at Dover Motorsports, Inc., which owns and operates Dover International Speedway in Dover, Delaware. "The person who was coaching me said, 'If you were them, would you do this? Would you invest in this? Would you buy what you're trying to sell?' That made me ask myself if I was just trying to get a commission, or did I believe in what I was selling. He would always make me put myself in their situation. People buy people." As mentioned earlier, if you want to be convincing, you have got to be convinced.

Be Yourself

"You are missing you." That's the advice Pat Haneman, national sales manager for the forensic business unit at NMS Labs, received early in her career. "You are technically accurate," she was told. "You do everything by the book. What you are missing is just allowing yourself to come through a little bit more." After that, Haneman says she relaxed and actually had more fun. And her clients responded.

No Business Is Better than Bad Business

"We look for people who understand what we do, appreciate it, and want to grow with us. If they don't, that's fine," says Gary Ramey, vice president of sales for Beretta U.S.A. His point is simple: If a buyer's strategies and tactics aren't aligned with those of the seller, it's better to hold off. This, of course, is antithetical to practically every piece of advice ingrained in sales professionals for generations. They want the deal. But Ramey thinks it's a mistake. "There's nothing personal about moving on," he says. "If we're more aligned next year, then wonderful, let's partner and grow together. If not, let's go have a cappuccino and call it a day."

Sell from a Position of Strength

"It's a lot easier to make your next sale when you're already at quota," says John Duffy, CEO of 3Cinteractive. That confident mind-set permeates everything from your body language to the sound of your voice, to the look in your eye. "If it's the second day of the month, and you've got your number in the bag, you're going to have a better month than if it's the 29th and you're only 10 percent of the way there. Being in a position where you don't create desperation is most important. I work in businesses where relationships and selling from a position of strength are *everything*."

Push Aside Your Ego

Probably the toughest piece of advice to take comes from Mark Rossi, vice president of sales for Dover Motorsports. He instructs salespeople to push aside their egos and let the buyer assume the primary role. "I'm not trying to impress buyers and show them how smart I am," Rossi admits. "I want to truly learn about their business. I don't want to just make the sale; I want to establish a relationship."

Do Your Homework

My own favorite piece of whispered wisdom came to me at the unlikely age of eight, from as unlikely a source for sales advice as you can imagine: my paternal grandfather. A blue-collar working man from the Anthracite region of Pennsylvania, he started his career at 12 years old as a breaker boy in the local coal mines. (If you'd like to learn more about a job you'd *never* want, Google "breaker boy.") He was opinionated, known to utter a profanity or two, and smoked filterless Lucky Strikes.

I was sitting at our dining room table one night, doing my math homework, when my grandfather paused while walking by. I can still feel his hands, calloused from a lifetime of arduous manual work, as he gently placed them on my shoulders. "Mark, it's going to take one of two things to make it in this world," he intoned. "A strong mind or a strong back, so always do your homework." His lesson was clear: "You don't want to wind up working the jobs I did." I didn't always do my homework in school, but I sure do now. I prepare, I research, and I plan. (To share your greatest piece of sales advice, go to—where else?—www.AcceleratetheSale.com.)

Greatest. Sales. Ever.

What was your greatest sale ever?

That's another question I asked every single person I interviewed for this book.

Some answered that it was the one with the highest dollar amount, but most didn't. Anne Ponzio-Shirley from the inScope Consulting Group cited her jaw-dropping $15-million sale in the tech sector during 2009—when there were few deals to be made. But the Retail Ready Group's Pete Scholovich talked about his contribution to helping repair relationships between Iomega and Office Depot. Zillow.com's Doug Slotkin remembered hanging tough with a real-estate agent who ultimately enjoyed success.

John Duffy spoke proudly about 3Cinteractive's partnership with AT&T on Text Collect, a platform enabling collect calls to mobile phones. It sounds simple, but it's actually a complex arrangement, and Duffy's company is the only one in the United States to offer something like it. Duffy is so proud of that project that he sometimes dials 1-800-CALL-ATT just so he can hear the message, "We now offer collect calls on cell phones."

"The sale I take the most pride in is not necessarily the largest-revenue sale, but it was the one that took a lot of tenacity," says Pat Haneman of NMS Labs. Despite her best efforts to secure the business of a government agency that couldn't afford the product, Haneman maintained a positive relationship with the entity and returned to its officials each time NMS refined the product and reduced its deliverable cost to the client. Four years later, she made the sale. "It taught me not to give up," she says. "You try different approaches, you try different levels, you listen to the client. You just keep trying. The end result was a client who improved the quality of their own operation by using our services."

Perhaps my favorite "greatest sale" story comes from the CEO of the Glowac + Harris marketing firm. Wayne Glowac has been selling for more than 30 years and told me how he—still—is constantly learning, growing, and improving as a salesperson.

"Wayne," I asked, "what was your greatest sale ever?"

His answer was simple, elegant, and, in a word, *perfect.*

Glowac paused thoughtfully before responding.

"My next one," he said.

Then his voice began to rise, which you wouldn't necessarily expect in a hardened sales veteran. "I'm going to be better," he promised. "So my clients will be better. That way, it's going to be more fun for both of us. I love this business, and for me, it's about the next challenge."

What will be your greatest sale ever? The answer is still ahead of you.

Appendix

ACC*SELL*ERATION ASSESSMENT:
ARE YOU HEADED FOR THE CHECKERED FLAG?

A: Offering Expertise

1. You can tell you clearly and concisely what our offering does for buyers.

NO WAY				SOMETIMES				ABSOLUTELY	
1	2	3	4	5	6	7	8	9	10

2. There are at least three statistics or specifications you can relate about our offering.

NO WAY				SOMETIMES				ABSOLUTELY	
1	2	3	4	5	6	7	8	9	10

3. You can explain mechanically, procedurally, or physically how our offering works.

NO WAY				SOMETIMES				ABSOLUTELY	
1	2	3	4	5	6	7	8	9	10

4. You can name at least five ways our buyers are improved with our offering.

NO WAY				SOMETIMES				ABSOLUTELY	
1	2	3	4	5	6	7	8	9	10

5. Working with others, you've completed the Sales Acc*sell*eration Exercise in Chapter 3.

NO WAY				SOMETIMES				ABSOLUTELY	
1	2	3	4	5	6	7	8	9	10

Total numbers 1–5: _____

B. Language Skills

1. Your industry has a specific vernacular, and you use this with buyers.

NO WAY				SOMETIMES				ABSOLUTELY	
1	2	3	4	5	6	7	8	9	10

2. You can ask interesting and thought-provoking questions about a variety of topics.

NO WAY				SOMETIMES				ABSOLUTELY	
1	2	3	4	5	6	7	8	9	10

3. You have almost completely removed the word *like* from your vocabulary.

NO WAY				SOMETIMES				ABSOLUTELY	
1	2	3	4	5	6	7	8	9	10

4. You can weave a great, real, client acquisition story in 15 seconds or less.

NO WAY				SOMETIMES				ABSOLUTELY	
1	2	3	4	5	6	7	8	9	10

5. You can use your voice effectively to communicate everything from energy to sincerity.

NO WAY				SOMETIMES				ABSOLUTELY	
1	2	3	4	5	6	7	8	9	10

Total numbers 1–5: _____

C. Process Proficiency

1. You can prove (show, demonstrate) the results of each step of your sales process to others quickly and easily.

NO WAY				SOMETIMES				ABSOLUTELY	
1	2	3	4	5	6	7	8	9	10

2. When you work with buyers you serve as a guide, always knowing "what's next."

NO WAY				SOMETIMES				ABSOLUTELY	
1	2	3	4	5	6	7	8	9	10

3. You set expectations and gain buyer commitment for referrals and/or testimonials early in your exchanges.

NO WAY				SOMETIMES				ABSOLUTELY	
1	2	3	4	5	6	7	8	9	10

4. You are able to involve your buyer physically and/or mentally in the purchase process.

NO WAY				SOMETIMES				ABSOLUTELY	
1	2	3	4	5	6	7	8	9	10

5. You have options for when your buyers say, "No."

NO WAY				SOMETIMES				ABSOLUTELY	
1	2	3	4	5	6	7	8	9	10

Total numbers 1–5: _____

D. Resiliency

1. You often say or think, "I made the sale because I'm good at what I do."

NO WAY				SOMETIMES				ABSOLUTELY	
1	2	3	4	5	6	7	8	9	10

2. When you don't know something or feel uncomfortable, you seek to rectify that knowledge gap.

NO WAY				SOMETIMES				ABSOLUTELY	
1	2	3	4	5	6	7	8	9	10

3. When a buyer says, "No," you move on and realize it's his or her loss.

NO WAY				SOMETIMES				ABSOLUTELY	
1	2	3	4	5	6	7	8	9	10

4. You celebrate your successes and shake off your losses.

NO WAY				SOMETIMES				ABSOLUTELY	
1	2	3	4	5	6	7	8	9	10

5. Every sale makes you better for the next one.

NO WAY				SOMETIMES				ABSOLUTELY	
1	2	3	4	5	6	7	8	9	10

Total numbers 1–5: _____

Acc*seller*ation Scorecard

Use the numbers on the bottom of each page.

A. Offering Expertise   _____

B. Language Skills   _____

C. Process Proficiency   _____

D. Resiliency   _____

Total   _____

0–50: You might as well be walking; consider doing something else. No, really, the profession of sales may not be for you.

51–100: You're driving a moped; don't take that thing on the highway without a helmet. You've got potential, but you have more work to do. Review this book in its entirety. Build your fundamentals.

101–150: Nice! You can think of yourself as the new Chevy Camaro. Fast, good-looking, and able to do well off the line. Concentrate on "higher level" ideas—shifting, referrals—and concentrate on peak sales performance skills.

151–200: Are you familiar with the Bugatti Veyron Super Sport? You should be because it's the fastest production car on the planet, kind of like you. You're ready for your next win!

Index

About the Author

Mark Rodgers is a principal partner of the Peak Performance Business Group, which helps clients dramatically accelerate their sales along with marketing and management efforts, achieving astonishing results.

Working in both business-to-business and business-to-consumer environments, Rodgers has helped clients:

» Considerably increase market share through competitive strategy creation and tactical implementation
» Develop competition-crushing marketplace superiority
» Significantly accelerate cash flow via comprehensive sales and marketing initiatives
» Greatly increase organizational synergy by improving internal communication
» Reduce workforce attrition, streamline processes, and speed management decision making
» Seize advantage of quickly unfolding market opportunities
» Fire on all cylinders by generating long-lived enthusiasm and uncommon alignment and ensuring essential skill acquisition

His coaching, speaking, and consulting work attracts clients as diverse as the Harley-Davidson Motor Company and the Executive Education Program at the University of Wisconsin-Madison.

An award-winning author, engaging communicator, and world-class speaker, Mark Rodgers has published more than 100 articles and holds the National Speakers' Association Certified Speaking Professional designation; he is one of 500 people on the planet to have earned this coveted achievement.

Rodgers lives in Milwaukee, Wisconsin, with his wife, Amy. For more information, and to access the enhanced content for this book, go to www.Acceleratethe Sale.com

    User name: acceleratethesale

    Password: MRDI24680

    Contact Mark via e-mail (Mark@AcceleratetheSale.com) to see how quickly he can improve your business.